SURVIVAL MIGRATION

Failed Governance and the Crisis of Displacement

Alexander Betts

CORNELL UNIVERSITY PRESS   ITHACA AND LONDON

First published 2013 by Cornell University Press
First printing, Cornell Paperbacks, 2013

Printed in the United States of America

Library of Congress Cataloging-in-Publication Data

Betts, Alexander, 1980–
    Survival migration : failed governance and the crisis of displacement / Alexander Betts.
        pages cm
    Includes bibliographical references and index.
    ISBN 978-0-8014-5106-5 (cloth : alk. paper) —
    ISBN 978-0-8014-7777-5 (pbk. : alk. paper)
    1. Refugees—Africa, Sub-Saharan—Case studies. 2. Political refugees—Africa, Sub-Saharan—Case studies. 3. Forced migration—Africa, Sub-Saharan—Case studies. 4. Human rights—Africa, Sub-Saharan—Case studies. 5. Africa, Sub-Saharan—Emigration and immigration—Political aspects—Case studies. 6. Africa, Sub-Saharan—Politics and government—21st century. I. Title.
    HV640.5.A3B48   2013
    362.870967—dc23   2013000077

Cornell University Press strives to use environmentally responsible suppliers and materials to the fullest extent possible in the publishing of its books. Such materials include vegetable-based, low-VOC inks and acid-free papers that are recycled, totally chlorine-free, or partly composed of nonwood fibers. For further information, visit our website at www.cornellpress.cornell.edu.

Cloth printing   10 9 8 7 6 5 4 3 2 1
Paperback printing   10 9 8 7 6 5 4 3 2 1

Contents

Preface

This is a book that began as a digression and quickly became an obsession. In early 2009, when I first traveled to southern Africa, I had originally planned comparative research on regional cooperation on migration in Africa. My intention had been to undertake a few elite policy interviews in Pretoria and Gaborone and then leave. But I got distracted by something more interesting and, frankly, more important.

I arrived in the region just after the peak of the mass influx of Zimbabweans from Robert Mugabe's rapidly collapsing state. Without the means to survive at home, hundreds of thousands of people were fleeing across the border into neighboring states. And yet, what was most striking was that despite their situation back home—where they faced economic collapse, famine, drought, and generalized violence—most were not recognized as refugees. They received almost no assistance from the government or international organizations and were frequently rounded up, detained, and deported.

Even though most arrived because they could not maintain the most basic conditions of life in their own country, they fell outside the boundaries of an international refugee framework, which generally defines a refugee as someone fleeing targeted persecution. Most of the Zimbabweans were fleeing very serious human rights deprivations, but only a small number faced targeted persecution that met the threshold of the refugee definition established by states after the Second World War. The UN refugee agency described the Zimbabweans as in a "neither/nor" situation, not refugees but not voluntary economic migrants either.

While I was in Johannesburg, I visited some of the main areas where Zimbabwean migrants were based. On one such visit, Elina Hankela, a Finnish volunteer doing PhD research, took me and my colleague, Esra Kaytaz, to the overcrowded Central Methodist Church in downtown Johannesburg, where some 3,400 Zimbabweans had spent many months living and organizing their community, despite constant attempts to evict them by the authorities.

At the church, among the people I spoke to was Michelle, a bright and articulate fifteen-year-old Zimbabwean girl who approached me and said, "A lot of people come here and ask us questions, but nobody ever does anything, and nothing changes. What are you going to do?" I explained that I was just a researcher and I would not be able to do very much. But I said that I would try to write something.

Four years later, this book is the best response I have to her question. It is too little and too late. It is, however, an attempt to make sense of what happened not only to Zimbabweans in South Africa but also to the many millions of people around the world who flee similarly serious human rights deprivations in failed and fragile states and yet fall outside the international refugee framework created in the aftermath of the Second World War.

Following my return from the region, it occurred to me that the situation of Zimbabweans in southern Africa was not unique but was part of a broader pattern. Across many African states—and others around the world—increasing numbers of people are fleeing serious rights deprivations in fragile and failed states rather than targeted persecution. Yet the international community has struggled to conceptualize such populations. In response to this conceptual challenge, "survival migration" was born, the term reflecting the language used by many of the people I interviewed. I spent the next two years researching survival migration in a range of other contexts across sub-Saharan Africa. I explored the situation of Zimbabweans in South Africa and Botswana, Congolese in Angola and Tanzania, and Somalis in Kenya and Yemen. My case selection reflects the variation in national and international responses across host states. Some offer protection for survival migrants as if they were refugees, and others do not. This inconsistency matters for its own sake, and it also poses an important puzzle for our understanding of international institutions: How is it that host states with the same or similar institutionalization of international norms relating to refugees could have such radically different practices in response to cross-border displacement?

In relation to each of the six cases, I therefore set out to explore three basic questions: (1) Why have people been leaving these fragile and failed states? (2) What national and international institutional responses have they encountered in the host country? and (3) What explains variation in these responses? My purpose in posing these questions has been both practical and academic. On one level, I have set out to highlight the situation of people fleeing serious rights deprivations that fall outside the refugee regime. On another, I have set out to explore a particular academic question: to understand how international institutions work in practice—when and why do international institutions adapt to new circumstances at national and local levels and when and why do they not?

This dual imperative, speaking simultaneously to policy and practice, on the one hand, and to academic debates in political science and international relations, on the other hand, is often a fine balance. I hope I have done both goals justice, not least because of the vast numbers of people who have assisted me in my work along the way. This has been a very ambitious project in both theoretical and empirical scope. It has taken me outward from my disciplinary comfort zone of international relations into comparative politics, political philosophy, law, and African studies. In doing so, I have ventured far beyond my own areas of expertise and research networks, and I am greatly indebted to the grace, goodwill, and patience of the many people who have assisted me.

This book would not have been possible without fieldwork and interviews, conducted in the Democratic Republic of Congo, Tanzania, South Africa, Botswana, Kenya, Ethiopia, Geneva, Brussels, and New York, as well as through numerous phone interviews and conversations. The work was possible only because of the logistical support of a number of international organizations and nongovernmental organizations (NGOs). Above all, the United Nations High Commissioner for Refugees (UNHCR) has put significant amounts of time and resources into enabling me to conduct this research, revealing itself once again to be extremely open to and supportive of the research community. Aside from the many UNHCR staff who responded to my questions, I am especially grateful for the support of Jeff Crisp, Ann Encontre, Geoffrey Carliez, Sanda Kimbimbi, Kamini Karleker, and Eveline Wolfcarius for facilitating my research. Médecins Sans Frontières–Belgium also provided significant support for my work, and I am especially indebted to Liesbeth Shockeart, Katherine Derderian, and Aurelie Ponthieu. Institutionally, I also received notable logistical assistance from the International Organization for Migration, the International Committee of the Red Cross, and a range of local NGOs including Ditshwanelo, Kituo Cha Shariya, and Lawyers for Human Rights.

The ideas in the book did not come prepackaged. Rather, they emerged as the outcome of debate, deliberation, and constant refinement. Many people played an important role. I am especially grateful to the participants in a September 2009 workshop in Oxford, who sat for a day and helped deconstruct and rebuild the concept of survival migration. My initial thoughts were subjected to a thorough workout in numerous public lectures and seminars at universities between 2009 and 2012, including Georgetown, Stanford, Oxford, University of Texas at Austin, Southern Methodist University, Sussex, and the Université Libre de Bruxelles. Different sections of the book were also presented at professional associations, including the New Orleans and Montreal meetings of the International Studies Association in 2010 and 2011 and the Kampala meeting of the International Association for the Study of Forced Migration in 2011.

I was privileged to benefit from the feedback and insights of policy audiences at the U.S. Department of State, the World Bank, the Canadian Department of Foreign Affairs and International Trade, and the Commonwealth Secretariat. All these presentations at universities, to governments, and at international organizations were possible thanks to people unlocking doors or extending invitations. In particular, I am grateful to Sarah Cross, Michael Bonser, Beth Mercurio, Kate Weaver, Jim Hollifield, Roli Degazon-Johnson, James Vreeland, Michael Collyer, Margarita Puerto Gomez, and Jean-Frederic Morin.

My home institution, the University of Oxford, played a central role in nurturing this project. The book is in many ways the product of my three different Oxford worlds—the Department of Politics and International Relations (DPIR), the Refugee Studies Centre (RSC), and the Global Economic Governance Programme (GEG), which has recently become part of the new Blavatnik School of Government. Colleagues in each of these contexts contributed to different aspects of the work. DPIR was a source of intellectual engagement on international relations theory, the RSC offered a unique environment for thinking through the empirical focus on refugees, and the GEG helped me develop a policy-oriented interest in international institutions. Across those institutions, I am immensely grateful to Andrew Hurrell, Jennifer Welsh, Noa Schonmann, Emily Paddon, Matthew Gibney, Gil Loescher, Jean-François Durieux, Ngaire Woods, and Devi Sridhar for having been a constant source of dialogue and inspiration. Other Oxford colleagues, notably Guy Goodwin-Gill, Nick Van Hear, Oliver Bakewell, David Anderson, and Hein de Haas, also generously offered their ideas and responses as the work evolved.

During my writing of the book, I was privileged to spend a year at Stanford University, at the Center for International Security and Cooperation at the Freeman Spogli Institute for International Studies. I cannot imagine a more idyllic base from which to write a book; it was a wonderful experience and I miss it every day. I am grateful to Lynn Eden, Mariano-Florentino Cuéllar, Scott Sagan, Steve Stedman, Eric Morris, Brenna Powell, and Steve Krasner for having been so generous with their time and comments on my work. I am also thankful to the students in my Stanford graduate class on refugees, migration, and security, who probably endured more survival migration than they bargained for. I am grateful to Kay Culpepper and Rob Ruether, who welcomed me into their home and became my adopted family while I wrote from Palo Alto, and to Erica Grieder for trying to teach me how to write and for being the biggest source of inspiration for just about everything I did during my year in America.

Away from Oxford and Stanford, a range of other people offered insightful and important comments and suggestions. I thank Erik Abild, Matthew Albert, Michael Barnett, Josh Busby, Ale Delano, Alan Gamlen, Kelly Greenhill, Jennifer Hyndman, Khalid Koser, Loren Landau, Anna Lindley, Katy Long, Susan Martin, Jane McAdam, James Milner, Dan Nexon, Calum Nicholson, Phil Orchard, Justin Pearce, Tara Polzer, Anna Schmidt, Andrew Shacknove, and Tamara Wood.

I also thank my brilliant DPhil students for being a constant source of inspiration through their work and ideas: Rebecca Brubaker, Georgia Cole, Erin Court, Francesca Giovannini, Nina Hall, Sarah Miller, Angela Pilath, Henning Tamm, and Clara Weinhardt.

Research on this scale is impossible without funding. This work would not have been possible without a generous grant from the John D. and Catherine T. MacArthur Foundation. I am especially grateful for the ongoing support of John Slocum and Milena Novy-Marx, who were extremely adaptable in allowing me to stretch the boundaries of the Global Migration Governance project to focus so much on the human rights dimensions of global migration governance in general, and survival migration in particular.

In addition to supporting field research and workshops, that funding enabled me to benefit from the work of a small group of research assistants, who have done an excellent job on a whole range of tasks: Shea Houlihan, Janosch Kullenberg, Patrycja Stys, Dominic Burbidge, and Kristina Sandesjo. Perhaps most important, I am immensely grateful to Esra Kaytaz, who, as Research Officer on the Global Migration Governance project and co-author of the original UNHCR policy paper on Zimbabwean survival migration, accompanied me on research trips to South Africa, Botswana, Kenya, Ethiopia, and Djibouti, and provided logistical support, ideas, and editing that directly helped shape this book. I must acknowledge my editor, Roger Haydon, for his outstanding work in nurturing this project from its inception. Finally, and just because I can, I want to thank my closest friends—Ben, Caroline, Andy, Mark, Emily, Wouter, Noa, Esra, Francesca, Calum, Anna, Laura—and my mum, Hilary, for being a constant source of support and welcome distraction.

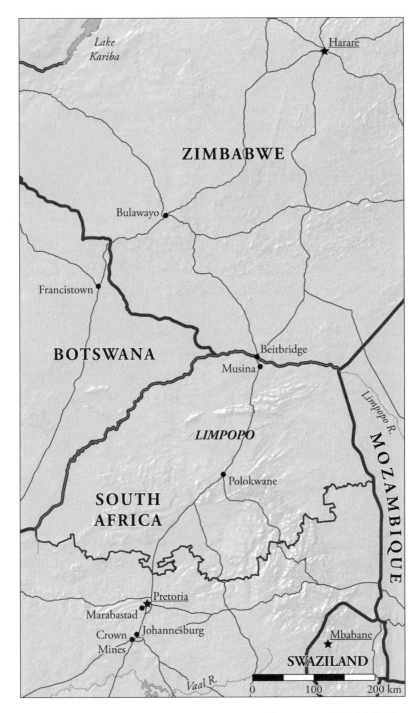

MAP 1. Zimbabwe–South Africa border region. Map prepared by Michael Borop, using road data courtesy of and © DeLorme.

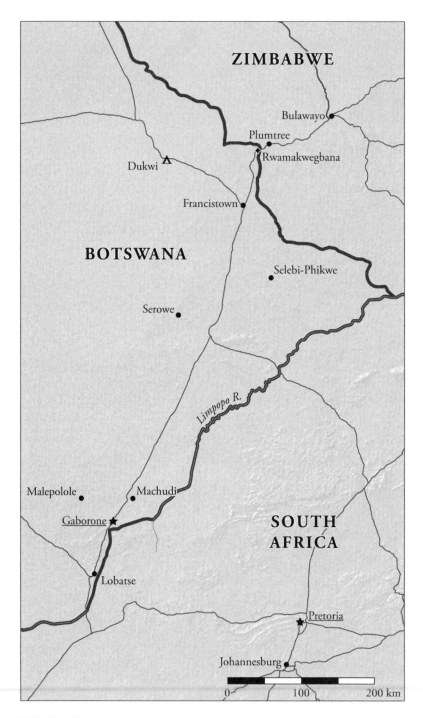

MAP 2. Zimbabwe-Botswana border region. Map prepared by Michael Borop, using road data courtesy of and © DeLorme.

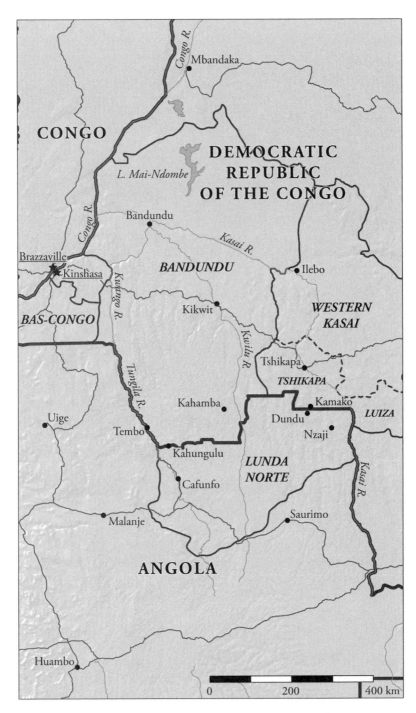

MAP 3. Democratic Republic of Congo–Angola border region. Map prepared by Michael Borop, using road data courtesy of and © DeLorme.

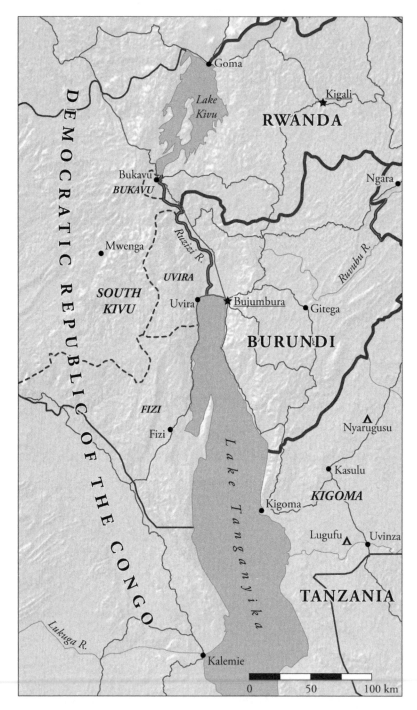

MAP 4. Democratic Republic of Congo–Tanzania border region. Map prepared by Michael Borop, using road data courtesy of and © DeLorme.

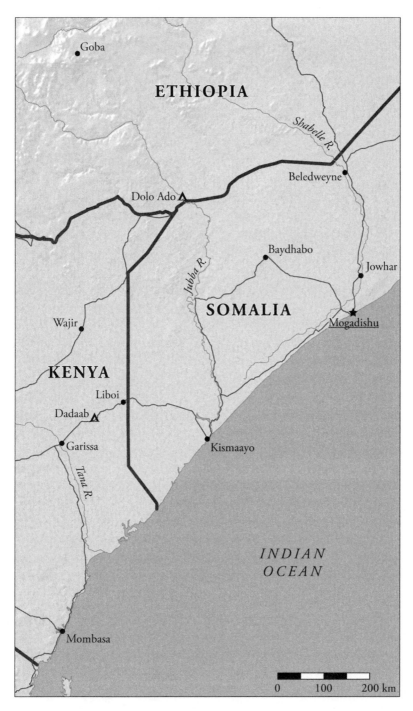

MAP 5. Somalia-Kenya border region. Map prepared by Michael Borop, using road data courtesy of and © DeLorme.

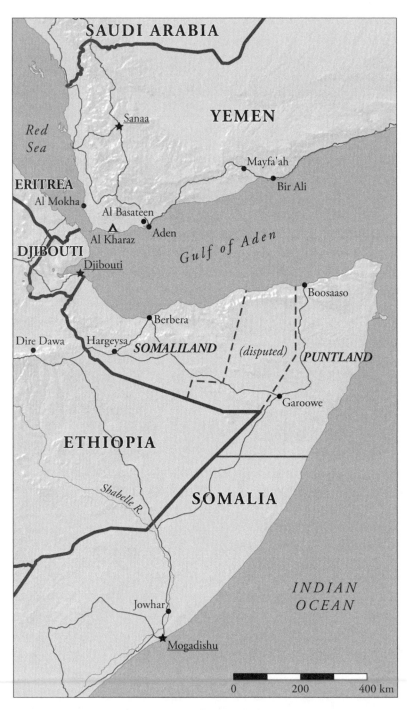

MAP 6. Somalia, Yemen, and the Gulf of Aden. Map prepared by Michael Borop, using road data courtesy of and © DeLorme.

SURVIVAL MIGRATION

Introduction

States are primarily responsible for ensuring the human rights of their own citizens. Sometimes, though, the assumed relationship between state and citizen breaks down and states are unable or unwilling to provide the rights of their citizens. Through malevolence, incompetence, or lack of capacity, many governments cease to ensure that their citizens have access to the fundamental conditions for human dignity. That people who cannot access basic human rights in their own country are entitled to run for their lives is widely recognized and accepted as an important part of what makes the international society of states both legitimate and civilized. It provides a valuable safeguard against the possibility that a government may turn against its own people, conflict may break out, a country's institutions may fail, famine or drought may strike, or a natural disaster may make the territory uninhabitable.

The international society of states created the international refugee regime to address the reality that some states fail to provide for the fundamental human rights of their citizens. The modern refugee regime was formalized in the aftermath of the Second World War, following the experience of the Holocaust.[1] To ensure that states would henceforth have a reciprocal obligation not to forcibly return refugees present on their territory, the international society of states created the 1951 Convention on the Status of Refugees to define refugees and their entitlements, and an international organization, the Office of the United Nations High Commissioner for Refugees (UNHCR), to oversee states' implementation of the convention (Haddad 2008; Loescher 2001). The purpose was to ensure that people who cannot get access to their most basic rights within their country of origin would have the right to flee their own country and seek access to those rights in another country.

Given the era and geographical context in which the modern refugee regime was created (post–Second World War Europe), "refugee"—and hence who qualified for access to asylum—was given a very specific meaning. The definition of a refugee was mainly limited to people fleeing targeted persecution by their own governments. Yet after the creation of the refugee regime in the 1950s, the circumstances that shape flight changed. New drivers of cross-border displacement emerged, especially outside Europe. Factors such as generalized violence, environmental change, and food insecurity—and their interaction—underpin a significant and growing proportion of cross-border displacement in many parts of the world. In strong states, people are able to seek remedy for these threats from their own governments. In states with weak governance, the only available means to acquire protection from these threats may be to leave the country. This opens up the question of who should be entitled to cross an international border on the grounds of human rights.

From Persecution to Deprivation

The creators of the refugee regime envisaged that the definition of a refugee would evolve over time, through either the jurisprudence of particular states or supplementary agreements. In some regions and states, the legal-institutional category of a refugee has partly expanded beyond its original focus on persecution. However, state practice has generally adapted much more slowly than the changing reality of cross-border displacement. While there has been a decline in the kinds of repressive or authoritarian states of the Cold War era, there has been an increase in the number of fragile states since the end of the Cold War. This trend means that fewer people are fleeing persecution resulting from the acts of states while more are fleeing human rights deprivations resulting from the omissions of weak states that are unable or unwilling to ensure fundamental rights. Yet although states' obligations to those fleeing persecution are based on a relatively high degree of legal precision, those relating to states' obligations to people fleeing deprivations are based on legal imprecision. The result is that while the former is characterized by relative consistency in host state practice,[2] the latter is characterized by inconsistency (see table 1).

The consequence is that many people who are forced or who feel forced to cross international borders today do not fit the categories built in 1951. Many people fleeing human rights deprivations in fragile or failed states such as Zimbabwe, Somalia, and the Democratic Republic of Congo in Africa—or Haiti,

TABLE 1.1   Contrasting causes of and responses to cross-border displacement resulting from persecution versus deprivation

	PERSECUTION	DEPRIVATION
State of Origin Role in Rights Violations	**Acts** (e.g., civil and political rights violations)	**Omissions** (e.g., inability or unwillingness to mitigate serious threats to human security)
Empirical Trend	**Declining number of repressive states** (e.g., Soviet Union)	**Growing number of fragile states** (e.g., Haiti, Libya)
Quality of Legal Protection	**Legal precision** (1951 Refugee Convention)	**Legal imprecision** (regional conventions; human rights law)
Host State Practices	**Consistency** (based mainly on law)	**Inconsistency** (based mainly on politics)

Afghanistan, and Libya elsewhere in the world—look very much like refugees and yet fall outside the definition of a refugee, often being denied protection. They are not fleeing state persecution, though many are fleeing state incompetence. They are not migrating for economic betterment, unless you call finding enough to eat an economic motive. Yet these people have no guaranteed source of international protection, and the help they desperately need is not clearly mandated by any institutional mechanism. The help they occasionally receive is patchy and inconsistent and unpredictable and, even at best, terribly inadequate. They are more likely to be rounded up, detained, and deported than to receive protection.

In theory, there are sources of law that might protect many of these people. In Africa, Latin America, and Europe supplementary regional conventions have been developed that expand the definition of a refugee. For example, the 1969 Organization of African Unity (OAU) Convention on Refugee Problems in Africa extends the definition to cover people fleeing external aggression, occupation, foreign domination, and events seriously disturbing public order (Goodwin-Gill and McAdam 2007, 37; Sharpe 2012). Likewise, international human rights law standards have gradually been recognized as a potential source of "complementary protection" to protect people fleeing desperate circumstances that fall outside the framework of the 1951 convention (McAdam 2007).[3] In practice, though, these supplementary standards are applied in a limited, regionally varied, and highly inconsistent way.

The gaps in protection for people fleeing very serious human rights deprivations in failed and fragile states matter for human rights. To take one prominent example explored in the book, large numbers of Zimbabweans fled Robert Mugabe's regime between 2000 and 2010. Although there are no precise statistics, it is estimated that around 2 million Zimbabweans entered South Africa alone during that period. They were fleeing a desperate situation of economic and political collapse, in which almost no viable livelihood opportunities existed to sustain even the most basic conditions of life. Yet because only a tiny minority has faced individualized persecution on political grounds, the overwhelming majority has fallen outside the definition of a refugee under the 1951 convention. Even though South Africa is a signatory of the OAU convention, which could have been applicable, it was not used in practice. Rather than receive protection, the majority have therefore received limited access to assistance in neighboring countries; instead, hundreds of thousands have been rounded up, detained, and deported back to Zimbabwe.

These protection gaps also matter for international security. We know from the refugee context, that there is a relationship between cross-border displacement and security, and that where international responses are inadequate, displacement can exacerbate conflict or create opportunities for recruitment by armed groups. In the 1950s, states' motivation for creating a refugee regime was not exclusively rights-focused. It was also based on the recognition that a collective failure to provide sanctuary to people whose own states were unwilling or unable to provide their most fundamental rights could have destabilizing effects. A similar logic applies to people fleeing serious rights deprivations. Without coherent collective action, forced population movements—not least from failed and fragile states—can have implications for regional security and the potential to create spillover effects for the entire international community (Greenhill 2010; Lischer 2005; Salehyan 2009).

Survival Migration

Part of the problem is that there is an analytical gap. Beyond identifying people as refugees or voluntary economic migrants, we lack a conceptual language to clearly identify people who should have an entitlement not to be returned to their country of origin on human rights grounds. Although a debate has emerged on new drivers of cross-border displacement and what they mean for protection, it has mainly focused on particular causes of displacement such as environmental change or climate change. However, an approach based on identifying and privileging particular causes risks repeating the same mistake of the refugee definition: focusing on causes rather than on the underlying threshold of rights, which when unavailable in the country of origin require border crossing as a last resort.

To highlight the situation of people fleeing basic rights deprivations rather than just persecution, I develop the concept of survival migration. It refers to people who are outside their country of origin because of an existential threat for which they have no access to a domestic remedy or resolution. The concept does not focus on a particular underlying cause of movement—whether persecution, conflict, or environment, for example. Instead, it is based on the recognition that what matters is not privileging particular causes of movement but rather clearly identifying a threshold of fundamental rights which, when unavailable in a country of origin, requires that the international community allow people to cross an international border and receive access to temporary or permanent sanctuary. Refugees are one type of survival migrant, but many people who are not recognized as refugees also fall within the category.

The gap in rights and entitlements available to refugees compared with survival migrants fleeing serious deprivations is arbitrary. In theory, all survival migrants have rights under international human rights law. In many cases, these rights amount to an entitlement not to be returned to the country of origin when this implies the deprivation of certain rights. Yet, in contrast to the case of refugees, institutional mechanisms do not exist to ensure that such rights are made available in practice. No international organization takes on formal responsibility for protecting people with a human rights–based entitlement not to be returned home if they fall outside the refugee definition.

The arbitrariness of distinguishing between persecution and other serious human rights deprivations as a cause of displacement is implicitly recognized in other areas of the practice of the international community. For example, since the late 1990s, states have developed a normative and institutional framework to protect internally displaced persons, often referred to as "internal refugees." Rather than limit the definition to those fleeing persecution, the international community chose a more inclusive and less arbitrary approach. People fleeing fundamental human rights deprivations resulting from state fragility, environmental change, and food insecurity within their own country have a recognized entitlement to receive international protection. Yet, in contrast, when people cross an international border, we continue to draw an arbitrary line in terms of the causes of rights deprivations that we believe matter—simply because of the contingency of history.

The concept of survival migration in this book serves to highlight the situation of people whose own countries are unable or unwilling to ensure their most fundamental human rights and yet who fall outside the framework of the refugee regime. The book explores the dimensions of the problem in the context of sub-Saharan Africa by looking at survival migration from three of the most fragile and failed states in the world: Somalia, Zimbabwe, and the Democratic Republic of Congo. It examines variation in national and international institutional responses in six different host states in the region of origin. In each case, it describes the underlying causes of survival migration in Africa and examines how states and the international community are currently responding. By doing so, it offers insights into how the international community can best respond to the human rights and security implications of survival migration.

Explaining Variation in Institutional Adaptation

The book examines six host country cases: Zimbabweans in South Africa and Botswana; Congolese in Angola and Tanzania; and Somalis in Kenya and Yemen. While the populations and the countries of origin have some variation, they have in common the central characteristic that matters for the analysis: they are all fleeing serious human rights deprivations that could be argued to make them nonreturnable (on either ethical or international human rights law grounds), and yet the majority fall outside the 1951 Refugee Convention. What is interesting, though, is that in spite of this commonality in the underlying causes of movement, the responses of host states to those populations have varied radically—across the populations and even toward the same populations. All the responses have been imperfect from a human rights perspective, but some have been far more imperfect than others.

Africa has been chosen as the main focus because it is the continent that arguably faces the greatest level of survival migration that falls outside the 1951 convention. Selecting countries of origin and host states from broadly the same region also helps to hold a number of factors constant while introducing some controlled variation. For example, all six states have signed and ratified the 1951 convention and incorporated it into domestic law or policy. Four of the six states have signed and ratified a supplementary regional refugee convention, the 1969 OAU convention, the exceptions being Botswana and Yemen (because it is outside Africa). While that convention has particular relevance to survival migration because of a clause on "events seriously disturbing public order," it has generally been avoided, and with the exception of Kenya, the OAU convention is rarely invoked in practice. In practice, then, the states have broadly similar levels of adoption of legal standards relating to refugee protection.

In some cases, the refugee regime has "stretched" to provide protection to survival migrants. The six host countries have been chosen because they exhibit variation in the regime stretching that this book is trying to explain. Two of the countries (Tanzania and Kenya) represent cases of regime stretching, two represent nonstretching (Angola and Botswana), and two represent an intermediate response (South Africa and Yemen). What is puzzling about the cases is that despite all the host states having adopted, signed, and ratified broadly similar refugee norms, there is significant variation in what happens in practice. This is an observation that existing top-down approaches to international institutions struggle to explain. The book therefore seeks to explain this variation in practice: why is it that in some cases national refugee regimes stretch to protect survival migrants and others do not?

The question matters for thinking about survival migration because it tells us whether—and if so, to what extent—the existing refugee regime can adapt to survival migration or, alternatively, whether more formal renegotiation of the international regime is required. If we can understand the causal mechanisms through which international institutions adapt at the national level, then this may empower international public policymakers to close protection gaps without fundamental institutional reform.

The question also matters because it tells us something more general about how international institutions work in practice. Rather than look at international institutions as abstract top-down entities that exist exclusively in Geneva or New York, as international relations scholars tend to do, I explore the refugee regime from a bottom-up perspective, examining what the refugee regime means and how it varies in particular national contexts. In looking at this question, I show how and why international institutions sometimes adapt—and sometimes do not adapt—to new challenges at the national level.

By taking this approach, the book situates itself in a broader research agenda relating to the national politics of international institutions (Acharya 2004; Checkel 1997, 1999; Cortell and Davis 2000; Diehl, Ku, and Zamora 2003; Simmons 2009; Weiner 2009). Some of these ideas have been applied to some extent to the context of forced displacement in the work of Anna Schmidt (2006) on how global refugee norms translate into national and local refugee status determination practices in Uganda and Tanzania and the work of Phil Orchard (2013) on how global IDP norms translate into practice in Uganda and Nepal.

I take the existing work on the national politics of international institutions in a different direction by focusing on the national and local dynamics of international institutional adaptation—in terms of both the norms and the international organizations that make up an international regime. These national and local dynamics of international institutional adaptation have yet to be explored in the existing literature on institutional change, in which the temporal dynamics of change are generally privileged over the spatial dynamics of change (Blyth 2002; Hall and Thelen 2009; Mahoney and Thelen 2010; Pierson 2004; Koremenos et al. 2001).

Methodology

In order to explore these questions, I draw on a methodology that attempts to strike a middle ground between in-depth fieldwork and multicountry comparative analysis. On the one hand, international relations research has conventionally been based on remote methodologies such as secondary data or archival investigation. The benefit of this approach is that it allows rigorous quantitative or qualitative analysis beyond single case study analysis. The limitation is that it has often precluded engaging in research in contexts—such as Africa—in which data may be patchy or limited. On the other hand, in response to the recognition that some of these armchair methodologies may be too remote to acquire empirical depth, some scholars have engaged in what might be considered an ethnographic turn in international relations methodology, using a combination of participant observation and semi-structured interviews to acquire greater granularity and more in-depth empirical insights (Vrasti 2008). Fieldwork, long embraced by other social sciences, has become an increasingly common part of international relations research.

This embryonic ethnographic turn in the study of world politics has particular potential for the study of international institutions, at both the global and local levels (Autesserre 2010; Hopgood 2006). However, one of the challenges with such ethnographic work is how to move beyond single case studies and draw the benefits of in-depth fieldwork into comparative analysis. This book is an attempt to strike a balance between the in-depth ethnographic work of, for example, Severine Autesserre (2010) on the politics of peace-building in the Democratic Republic of Congo and the desire within mainstream international relations for rigorous, multicountry comparative analysis.

The book is based mainly on fieldwork in Africa. It uses a combination of participant observation and semi-structured interviews with representatives of states, international organizations, and nongovernmental organizations (NGOs), and with migrants and refugees. It draws on data gathered during numerous short fieldwork visits of ten days to three weeks in the relevant host countries of asylum in the region, mainly during 2009 and 2010. Fieldwork was conducted in South Africa, Botswana, Tanzania, Democratic Republic of Congo, Kenya, Ethiopia, and Djibouti; further interviews relating to Yemen and Angola were conducted by telephone (due to restrictions on access and safety); and additional interviews were conducted in Brussels, Geneva, and New York.

Main Argument

My central argument is that, in the absence of legal precision, there is massive inconsistency in how states respond to survival migrants fleeing serious human rights deprivations. In some contexts people fleeing similarly severe thresholds of rights deprivations may be protected as though they were refugees; in others they may be rounded up, detained, and deported. This inconsistency, as well as being arbitrary from a normative perspective, has serious human rights and security implications.

To explain this inconsistency, I offer an interest-based account of variation in national and international institutional responses. I argue that what determines whether the refugee regime stretches to protect survival migrants is not variation in how legal norms are incorporated in particular states but whether doing so is ultimately in the interests of elites within the host state government. This in turn depends on the set of incentives for inclusion or exclusion that emerge from the domestic and international level. Where there are positive incentives on elites, the regime will stretch. Where there are negative incentives on elites, the regime will not stretch. In other words, in the absence of precision in international law, incentives matter for determining whether or not the regime adapts at the national level.

This argument has important implications for theory and for international public policymakers interested in influencing the national politics of international institutions. It tells us that there is a national politics of international institutions, in which the very meaning of international norms and the work of international organizations are often recontested and may adapt based on national politics. Far from just being a distortion, these processes of adaptation may represent an opportunity. By understanding the mechanisms through which international institutions adapt at the national level, public policymakers may be better placed to influence outcomes at the national level. Even when international institutions cannot be renegotiated at the global level, there may be alternative options for improving how old international institutions adapt to emerging challenges at the national level.

SURVIVAL MIGRATION

In the context of the changing nature of forced displacement, who should have an entitlement to cross an international border and seek asylum? Given that the refugee regime was a product of its time and mainly provides protection to only a narrow group of people fleeing targeted persecution, how can we conceptualize the broader category of people who today cross an international border and are in need of protection because of serious human rights deprivations? If "refugee" is a legal-institutional category defined by state practice, how can we stand apart from that and render visible the situation of the many millions of people crossing borders in failed and fragile states such as Zimbabwe, Democratic Republic of Congo, and Somalia, people who are often in desperate need of protection and yet frequently fall outside the refugee framework? Should these people also be entitled to asylum? In order to address these questions, this chapter sets out the core concept of survival migration on which this book is based. It is intended to serve as both a conceptual category for highlighting the situation of people fleeing desperate situations that fall outside the dominant legal interpretation of who is a refugee, and a normative framework for thinking about who should be entitled to asylum in a changing world.

The Purpose of Refugee Protection

Since the Peace of Westphalia in 1648 divided Europe into clearly bounded religious and administrative units, the nation-state has become the dominant unit of collective organization. State sovereignty is the main organizing principle in world politics. The legitimacy of this system comes from the belief that states are able to uphold the rights of their citizens. Today this is recognized in the idea that states have ultimate responsibility for ensuring the human rights of their own citizens. By ensuring that everyone in the world has membership in a state that guarantees his or her access to these rights, the state system represents a legitimate and valid way of ensuring human welfare.

Occasionally, however, this state system breaks down and fails to live up to the assumed ideal of a seamless nexus between state, citizen, and territory in which people can live in dignity and get access to their fundamental human rights (Haddad 2008, 47–69). Sometimes states are unable to guarantee the human rights of their own citizens (as in Somalia). This may be due to a lack of state capacity or because of conflict or a serious natural or man-made disaster. In other cases, states are simply unwilling to guarantee the rights of citizens, as when an authoritarian or dictatorial government seizes control of a country (for example, North Korea).

International protection is intended to ensure that even when this kind of malfunction takes place, people can have their fundamental human rights respected (Martin 2010). The idea is contested but generally refers to "all activities aimed at respecting the rights of the individual in accordance with the letter and spirit of all relevant bodies of law, including international humanitarian law, international human rights law, or international refugee law."[1] The basic idea is that when a state fails its citizens, a substitute provider of rights can stand in, and responsibility transfers to the international community or to another state or group of states.[2]

Asylum is part of international protection (Goodwin-Gill and McAdam 2007, 355–417). One of the principal ways in which people in states unable or unwilling to ensure their human rights can access protection is by crossing an international border. In doing so, a person has access to a state that has assumed international obligations, enabling that state to serve as the substitute provider of rights. Asylum is a mechanism for providing international protection insofar as it creates a norm that states will not forcibly return people who are in need of protection—at least until the country of origin is willing and able to resume responsibility for guaranteeing that person's most fundamental human rights.

Using asylum to enable people to access substitute protection serves as the basic logic underlying the international refugee regime. Where a country of origin is unable or unwilling to provide certain entitlements, the refugee regime theoretically presents a uniform and reciprocal basis on which other states identify those people and the rights to which they are entitled. Most fundamentally, it guarantees the right not to be forcibly returned to any state where he or she will be at risk of persecution. Reflecting its role as a corrective to the inevitable limitations of that system, the refugee regime has evolved in a dialectical relationship with the state system (Haddad 2008). Beginning in 1648, as people fled religious intolerance, revolutions, and state formation, an informal conception of asylum emerged in Europe. With the collapse of European empires following the First World War, a more formalized system was created as part of the League of Nations (Skran 1995). And finally, the modern global refugee regime emerged after the Second World War in order to guarantee that people fleeing desperate situations would henceforth have a right to seek international protection and asylum (Loescher 2001). The refugee regime as we know it was created as a safeguard against the inevitable limitations of the state system, to ensure that even when someone's own state was unwilling or unable to provide most of its citizens' most basic rights, there would be an alternative provider of those rights.

Limitations of the Existing Refugee Framework

The modern refugee regime is a product of its time. Today the regime only partly fulfills its underlying function. It protects people who flee the kinds of situations that required international protection and asylum in Europe in the 1940s and 1950s: targeted persecution by governments and by non-state actors when governments turn a blind eye. But it does very little to ensure that substitute protection is available in the kinds of situations that many people in the developing world flee today.

The modern refugee regime has two core elements: a multilateral treaty (the 1951 Convention on the Status of Refugees) and an international organization, the Office of the United Nations High Commissioner for Refugees (UNHCR). The convention defines who is a refugee and the rights to which people in that category are entitled and hence also the obligations that signatory states have toward refugees on their territory. The core norm within the convention is *nonrefoulement*—the idea that states cannot forcibly return a refugee to his or her country of origin and should instead provide sanctuary to that person in the form of asylum, at least until a viable long-term solution can be found. UNHCR's role—as set out in its 1950 statute—has been primarily to oversee and support states' ratification and implementation of the 1951 convention.

This regime was created for a particular era and geographical context. It was designed to protect people who fall into this narrow definition of who is a refugee—as a person who "owing to a well-founded fear of being persecuted for reasons of race, religion, nationality, membership of a particular social group or political opinion, is outside the country of his nationality and is unable or,

owing to such fear unwilling to avail himself of the protection of that country"—
a definition that was intended to fit with the circumstances of displacement in
postwar Europe.[3] Consequently, the scope of the convention was originally limited to events prior to 1951 and many of the signatory states chose to adopt
a geographical limitation on the treaty, effectively confining its initial scope to
Europe. Its creators did not anticipate that its obligations would be spread to the
rest of the world. In fact, UNHCR's own role was originally intended by the UN
General Assembly to be time-limited, in anticipation that the refugee problem in
Europe would eventually be resolved.

During the Cold War, however, the refugee regime proved to be relevant and
politically expedient for Europe and the United States. It served to discredit Communist regimes by enabling those fleeing from East to West to "vote with their
feet." This led states to support an extended mandate for UNHCR and to expand
its work. Furthermore, as refugee challenges began to emerge in other parts of the
world, the UN General Assembly decided to expand the geographical scope of the
convention to the rest of the world through a protocol to the convention in 1967.
A treaty created for Europe was suddenly meant to cover the world.

The people who drafted the 1951 convention had envisaged that change would
be needed over time. They foresaw a "living" regime, capable of adaptation and
interpretation in context (Goodwin-Gill and McAdam 2007, 74). Rather than
being indefinitely fixed, the meaning of a refugee was intended by the convention
drafters to be something organic that could evolve over time if necessary, through
the jurisprudence and decision making of national courts or supplementary international agreements. In different countries and regions, the precise meaning
of a refugee therefore varies, and some countries have adopted more open or
restrictive interpretations than others. Yet although the definition of a refugee
has evolved, it has generally adapted conservatively and slowly. In practice, the
dominant interpretation has remained closely aligned to the 1951 convention's
focus on persecution. As a result, access to asylum has been decided primarily on
whether or not a person has been actively pursued by a malevolent or persecuting government.

The problem with this definition is that it simply ignores many of the drivers
of cross-border displacement in most of the developing world. Many people are
in exile for reasons that are not reducible to individualized—or even group—
persecution, and as a result they are denied access to international protection for
reasons that are arguably arbitrary. This is nothing new—the refugee definition
has for a long time left out many desperate people. But it is a problem that has
renewed salience through growing recognition of new drivers of cross-border
displacement, notably the complex interaction of factors such as environmental change, natural disaster, food insecurity, famine and drought, state fragility,

and collapse of livelihoods. All these can contribute to situations in which cross-border movement is the only available recourse and yet they all fall outside the 1951 refugee definition. Put most simply, the existing regime privileges asylum for people fleeing targeted persecution by governments over and above those fleeing other serious human rights deprivations, even where people may suffer the same threshold of underlying rights violations (Foster 2009, 5–20). This arbitrariness has major implications for human rights. It is increasingly acknowledged but has yet to attract a sustained and rigorous debate on what should be done to fill the gap.

States have been gradually trying to fill some of these gaps, but they have been doing so in very particular rather than overarching ways. In practice, the refugee regime has adapted in some geographical contexts to better fit today's circumstances. Sources of "complementary protection" have emerged to address the gray area between the extremes of "voluntary economic migrant" and "refugee" (McAdam 2006). The two main examples are regional normative frameworks and international human rights law treaties. Both, however, have enormous limitations—in terms of geographical scope, normative coverage, and implementation.

First, at the regional level, the 1969 Organization of African Unity (OAU) Convention on Refugee Problems in Africa incorporates people fleeing "external aggression, occupation, foreign domination or events seriously disturbing public order."[4] The 1984 Cartagena Declaration for Latin America incorporates people "fleeing generalized violence, foreign aggression, internal conflicts, massive violation of human rights or other circumstances which have seriously disturbed public order."[5] The 2004 European Union Asylum Qualification Directive provides subsidiary protection to people fleeing "serious harm," which consists of (a) death penalty or execution, (b) torture or inhuman or degrading treatment or punishment of an applicant in the country of origin, or (c) serious and individual threat to a civilian's life or person by reason of indiscriminate violence in situations of international or internal armed conflict.[6] However, these three supplementary conventions have major limitations, even beyond their confined geographical scope. The African and Latin American conventions, although incorporated in national legislation, are often not applied in practice. The coverage for the potentially broader "events seriously disturbing public order" has almost never been invoked, and UNHCR remains reluctant to use it as a basis for recognition. Meanwhile, the Europe Union directive mainly serves to ensure that people who may not be refugees but face extreme forms of inhuman or degrading treatment are not forcibly returned, rather than to significantly expand the availability of protection to a much broader category of people.

Second, aspects of international human rights law have been applied to address the protection needs of people who may fall outside the 1951 convention but may be nonreturnable to their country of origin. A range of jurisprudence has emerged, drawing notably on the European Convention on Human Rights (ECHR), the American Convention on Human Rights (ACHR), and the Convention against Torture (CAT). The most high-profile cases have found that those who are not covered by international refugee law may nevertheless be entitled to international protection if they face, for example, the prospect of torture or cruel, inhuman, and degrading treatment on their return.[7]

Despite its potential, complementary protection derived from international human rights law remains limited in its scope and application. First, its jurisprudence has been limited to the right to life and to situations in which people will face torture or inhuman and degrading treatment on return. Second, its application remains regional; most jurisprudence has emerged in the ECHR and ACHR regions, having almost no application to the African context, for example. Third, its application to economic and social rights has been limited and so this jurisprudence tends to exclude economic and environmental causes of flight (Foster 2009).[8] While complementary protection, along with jurisprudence by particular states and particular regions, fills some of the gaps, it represents an inadequate response to the scale of the problem.

New Drivers of Displacement

States still generally view people who cross international borders as being 1951 convention refugees or voluntary economic migrants (Richmond 1993). Yet there is growing recognition of new drivers of cross-border displacement. In recent years, UNHCR has begun a debate about the complexities of protection in the context of migration, at different times subsuming the debate under labels such as the "asylum-migration nexus," "mixed migration," and "migration and refugee protection" (Crisp 2008). This debate has partly considered how to protect refugees in the context of wider migratory flows, given that many asylum seekers now use the same routes as other migrants. The same debate has also begun to recognize groups of people in need of asylum and international protection who may fall outside the refugee framework. These new drivers, increasingly recognized in public debates, include environmental change, food insecurity, and state fragility.[9]

However, the current debate on some of the new drivers risks missing the point. Although it is perfectly possible to highlight a range of emerging proximate causes of displacement that are excluded by the current refugee framework, it is important that those emerging causes are interpreted appropriately in relation to the broader question of who should be entitled to asylum. In particular, two problems arise with focusing in isolation on any specific new driver.

First, *attribution*: in many cases it will be challenging to assign movement to a single cause. Migration decisions are complex, and proximate causes of movement will often be hard to isolate. In some cases of acute crisis with sudden onset, the most proximate cause of movement may be discernible, but with more chronic, structural challenges, there is likely to be complex causality based on the interaction of a range of proximate causes. Second, *relevance*: if the aim is to identify who should be entitled to asylum, then isolating a particular cause of movement is unimportant. What should matter for allocating asylum is not identifying and privileging any particular proximate cause of movement but rather the underlying threshold of rights that, when unavailable in the country of origin, necessitate border crossing as a last resort.

Environmental Change

The most widely discussed new driver of displacement is climate change. As the global discussion of climate change has shifted from an exclusive focus on mitigation toward adaptation, it has incorporated a debate on the humanitarian and migration implications.[10] Academics, policymakers, and the media have made suggestions about the impact of environmental change on cross-border displacement, and the creation of so-called climate change refugees or environmentally displaced people. The literature on environmental migration divides between those who make alarmist claims about the migratory implications of climate change (Myers 1993, 1997, 2005; Myers and Kent 1995) and those who are more skeptical about attributing causality for migration directly to environmental factors, let alone climate change (Black 2001; Brown 2008; Castles 2002; Kibreab 1994, 1997; Suhrke 1994). In either case, though, it is clear that rapid-onset and slow-onset environmental change will have human consequences, including for the choices people make in terms of their mobility within states and across international borders.

Nevertheless, in looking at the new drivers of displacement, we must broaden our view beyond just environmental displacement. There are two reasons why it would be a mistake to focus narrowly on environmental displacement: it is rarely possible to attribute cross-border displacement exclusively to an environmental cause, and it is not desirable to allocate access to asylum on the basis of a singular cause of movement.

First, most cross-border displacement connected to environmental change will not be easy to attribute solely to environmental change, let alone climate change. While it may be possible to infer a significant environmental role in extreme cases of "sinking islands" (which will require resettlement) or rapid-onset natural disasters (which are more likely to require in-country humanitarian assistance), the kind of slow-onset environmental change that is likely to result in cross-border displacement will rarely be attributable to a single causal factor. Rather, it will in nearly all cases be mediated through the complex interaction of environmental change with other factors such as livelihoods collapse and state fragility (Betts 2010a; Boano, Zetter, and Morris 2008; Gemenne 2009; Martin 2010; McAdam 2012; Piguet 2008).

Second, and more important, it is arbitrary to allocate asylum based on the underlying causes of movement, whether environmental or otherwise. Instead, it makes more sense to focus not on causes but on the underlying rights that are not available in the country of origin and so can be restituted only in another state—irrespective of what the underlying cause may be. Whether someone's displacement is predominantly attributable to environmental change, state fragility, or livelihoods collapse is unimportant from a human rights perspective. What matters is whether certain sets of fundamental rights are not available in the country of origin.

Food Insecurity

According to the Food and Agricultural Organization (FAO), nearly 1 billion people around the world are chronically hungry due to extreme poverty, and up to 2 billion people lack food security intermittently due to varying degrees of poverty. This frequently contributes to chronic or acute malnutrition, often with significant health consequences. Whether alone or in interaction with other factors such as dictatorship, environmental change, and state fragility, food insecurity can be a significant cause of displacement. Zimbabwe is an example of a country in which famine, drought, sanctions, and political instability have contributed to chronic food insecurity in ways that have impelled large numbers of people to cross international borders in search of livelihood opportunities. In the Horn of Africa, the 2011 famine and drought led more than half a million Somalis to flee their country.

Historically, however, international protection has rarely been provided to people fleeing across borders for reasons predominantly relating to food insecurity or the absence of livelihood opportunities. Refugee protection has been based mainly on protecting people's civil and political rights rather than their economic and social rights (Price 2009). Yet from a human rights law perspective, one can argue that this is an arbitrary distinction because, beyond a certain threshold, those fleeing food insecurity will be equally in need of international protection (Foster 2009). Similarly, from an ethical perspective, those fleeing the absence of basic liberty or basic security cannot be privileged over those fleeing the absence of basic subsistence, since all represent "rights without which it is impossible to enjoy any other rights" (Shue 1980; Shacknove 1985).

This challenge is not a new one, but it is likely to be exacerbated by the interaction of food insecurity and livelihoods collapse, on the one hand, with environmental change and state fragility, on the other. The current delineation of refugee/migrant is based partly on a political/economic distinction in underlying motives, but there are many situations in which large-scale deprivations of economic and social rights—in Zimbabwe, for example—can be understood as economic consequences of an underlying political situation.

State Fragility

In most cases, however, what ultimately determines whether factors such as environmental change and food insecurity—and their complex interaction—necessitate cross-border movement is the quality of governance in a country. Strong governments will have the means to provide domestic remedy or resolution for a whole variety of threats to human security. People will be able to get access to their most fundamental rights without needing to leave the country. In states with weak governance, in which the most fundamental institutions of government have collapsed and neither property rights nor the judiciary function, domestic remedy or resolution may simply be unavailable, and so movement across an international border may be the only means for people to access fundamental rights necessary for survival.

The designation of states as "fragile" or "failed" is often criticized for lacking clarity, encompassing a disparate variety of situations, and being an overused political label that measures states against idealized Western standards of governance (Patrick 2011, 19–21). However, it highlights an emerging trend in weak states in developing countries. Fragility is often measured by a range of indicators of weak governance. The Fund for Peace's Failed State Index, for example, ranks states according to a variety of social, political, and economic indicators, highlighting Somalia, Zimbabwe, Chad, Sudan, and the Democratic Republic of Congo (DRC) as the world's most failed states. Stewart Patrick (2011, 51) ranks Somalia, Afghanistan, the DRC, Iraq, and Burundi as the top five weak states.

Patrick (2011) shows how failed states matter because of the implications they have not only for the welfare of their own citizens but for transnational security. He highlights how fragility correlates strongly with gross human rights abuses and refugee movements (2011, 46). Yet the 1951 Refugee Convention did not envisage state fragility to be a significant cause of external displacement. While the "events seriously disturbing public order" aspect of the OAU Refugee Convention may be argued to cover aspects of state fragility as a cause of cross-border displacement, its patchy use and weak jurisprudence continue to make its application to fragile states ambiguous and unreliable.

Recognizing state fragility as the most important underlying source of new drivers of cross-border displacement is crucial to the future of the refugee protection regime. Ultimately, it will not be factors such as environmental change that drive cross-border displacement and international protection but rather the governance capacity of particular states to domestically respond to those threats.[11] However, state fragility poses a conceptual challenge to the refugee regime. In addition to protecting people fleeing the acts of states against their own populations, the refugee regime must also protect people fleeing the omissions of states, whether due to the unwillingness or the inability to provide for their citizens' most fundamental human rights (Foster 2009; Martin 2010).

Beyond Arbitrary Causality

Recognition of the emergence of new drivers of cross-border displacement poses a dual challenge: to conceptually make sense of contemporary patterns of displacement and to normatively consider the basis on which asylum should be granted. As it stands, debate on how to respond to the emergence of new drivers of displacement is falling into an analytical trap of privileging particular causes of displacement. A central contention of this book is that the allocation of asylum should be based not on privileging particular causes of displacement—whether old or new—but rather on the underlying threshold of human rights, which when not available in the country of origin are available only through crossing an international border. The arbitrary privileging of particular causes of rights deprivation and displacement underlies both the existing refugee regime and current attempts to grapple with the new drivers of displacement.

Weak governance and state fragility are a qualitatively different kind of driver of forced displacement than other causes. Unlike, say, environmental change or food insecurity, state fragility creates the conditions under which wider threats come to be relevant to asylum. Where strong governance exists, people are usually able to seek domestic remedy or resolution for those threats. However, in chronically weak states, with governments that are unable or unwilling to ensure even the most fundamental rights, wider sets of threats may lead to very severe levels of rights deprivation that simply cannot be met without—as a last resort—leaving the country. Weak governance is the filter through which all other sources of rights deprivation beyond persecution do or do not become relevant to asylum.

Yet while there is relative legal precision relating to people fleeing persecution, there is legal imprecision relating to people fleeing deprivations. The 1951 convention offers a relatively unambiguous source of protection to people fleeing persecution. In contrast, sources of protection in international law for those fleeing rights deprivations are less clearly defined and more contested. This means that people fleeing deprivations rather than persecution, the omissions rather than the acts of states, and humanitarian rather than clearly political causes, are less likely to get access to protection. They may be fleeing the same underlying rights violations, but the different proximate causes will shape the response of host states and international institutions. While international law at least offers some clarity on flight from persecution, the relative legal ambiguity in relation to flight from deprivation means that politics rather than law determines what happens to many desperate people with severe rights deprivations in fragile and failed states.

This recognition opens up the question of whether or not asylum should be available to people fleeing very serious human rights deprivations as well as those fleeing targeted persecution. Is the distinction arbitrary or does it have a valid normative basis? Matthew Price (2009) and James Hathaway (1997) are among the most prominent authors to defend the privileging of persecution as grounds for asylum. Price (2009) argues against widening who should qualify for asylum beyond those fleeing persecution. He suggests that persecution has a particular status because those who are specifically victimized or pursued by their own governments are in a normatively distinct position from those fleeing wider sets of deprivations caused by, for example, poverty or insecurity. His distinction rests on two core claims.

First, he argues that asylum has a particular meaning, being closely related to citizenship and providing surrogate political membership. For Price, people fleeing persecution need a form of membership because of the way in which discriminatory targeting by the state leads to severance of political membership. Price does not deny that other people fleeing other forms of human rights deprivations could still be entitled to assistance from other forms of humanitarian aid including temporary forms of protection and access to territory. Indeed, he is correct to observe that different groups of people fleeing different rights deprivations will obviously have different needs. Of course this is the case; someone fleeing torture will have different needs than someone fleeing a large-scale famine. However, if one conceives of asylum more broadly than Price, not as a form of political membership related to citizenship but simply as access to territory and juridical status on human rights grounds, then the privileged status of persecution over deprivations begins to look rather more arbitrary.

From an individual's perspective, whether one's source of human rights deprivation comes from a persecuting state or another source makes no difference. If one cannot survive or maintain the fundamental conditions of human dignity without leaving a country, then distinguishing between persecution and other causes is normatively meaningless. Whether the fundamental human rights deprivation comes from acts or omissions by the state does not change the implications it has for an individual's access to rights. The only thing that matters is that a particular threshold of human rights is unavailable in the country of origin and the only means to access them is to cross an international border and seek territorial asylum.

Second, his argument rests on a claim about the nature of severance in the relationship between state and citizen that arises from persecution. Price suggests that persecution represents a particular form of severing of the state-citizen relationship and so—unlike other categories of rights deprivation—requires a form of surrogate political membership. However, this view is based on implicit distinctions between violations and deprivation, acts and omissions, and civil and political and socioeconomic rights. Irrespective of whether a state actually engages in persecution, it may—through inability or unwillingness to positively provide the minimum conditions for life—undermine the assumed relationship between state and citizen. Indeed, if one holds a conception of the state as having positive as well as negative obligations toward its citizens (however minimalist), then temporary or permanent surrogate protection may equally be required for those fleeing serious human rights deprivations for which there are no domestic alternatives.

Yet because weak governance tends to lead to omissions as well as acts, deprivations in addition to violations, and socioeconomic abuses as much as civil and political abuses, many of the sources of the human rights–related reasons for flight fall outside the persecution focus of the 1951 convention. This is an arbitrary distinction because the inability or unwillingness of a state to safeguard certain fundamental human rights can be just as much of a severance of the relationship between citizen and state as persecution. What should matter is not privileging any particular cause of displacement but rather focusing on the particular threshold of human rights which, when unavailable in the country of origin, necessitates substitute protection in another state.

Hathaway (1997) presents a slightly different defense of the persecutory bias of the status quo. His argument is based on the claim that any attempt to expand the entitlement to asylum would risk undermining the refugee regime. Given his observation that states are increasingly reluctant to provide asylum or admit immigrants onto their territory, he argues that it makes sense to safeguard the status quo rather than risk expanding in ways that might undermine protection for all.

There are a number of problems with Hathaway's position. First, it risks confusing "is" with "ought." While criticality requires an element of feasibility, recognizing that something would be politically challenging to achieve is not the same thing as arguing that it is not the right thing to do. Even if Hathaway's preservationist argument is based on an underlying recognition that asylum is a finite commodity and there are limits to how many people states can admit onto their territory, his argument does not offer a compelling reason why the line should be drawn where it currently is and why persecution should always trump deprivation.

Second, the argument is based on the claim that we already have a legal framework relating to one group but not the other. Yet in reality, people fleeing persecution and people fleeing serious human rights deprivations both have rights under current international law. People fleeing serious rights deprivations have rights under international human rights law, even if they fall outside the framework of international refugee law. While the jurisprudence on the application of international human rights law to *non-refoulement* may be underdeveloped, the human rights that those fleeing deprivations have qua human beings are every bit as much a part of the status quo as international refugee law (Foster 2009).

The Need for a New Concept

It has been argued that the distinction between persecution and other sources of serious human rights deprivations is arbitrary as normative grounds for asylum. There is a strong case for grouping people fleeing persecution and people fleeing serious human rights deprivations under a single label. This leaves us with a choice. We would need either to radically change the scope of the old term—refugee—or to introduce a new term. There are good arguments for expanding the scope of the refugee concept. International refugee law was conceived to be adaptable and has in some jurisdictions begun to expand to include some people fleeing certain forms of rights deprivations other than persecution. There is no logical reason why, over time, jurisprudence could not expand to include all categories of people fleeing the most serious human rights deprivations. However, the reality is that jurisprudence is expanding slowly and the concept of refugee is a legal-institutional category, the boundaries of which are defined by state practice.

This book therefore chooses to adopt a new term for the broader category of people who should have a normative entitlement to asylum based on human rights grounds. It does so in order to render visible a population that is not currently recognized as refugees within the dominant interpretation of a refugee in international law, and yet are outside their country of origin because of a very serious threshold of human rights deprivations. Furthermore, there is an additional logic to introducing a new term if it offers a normative benchmark against which to assess the predominantly legal-institutional category of refugee.

The idea that people fall between the gaps of the dichotomy between refugee and voluntary economic migrant is not new, and a range of labels have already been adopted in academic and policy circles to capture this gap: "externally displaced people,"[12] "people in distress" (Goodwin-Gill 1986), "distress migration" (Collinson 1999), and "vulnerable irregular migrants" (Betts 2010a). Others have argued that the concept of a "refugee" needs to be interpreted in a more expansive and inclusive way than is currently the case (Shacknove 1985). Despite the different labels to describe people who cross borders in broadly difficult situations and who may require some form of protection or assistance, there continues to be a lack of consensus on how to conceptualize those people who cross international borders who have a human rights-based entitlement not to be forcibly returned to their country of origin.

In order to address this conceptual gap, this book develops the concept of "survival migration" to highlight the conditions under which a person cannot get access to a fundamental set of rights in his or her country of origin and so (as a last resort) needs to seek those rights in another country.[13] Survival migrants can be defined as "persons who are outside their country of origin because of an existential threat for which they have no access to a domestic remedy or resolution."

This definition has three elements. First, people are "outside their country of origin." This is important because it implies that the people have access to the international community, and the international community has access to them (Hathaway 2007). Second, they face "an existential threat." This need not be reduced to the literal right to life but includes the core elements of human dignity, and could be grounded either ethically or legally. Third, "access to a domestic remedy or resolution" implies the inability to find a solution in the domestic courts or through an internal alternative, making cross-border migration the only viable source of protection.[14] The point here is that border crossing is a last resort.

The most important element of this definition is the way one conceives of the threshold that defines an existential threat in the country of origin. From an ethical perspective, one way in which it could be grounded is in the concept of "basic rights" developed by Henry Shue (1980). A basic right can be defined as a right without which no other right can be enjoyed. Shue's (1980, 5) main concern in developing basic rights is to identify a nonarbitrary basis on which to prioritize human rights. The idea of basic rights was first applied to the refugee context by Andrew Shacknove (1985) to develop an ethical definition of a refugee distinct from the legal-institutional definition.

In developing basic rights, Shue (1980, 18–19) is attempting to identify what he regards to be the minimum conditions for human dignity and self-respect: basic rights are "the morality of the depths. They specify the line beneath which no one is allowed to sink . . . [they] are everyone's minimum reasonable demands upon the rest of humanity." He grounds the logic of basic rights by arguing along the following lines: (1) Everyone has a right to something; (2) Some things are necessary for enjoying the first thing as a right, whatever the first thing is;

(3) Therefore, everyone also has rights to the other things that are necessary for enjoying the first as a right (1980, 31). In other words, basic rights are the basic conditions for anyone to enjoy any other right. For Shue, there are three kinds of basic rights: basic liberty, basic security, and basic subsistence.

At the moment, the refugee definition focuses on basic security and to some extent basic liberty but excludes basic subsistence. Shue (1980, 36–40) is able to explain why the distinction between security and subsistence, between positive and negative rights is arbitrary. He explains how very commonly in rights frameworks—such as international refugee law—there is an implicit assumption that the distinction between subsistence rights and security rights is sharp and significant, because the former are positive rights, imposing a correlative obligation on someone else to "do something," whereas the latter are negative nights, simply requiring others to refrain from a particular course of action. As Shue (1980, 37) explains, though, "the moral significance, if any, of the distinction between positive rights and negative rights depends upon the moral significance, if any, of the distinction between action and omission." When they are unpacked, though, he argues that there is no contrast of any moral significance. Security rights can rely on positive correlative duties of others while subsistence rights are equally often the result of human action rather than inaction.

To add conceptual clarity, figure 1 highlights the conceptual relationship of survival migrants to refugees and international migrants. It is adapted from a diagram presented by former International Federation of the Red Cross and Red Crescent Societies (IFRC) Special Envoy on Migration, Trygve Nordby. As we see, refugees are survival migrants, but not all survival migrants are refugees, and survival migrants are international migrants, but not all international migrants are survival migrants.[15]

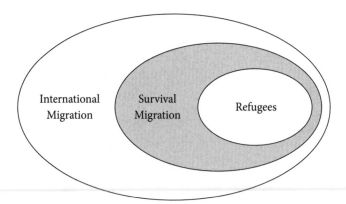

FIGURE 1.   The conceptual relationship of survival migration to refugees and international migration.

The population that this book is primarily concerned with is the middle segment of figure 1, survival migrants who fall outside the refugee framework. The inner dividing line in figure 1 cannot be understood as fixed—over either time or space. Exactly where it is drawn changes over time and is subject to significant variation across different states. In theory, given the organic nature of the refugee definition, all survival migrants could be recognized as refugees—either universally or in a specific state. In practice, though, there is a significant global gap and usually some degree of gap in the practice of most states. Usually, as has been argued, the inner circle of refugees is limited to those people fleeing persecution while the middle circle relates to those fleeing other sources of serious human rights deprivations. Nevertheless, there is huge variation and inconsistency in where and how the line is drawn in different states. As the next chapter explains, one of the most interesting questions relates to when and how the refugee regime stretches so that the gap between "refugee" and "survival migration" diminishes or expands.

The second dividing line, between "international migration" and "survival migration" (see figure 1), relates to a very serious threshold of human rights deprivations that necessitate border crossing as a last resort. It is important to emphasize that although the term "survival migration" is more inclusive than "refugee," it is not intended to offer a carte blanche for anyone in a weak or fragile state to seek asylum. Rather, it remains a high threshold based on a threat to an individual or group in which the fundamental conditions of human dignity simply cannot be obtained in their country of origin. On the other hand, the designation of a line between survival migration and other forms of international migration should not be taken to imply that there are no other grounds for admission or that other international migrants do not also have human rights qua human beings. Rather, the distinction is between those who need territorial asylum and those who do not.

Survival migration is therefore intended to be an inclusive protection framework that highlights the range of people who have a human rights–based entitlement not to be returned to their country of origin, irrespective of whether they are refugees and of whether that right derives from international refugee law or international human rights law. The purpose is not to create a new concept for the sake of it, but to give language to an analytically distinct group of people for whom there currently is no widely recognized language. While the category of refugee covers people who are recognized under international refugee law, it is widely recognized that many people who fall outside international refugee law also have an entitlement under international human rights law to not be returned to their country of origin (McAdam 2007). However, there is no widely accepted language to describe the larger group of people who have a human rights–based entitlement to nonreturn, whether or not they are refugees. Hence "survival migration" is used in order to fill that analytical gap—and to highlight the totality of people who might be considered to have a right to *non-refoulement* because of the absence of rights in their country of origin.

The use of the term "survival migration" is therefore not a neologism for the sake of novelty. Nevertheless, there are a number of possible objections to the concept, which are worth addressing up front.

First, *are there risks in developing new labels and policy categories?* Labeling has real-world effects. When a category of people is created and then used as the basis for bureaucratic decision making, it leads to exclusions and inclusions (Zetter 1991). The danger is that by including some people in a designated category, we exclude others from access to the resulting rights and entitlements. For example, in delineating the category of survival migration and using it as a basis on which to allocate asylum and the right to *non-refoulement*, one might be concerned that, at one end of the spectrum, this could dilute the rights of refugees while further marginalizing the human rights of other migrants at the other end of the spectrum. While this suggestion is not without foundation, two responses can be offered. First, all law and policy require drawing lines that distinguish people with different sets of entitlements and obligations based on their circumstances. It is better to develop frameworks for allocating entitlements that attempt to improve on the status quo than to persevere with old categories that are even more arbitrary. Second, the label itself need not necessarily undermine other categories. There is no inconsistency between highlighting that there is a broader category of people who have a human rights–based entitlement to *non-refoulement* and simultaneously working to uphold the human rights of all migrants.

Second, *why not include people who do not cross a border?* There are two reasons why survival migration focuses exclusively on cross-border displacement, one conceptual and the other institutional. Conceptually, borders matter. When people cross an international border, they have access to the international community, and the international community has access to them. This causes a host country to make a choice to make about whether to return a person to their country of origin or to recognize that person's right not to be returned. Institutionally, we already have an analogous framework for internally displaced persons (IDPs). While the "refugee" label is limited to people fleeing individualized persecution and generalized violence, the "IDP" label—defined with the so-called UN Guiding Principles on Internal Displacement—is much broader, including people who flee domestically because of, for example, the complex interaction of state fragility, livelihoods failure, and environmental change. The institutional gap is for groups of people who cross borders.

Third, *why ground the concept in rights rather than causes?* In much of the political debate on environmental displacement, there is discussion of developing legal and normative frameworks that are exclusively for people fleeing a particular cause. In contrast, survival migration is based on the underlying rights deprivation that cannot be addressed in the country of origin. This is important because from both an ethical and a human rights law perspective, the underlying cause is arguably irrelevant. To develop a supplementary institutional framework to allocate asylum on the basis of particular causes would simply risk perpetuating further arbitrary exclusions. Rather, it makes more sense to base any criteria for allocating asylum and the right to *non-refoulement* (whether temporary or permanent) on the sets of rights that are unavailable in the country of origin and can be restituted only in another country. Of course, causes are a proxy for underlying rights violations, which can and must be used to identify survival migrants, empirically or institutionally. However, it is the underlying rights that matter and are hence core to the definition of survival migrants. It is this suggestion to ground the concept in rights rather than causes that makes it more analytically useful and less arbitrary than increasingly common labels such as "cross-border environmental displacement."

Fourth, *could all survival migrants be better described as refugees?* The 1951 convention and other legal instruments relevant to defining the refugee in international law are "living" documents and are subject to reinterpretation and jurisprudence over time (Goodwin-Gill and McAdam 2007, 7–8). This means that the outer boundaries of who is a refugee are never normatively fixed but rather are inherently contested, both over time and across states. From this perspective, one might argue that many survival migrants who are not currently recognized as refugees might nevertheless be argued to be potential refugees. Similarly, some political theorists or social scientists might argue that away from a legal definition of a refugee, survival migrants might fit the vernacular definition of a refugee (Gibney 2004). This is true. However, the reality is that there is a significant group of people who are fleeing a serious threshold of human rights deprivation and yet are outside the dominant interpretation of a refugee within existing state practice. The concept of survival migration serves to draw attention to that gap. It is useful precisely because it highlights the fact that many people whom one might believe to be refugees fall outside the dominant legal interpretation of a refugee.

Fifth, *why use the word "survival"?* For some people, describing this type of movement as survival is problematic because it might be seen as a form of "miserabilism," in which people are portrayed as victims, lacking agency. Two responses can be given to this. First, the label is not as important as the underlying concept, and it could just as easily be described using another label. Second, however, the label is appropriate. Many survival migrants have agency, but they are, by definition, fleeing desperate conditions. The notion of survival thereby

reflects the reality. It is the word that many migrants themselves and the civil society organizations faced with these types of influx have used. Furthermore, the
label has begun to be used in advocacy, being recognized as valuable because it
makes visible a group of people who arguably have the right to *non-refoulement*
under international human rights law, even if they are not refugees.

The next chapter outlines the book's explanatory framework for understanding national and international responses to survival migration. Having developed a conceptual basis on which to distinguish between the legal-institutional
category of a refugee and the normative concept of survival migration, the book
turns to examine the question of when and why the refugee regime, created to
protect people fleeing persecution, stretches (or not) to protect people fleeing
the wider set of human rights deprivations that constitute survival migration. In
other words, what explains variation in the extent to which the inner line separating refugees and survival migration in figure 1 expands or contracts in different
national contexts, and with what consequences?

THE NATIONAL POLITICS OF INTERNATIONAL INSTITUTIONS

Survival migration represents an emerging challenge in world politics. It matters because of its implications for human rights and security. Yet there is no clearly defined international institutional framework to address the issue. The refugee regime exists to protect and assist people who cross borders in desperate circumstances, but it focuses on protecting only a very small proportion of those who flee desperate human rights deprivations, those defined as refugees. Nevertheless, sometimes people who fall outside the dominant legal interpretation of who is a refugee do receive protection from the refugee regime. The refugee regime has sometimes adapted at the national level to protect other survival migrants. In other cases, though, it has failed to adapt, leaving gaps in protection. This observation begs the question: under what conditions can the old refugee regime adapt (or not) to address the new challenge of survival migration?

This puzzle is important for practice because it tells us about whether or not the existing refugee regime is capable of adapting to the challenge of survival migration. But it is also of wider academic importance because it represents one case of a broader issue in world politics: under what conditions can an old regime stretch to meet new circumstances, even in the absence of formal renegotiation at the international level? This matters beyond survival migration because many international institutions have been created at a particular juncture of history. The UN system was mainly created in the aftermath of the Second World War. Since its creation, world politics and the nature of the challenges for which those institutions were created have changed, in some areas beyond recognition. In some contexts the original institutions have adapted, and in other cases they have not.

This necessitates a deeper understanding of how and why international institutions change and adapt. Within the field of international relations, international institutional change is currently understood as taking place at two levels: international negotiation and institutionalization. Either states renegotiate institutions or there is a change in how states sign on to, ratify, and adopt institutions. However, sometimes states with similar levels of institutionalization of the same international institutions have radically different practices. What is missing in order to explain this variation in practice is an account of how international institutions adapt at implementation. This chapter distinguishes between institutionalization as an international process and implementation as a domestic process, and shows how we must focus on implementation in order to understand how institutions adapt to address new challenges.

Implementation is particularly important for understanding how and why international regimes may adapt to new challenges that arise at the national level. In order to explore how norms and international organizations adapt to new problems and challenges at the implementation stage, the chapter develops the concept of "regime stretching," which it defines as the *degree to which the scope of a regime at the national or local level takes on tasks that deviate from those prescribed at the global level.* Such stretching may be regime-consistent (taking on tasks that are complementary to the underlying purpose of the regime) or regime-inconsistent (contradicting the underlying purpose of the regime).

Survival migration represents an especially salient case study for examining the conditions under which regime stretching takes place (or not). It highlights the case of an international institutional framework—the refugee regime—which has gradually been faced with new drivers of cross-border displacement that fall outside the scope of the original regime. Interestingly, in some countries the norm of who is a refugee and the work of UNHCR has stretched to include survival migrants who fall outside the 1951 convention definition, while in others it has not. This observed variation represents an interesting puzzle for international relations, and a paradox for the existing literature on the institutionalization of norms. On the basis of this literature, one would expect variation in who is a refugee to be explained by variation in institutionalization of the international norm. Yet in the cases explored by this chapter, we find that in states with very similar levels of institutionalization, there is nevertheless significant variation in the practice of who is a refugee. To explain this variation, we must turn to the level of implementation.[1]

Through the case of survival migration, it is argued here that national politics matters for how institutions adapt at implementation. In particular, variation in how regimes stretch on implementation is explained by national elite interests.[2] Where there is scope for interpreting the role of norms and organizations at the national level, this discretion results in domestic interests defining how regimes are implemented in practice. In the present context, variation in stretching in the refugee regime is explained by whether national elites in government are rewarded or punished for stretching the scope of the international norm by (1) the international system and (2) domestic politics. Where the net result of stretching is that the government is rewarded by the international system and domestic politics, stretching will occur. Where the net result is that the government is punished by the international system and domestic politics, stretching will not occur. In other words, incentives matter in defining how ambiguity in global norms translates into implementation at the national level.

In setting out this argument, this chapter has four sections. First, it outlines a theoretical framework for understanding how international institutions adapt (or not) at implementation. Second, it describes the dependent variable (the thing to be explained) that this book focuses on—regime stretching—summarizing how it applies to the six case studies developed in the ensuing chapters. Third, it identifies the independent variable (the thing that explains variation in the dependent variable): elite interests at the national level. Finally, it presents the alternative explanations for variation in regime stretching and explains why they are insufficient.

Theoretical Framework

The concept of a regime is often defined by its consensus definition of "principles, norms, rules, and decision-making procedures around which actor expectations converge in a given issue-area" (Krasner 1982, 2). Yet this definition is unwieldy and almost impossible to operationalize. It makes far more sense to see regimes as having just two core elements: norms and international organizations (both of which can be subsumed under the notion of international institutions).[3] Adaptation and change may take place in each of these two areas. Even in the absence of creating a new regime or formally renegotiating norms or international organizations, change and adaptation can and do take place. Yet in contrast to the comparative politics literature, which has examined processes of institutional change and adaption (Mahoney and Thelen 2010; Hacker 2004; Pierson 2004; Weyland 2008), international relations research has relatively neglected the issue of international institutional adaptation. Regime adaptation—in terms of both norms and international organizations—can be understood to take place at three levels: international bargaining, institutionalization, and implementation (see table 2).[4]

At the first level, *international bargaining*, norms may be changed through interstate (re)negotiation, and international organizations may be changed through statute (re)negotiation. For example, norms are sometimes adapted through additional protocols to a treaty, and international organizations may be formally changed through the UN General Assembly's decision to authorize the change in an international organization's mandate. This level of change is widely recognized in liberal institutionalist literature, which implies that when states change their demand for international regimes (for example, because of a change in preferences, power, or the nature of the problem), they will formally renegotiate the bargain on which the regime is based (Aggarwal 1998; Keohane 1982; Müller 2004).

At the second level, *institutionalization*, norms may adapt in how they are disseminated internationally, particularly in how they are signed, ratified, and adopted in national legislation. For example, if states change their ratification of a regime, whether or not the regime is incorporated within national legislation, this will represent an adaptation of the regime. This type of change is widely recognized in constructivist literature on institutionalization (Keck and Sikkink 1998; Risse-Kappen, Ropp, and Sikkink 1999; Simmons 2009). International organizations may adapt in terms of how they institutionalize (and interpret) their mandates. Many organizations' interpretation of their own mandates may change at the global level even in the absence of a formal General Assembly mandate. This type of change is explained in literature on principal-agent theory as applied to international organizations (Berle and Means 1932; Hawkins et al. 2006).

At the third level, *implementation*, the introduction of a norm's precepts into formal legal or policy mechanisms at the national level in order to routinize compliance (i.e., "policy") may vary between different national contexts (Betts and Orchard 2013). For example, even where two countries have the same degree of institutionalization of an international norm, there may be very different outcomes because of a state's willingness or ability to implement norms. In relation to international organizations, the way in which the organization's national representation interprets its mandate (i.e., "practice") may vary between different national contexts. For example, a national representation in one country may act differently from the same organization in a different country. In contrast to the other two levels, this third level of regime adaptation is almost entirely neglected in international relations. Yet it is important insofar as we observe variation (or change) in outcomes even in the absence of variation (or change) at the levels of international bargaining or institutionalization.

The implementation stage has been largely neglected by international relations. In explaining the dissemination of international norms, international relations scholars have traditionally had a tendency to look at how a given set of international norms—relating, for example, to human rights—is institutionalized

TABLE 2 Regime adaptation model

	NORMS	INTERNATIONAL ORGANIZATION
International Bargaining	Treaty negotiation	Statute negotiation
Institutionalization	Legislation	Mandate interpretation
Implementation	Policy	Practice

(i.e., how it emerges at the international level and comes to be signed, ratified, and adopted within national legislation). What scholars have focused much less on is why—in spite of similar levels of institutionalization—the implementation of those norms (i.e., the introduction of a norm's precepts into formal legal or policy mechanisms at the national level in order to routinize compliance) may vary between different national contexts. There is a vast social constructivist literature on the institutionalization of international norms. This literature can be divided into two broadly chronological waves of scholarship: (1) institutionalization as explained by international-level processes and (2) institutionalization as explained by domestic-level processes.

The first wave is based primarily on variations of Finnemore and Sikkink (1998)'s norm life cycle model. It shows how norms emerge and disseminate in three phases in which norms (1) emerge, (2) cascade, and (3) are internalized by states. In the norm emergence model, institutionalization is primarily international.[5] The norm is conceived as predefined and static, and the puzzle is to explain the conditions under which it is adopted, integrated, and complied with by an ontologically coherent state. In the second wave of scholarship, scholars have built on this early work, unpacking the "black box" of the state and looking to the domestic level in order to explain the conditions under which norms are institutionalized at that level. A range of domestic-level explanations for variation in norm diffusion and dissemination have been offered, including the role of veto players and domestic coalitions (Diehl, Ku, and Zamora 2003, 61; Busby 2007, 254; Cortell and Davis 2000, 66; Simmons 2009; van Kersbergen and Verbeek 2007; Deere-Birkbeck 2008), organizational structure and the identity of the state (Checkel 1999, 2005; Flockhart 2005; Legro 1997; Sundstrom 2005), and ideational and cultural factors (Acharya 2004; Merry 2006; Wiener 2009, 2010).

Both waves, however, are trying to explain institutionalization, notwithstanding that the definition of—and the line where institutionalization ends—varies across the literature. That line exists on a spectrum from signing and ratifying international treaties, at one end, to adopting domestic legislation, policies, and even standard operating procedures, at the other end (Diehl et al. 2003). In contrast, this book contends that it is useful (as Finnemore and Sikkink 1998 imply) to analytically distinguish between two distinct processes: institutionalization as an *international process*, which can be defined as "how a norm emerges at the international level and comes to be signed, ratified, and adopted within national legislation," and implementation as a *domestic process*, which can be defined as "the introduction of a norm's precepts into formal legal or policy mechanisms at the national level in order to routinize compliance." This distinction is important for two reasons. First, it enables us to separate two discrete phases of political contestation, and to recognize that even once a norm or international organization (IO) mandate is formally institutionalized, it will be subject to a new phase of political contestation (Jepperson et al. 1996, 56; Franck 2006, 93; van Kersbergen and Verbeek 2007, 218–19; Victor, Raustiala, and Skolnikoff 1998). Second, it allows us to explore why, in spite of similar levels of institutionalization, we may observe variation in how norms and organizations play out in practice (Deere-Birkbeck 2008).

Dependent Variable: Regime Stretching

In order to explore how the implementation stage matters for regime adaptation, the book develops the concept of regime stretching, which it defines as the *degree to which the scope of a regime at the national or local level takes on tasks that deviate from those prescribed at the global level.* Such stretching may be regime-consistent (taking on tasks that are complementary to the underlying purpose of the regime) or regime-inconsistent (contradicting the underlying purpose of the regime). The concept highlights the way in which a regime may adapt at the national level even in the absence of adaptation at the level of international bargaining or institutionalization.

This is a particularly important concept in the context of a world in which new problems and challenges are emerging but new formal institutions are created at a much slower pace, resulting in a need for old global institutions to adapt to new national challenges. As problems emerge that were not within the scope of a regime at its creation, the norms and organization may adapt, even without formal renegotiation. Dan Drezner (2007) has written about the "viscosity of global governance." He argues that one of the tragedies of global governance is the ease with which states can fluidly create new international institutions and so engage in forum shopping or regime shifting. However, he notes that the costs of forum shopping are likely to vary with issue areas, implying different degrees of "viscosity" (or resistance). The concept of regime stretching adds a dimension to the concept of viscosity. Where Drezner implies that adaptation to new problems takes place through movement to new or alternative institutions, regime stretching highlights an alternative method of adaptation—within the regime itself. In other words, rather than (1) creating a new institution (institutional proliferation) or (2) moving to another institution (forum shopping or regime shifting; Alter and Meunier 2009), states may (3) adapt an existing institution, not only through international bargaining or institutionalization but also at the level of implementation through regime stretching.

Furthermore, regime stretching adds a spatial dimension to how we think about regime adaptation. Comparative politics has explored temporal explanations of institutional change (Hall and Thelen 2009; Lieberman 2002; Pierson 2004). James Mahoney and Kathleen Thelen's (2010) work in particular shows the range of causal mechanisms (displacement, layering, drift, convergence) through which an institution changes between time period t1 and time period t2. However, exploring the relationship between the global and the local opens up a spatial dimension to the question of institutional change, highlighting how the same global regime can have different national manifestations (in states a, b, and c) at the same time period (whether t1 or t2).

The degree to which norms stretch can be assessed in relation to the benchmark of the formal global norms. In cases where a formal treaty, such as the 1951 Refugee Convention, exists, it offers a basis for identifying the aims and scope of the regime at the global level. In the case of the refugee regime, Article 1a of the treaty defines who is a refugee, limiting it to people who face a well-founded fear of being persecuted for reasons of race, religion, nationality, membership of a particular social group or political opinion. The rest of the treaty ascribes certain rights to people who fall within that category. This benchmark means that, in a given national context, if one can identify activity that falls on either side of that line—for example, the inclusion or exclusion of additional groups of people—this might be regarded as regime stretching. In the case of the refugee regime, that might be measured by looking at the number of additional people included in the refugee framework and the degree of rights they receive.

The degree to which an IO stretches can be assessed in relation to the benchmark of the mandate given to that organization. In many cases this will be formally outlined in a statute, such as the 1950 UNHCR Statute, which specifies that the scope and purpose of the organization is to protect and provide solutions for refugees who fall within the framework of the 1951 convention. This benchmark means that, in a given context, if one can identify activity that falls on either side of that line—for example, providing protection to additional groups of people—this can be regarded as regime stretching. In the case of the refugee regime, that might involve UNHCR's becoming involved in the protection of nonrefugee populations, as it has often done in the past in relation to internally displaced persons or stateless persons before taking on more formal roles for these additional groups.

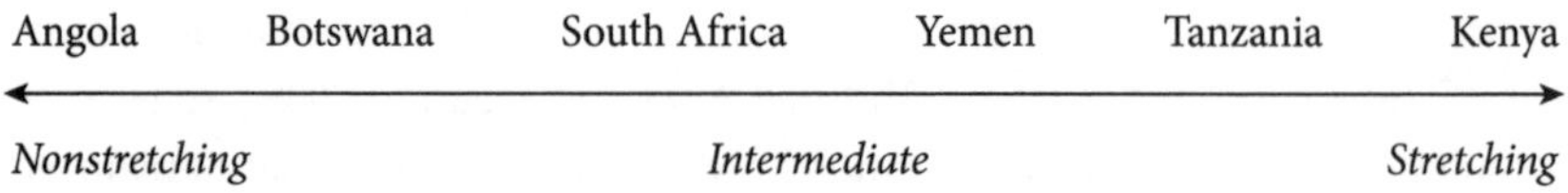

Angola	Botswana	South Africa	Yemen	Tanzania	Kenya

◄───►

Nonstretching   *Intermediate*   *Stretching*

FIGURE 2.   Regime stretching: spectrum of institutional responses to survival migration.

This book is concerned with explaining the conditions under which regime stretching has taken place to enable the norms and IO that make up the refugee regime to provide protection for the people who fall within the middle circle of the diagram in figure 1. In order to explain variation in regime stretching, the book examines national and international responses to three populations of survival migrants in six host states: Zimbabweans (in South Africa and Botswana), Congolese (in Angola and Tanzania), and Somalis (in Kenya and Yemen). The six case studies were selected on the basis of the dependent variable (King, Keohane, and Verba 1994, 129–136): two represent cases of regime stretching (Kenya and Tanzania), two of nonstretching (Botswana and Angola), and two of an intermediate response (Yemen and South Africa). This enables the reasons for variation to be inductively explored. In selecting cases from the same region, the book holds two important factors broadly constant: (1) the states are subject to the same regime at the intergovernmental level,[6] and (2) the states have roughly the same levels of institutionalization of those intergovernmental structures.[7] This allows adaptation at the level of implementation to be analytically isolated and explored as a dependent variable. The responses can be located on a spectrum in terms of the degree of regime stretching that has taken place, as shown in figure 2.

Somalis in Kenya: Stretching

After the collapse of the Siad Barre regime in Somalia in 1991, civil war led to the mass exodus of refugees from south-central Somalia into Kenya (e.g., Milner 2009). Kenya, informally after 1991 and through legislation since 2006, has recognized all Somalis as a group on a prima facie basis, without making them go through individualized refugee status determination (RSD). Kenya is the only country in Africa with a legislative and policy framework that allows for prima facie recognition on the basis of the regional OAU Refugee Convention refugee definition, which extends the 1951 Refugee Convention definition to include people fleeing generalized violence and public disorder (Albert 2010). Nearly all the other states in the region have signed, ratified, and institutionalized the OAU Refugee Convention, but Kenya is one of the only states in Africa that fully applies it at the level of implementation.

In contrast to the other cases, this means that survival migrants from south-central Somalia have been de facto protected by Kenya. Prima facie recognition has meant that all Somali survival migrants—irrespective of the underlying cause of their flight—have received the same standards of international protection. People from Somalia who may not be directly affected by individualized persecution or generalized conflict are still recognized as refugees.[8] Even during 2011, Kenya continued to accept Somalis fleeing famine and drought as though they were refugees. Implicitly, this means that those affected by, say, the economic or environmental consequences of the political situation—rather than by political persecution or conflict per se—nevertheless get access to protection.

The challenge in the case of Kenya, however, has been that although the refugee definition has been inclusive, the standards of protection available to all Somalis have been extremely minimal. The majority of refugees have been confined in the insecure, arid, and inhumane Dadaab camps close to the Somali border, where there were around 270,000 people at the end of 2009 and nearly 500,000 by early 2012 after the famine and drought. Despite massive overcrowding, the Kenyan government has refused to allow Dadaab to grow.[9] Nevertheless, unlike in the other cases, UNHCR and other international actors have provided material assistance in the camps. Meanwhile, a minority of Somalis have lived as urban refugees in the Eastleigh neighborhood of Nairobi, where international protection and assistance have remained more limited but still available through UNHCR on a more or less inclusive basis.[10] Consequently, although Kenya's response has been one of stretching, there has been a trade-off in terms of levels of rights and numbers.

Congolese in Tanzania: Stretching

More than 100,000 Congolese from South Kivu crossed Lake Tanganyika into the Kigoma region of western Tanzania between 1996 and 2003.[11] At the time, they fled the violence of the Congo Wars, primarily between the Banyamulenge and the Rwandan *génocidaires* (e.g., Prunier 2009). Given the generalized violence in South Kivu, all were recognized as refugees within the 1951 convention definition on a prima facie basis, and today the majority of those people remain as refugees in the Nyarugusu refugee camp in Kigoma. However, the response of the government and UNHCR is something of a paradox.

On the one hand, it has been argued by both UNHCR and the government of Tanzania that the original conditions of conflict and persecution in South Kivu that led to the exodus no longer apply.[12] Consequently, there is an increasing recognition that people who leave South Kivu are not in need of international protection. The government has thus shifted from initially recognizing all Congolese from South Kivu on a prima facie basis to using individualized refugee status determination (RSD). In the words of one representative of the Department of Refugee Affairs, "We reject them if they have socioeconomic reasons, any other aside from persecution."[13] In theory, then, RSD takes place through interviews coordinated by an ad hoc committee. However, as of September 2009, the regional commissioner's office in Kigoma has effectively suspended the work of the ad hoc committee and no new RSDs have taken place.[14] Furthermore, UNHCR openly acknowledged that the main problems in South Kivu no longer relate to conflict or generalized violence but rather stem from the lack of infrastructure and social services.[15]

On the other hand, there has been a general acknowledgment that conditions in South Kivu—in terms of livelihoods and social services—are too poor for UNHCR and the Tanzania government to actively promote return for those Congolese in the Nyarugusu camp who arrived in the late 1990s. Both the government and UNHCR have therefore fallen short of implementing the cessation clause and insisting on the return of the Congolese. In contrast to the Burundians in Tanzania, for whom "promoted return" is taking place, UNHCR and the government are engaging in only "facilitated return" for the Congolese from South Kivu through offering support items and "go and see" opportunities and allowing them the choice to return or to remain.[16] In the words of UNHCR's local head of field office, Kazuhiro Kaneko, "The reasons why they left may not exist anymore but the general situation—for example, in health and education—and the constant fear makes me agree that those that stay have to stay."[17]

Even though UNHCR and the government of Tanzania are denying that people arriving from South Kivu today are "refugees," they are continuing to offer protection to long-stay survival migrants on the ground that the situation—in terms of livelihoods and governance—is too poor for them to force people to return. In that sense, the norm of who is a refugee and the work of UNHCR have expanded to the protection of a broader category of survival migrants.

Somalis in Yemen: Intermediate

Yemen serves both as a country of asylum for many Somalis and as a country of transit for Somalis wanting to go to Saudi Arabia, the Persian Gulf States, or Europe. The country has traditionally been a tolerant host of Somali refugees and migrants. Today it is home to around 220,000 Somalis. As in Kenya, the government has recognized all Somalis on a prima facie basis. Unlike in Kenya, many of those refugees have been de facto locally integrated, albeit with limited assistance. Only a minority have been in camps; most Somalis are in urban areas, particularly the suburbs of Sana'a and the notorious Al-Basateen district of Aden.

However, there are at least two major caveats to Yemen's apparent generosity. First, there has been a gradual shift toward a more restrictive asylum policy. In the context of increasing political concerns about civil conflict, terrorism, and growing competition for resources, domestic attitudes have started to shift toward greater xenophobia. This has led to a change in the terms of the debate on policies toward Somalis. On January 18, 2010, the Yemeni authorities issued a two-month deadline for unregistered Somalis to register with UNHCR, threatening deportation for any Somalis who did not comply. Furthermore, interest has grown in introducing RSD for Somalis—as is currently the case for all other nationalities, such as Ethiopian asylum seekers.

Second, even with these shifts, protection for Somali refugees has been far stronger than for another numerically significant group seeking sanctuary in the country: Ethiopians. While Somalis fleeing a variety of causes of movement beyond persecution have received asylum in Yemen, the Oromo and Ogaden Ethiopians, often fearing persecution and insecurity at home, have sometimes been rounded up, detained, and deported. This contrast in responses to the two populations helps shed light on how, even within the same host state, the refugee regime may adapt differently to different populations, even when they have similar human rights–based reasons for fleeing.

Zimbabweans in South Africa: Intermediate

Between 2005 and 2009, large numbers of Zimbabweans fled the country in search of sanctuary (Betts and Kaytaz 2009; Polzer 2008), the majority to South Africa. It is difficult to estimate the precise number, but the NGO network Consortium of Refugees and Migrants in South Africa (CoRMSA) claims it could be anywhere from 1 to 9 million (CoRMSA 2008, 17), while South Africa's Department of Home Affairs (DHA) agrees that there likely have been up to 2 million Zimbabweans in the country.[18] In 2008, there were 250,000 Zimbabwean asylum seekers in South Africa, more than a quarter of the world's total number of asylum seekers.

Although all Zimbabweans who have crossed the border into South Africa have been allowed to remain on the territory for an initial period as "asylum seekers," only around 10 percent have received recognition, and the rest have been liable to be detained and deported. This is because, in the words of one South African NGO employee, "most are escaping the economic consequences of the political situation" rather than political persecution per se.[19] While a minority have faced direct government persecution as a result of their links to the opposition Movement for Democratic Change (MDC), the majority have been fleeing a combination of livelihoods failure, state fragility, and environmental pressure. Because of land invasions, international sanctions, capital flight, hyperinflation, and famine, very few Zimbabweans were able to maintain viable livelihood strategies without access to foreign exchange or remittances.[20]

In South Africa, the response by the government and UNHCR has been somewhat ad hoc, stretching the refugee regime to a certain extent in order to address this gap but providing only a limited response to the Zimbabweans. At the level of norms, the government of South Africa has in practice tolerated the presence of most Zimbabweans on its territory, and it announced a series of ad hoc measures to suspend deportations for a limited period, but without developing a coherent or consistent response or clear legal status for the Zimbabwean survival migrants. Meanwhile, at the level of the international organization, UNHCR has not developed any consistent policy toward the Zimbabweans in the country but has offered limited and ad hoc support in the border areas of Limpopo on the basis that, pending refugee status determination, all Zimbabweans can initially be considered asylum seekers (Betts and Kaytaz 2009). However, with few exceptions, Zimbabweans continue to lack refugee status or any other similar formal status, and neither the state nor UNHCR has adapted to ensure any systematic provision of material assistance.

Zimbabweans in Botswana: Nonstretching

The response to Zimbabweans in Botswana has been even more stark than in South Africa, being based on a sharp distinction between refugees and nonrefugees under the 1951 convention. In 2009, there were an estimated 40,000 to 100,000 Zimbabweans in Botswana, of which only around 900 were recognized as refugees.[21] The legal and policy framework requires that all asylum seekers remain in detention in Francistown during their refugee status determination process. If they receive recognition, they are entitled to live in the refugee camp in Dukwi, from where they can apply for a work permit if and when they find work. However, the majority of Zimbabweans remained outside the asylum system, facing detention and deportation.

According to the NGO Ditshwanelo, roundups are generally sporadic, and immigration officials will often tolerate the presence of Zimbabweans for long periods of time, knowing that deported migrants are likely to come back to Botswana. However, occasional roundups are carried out with large trucks. No NGO or independent agency has the capacity or access to oversee this process.[22] Beyond the asylum system, there is very little additional legal provision that relates to the situation of people who fall outside the refugee/voluntary economic migrant dichotomy.[23]

This dichotomous legal framework in turn changes the nature of the international response to undocumented migrants. Unlike South Africa, where the distribution of asylum seeker permits to all arrivals gives UNHCR a mandate to at least engage with the question of undocumented Zimbabweans as asylum seekers, no such nexus exists in the context of Botswana. This has made the international response to the exodus even less developed than in South Africa.[24] As the deputy representative of UNICEF said, "When people become refugees, a number of things kick in automatically. But for these undocumented, perhaps economic, migrants, it is not clear that we have any clear policies, structures, or guidelines."[25] All the UN agencies in Botswana have effectively been prevented from working with undocumented Zimbabweans who are outside the refugee framework.

Congolese in Angola: Nonstretching

There is a long history of livelihoods migration from the southern provinces of the DRC to Angola. However, with the collapse of diamond mines in the southern provinces of Bandundu and Western Kasai, the number of people crossing the border in search of work appears to have increased over the past decade. Although Bandundu and Western Kasai are not conflict regions in the way that other areas of the DRC such as North Kivu have been, the border regions of the southern provinces have the highest rates of food insecurity in the country, with extremely limited infrastructure, markets, or livelihood opportunities. Consequently, one of the principal survival strategies for people fleeing the combination of state fragility, livelihoods failure, and environmental degradation has been to cross into Angola to seek work in and around the diamond mining areas of the Lunda Norte region.

The response of the Angolan government has been brutal. According to Office for the Coordination of Humanitarian Affairs (OCHA), at least 300,000 Congolese have been forcibly deported from the Lunda Norte region of Angola to the DRC, in four main waves between 2003 and 2009 (Office for the Coordination of Humanitarian Affairs 2009). And beyond these waves, the deportations have continued up to the present day. There has been little documentation of these expulsions by academics, the media, or international organizations. However, the coverage that exists makes it clear that the roundup, detention, and deportation of the Congolese has been characterized by systematic human rights violations, which at times have bordered on crimes against humanity. In 2007, for example, MSF recorded one hundred testimonies from women who were deported. These testimonies highlighted systematic and state-sponsored rape, torture, and unsterile body cavity searches of those expelled, conducted by people who appeared to be acting as agents of the state (Médecins Sans Frontières 2007). Far from providing sanctuary, the government of Angola has systematically detained and deported Congolese survival migrants.[26]

Meanwhile, there has been very limited response from the international community as a whole and virtually no action by UNHCR. On the Angolan side of the border, the UN system has been constrained by the government's intransigence, and there has been almost no access to the deportation sites. On the DRC side of the border, UN agencies have engaged in occasional interagency missions to assess the condition of those deported, but there has been little concerted response. UNHCR, like the rest of the UN system, has remained largely on the sidelines. It has consistently argued that these people represent economic migrants and fall outside the scope of its mandate. Consequently, the main international response has come after deportation on the DRC side of the border, through assistance provided by "networked protection actors" such as the church, MSF, the Red Cross, and a variety of NGOs, which have been able to act through local contacts to offer very basic monitoring and assistance.[27]

Independent Variable: Incentives Matter

The six case studies therefore exhibit variation in the degree of regime stretching or nonstretching that takes place. This observation presents an interesting puzzle, given that all the cases relate to the same constant global regime, which has been broadly institutionalized in the same way across the six cases.[28] All the states have signed and ratified the 1951 convention and its 1967 protocol. All except for Yemen and Botswana have also signed and ratified the OAU Refugee Convention. Yet despite a broadly common level of institutionalization, the cases show variation in the regime at the level of implementation. How can we explain that variation? This section sets out and applies an explanatory framework, and the next section engages with alternative explanations.

The explanation that the book offers can be subsumed under a two-word story: incentives matter. Its argument is simple: incentives on national ruling elites shape how ambiguous norms are implemented. As Sandholtz and Stiles (2008, 101) suggest, norms cannot cover every contingency and hence "the inescapable tension between general norms and specific actions ceaselessly casts up disputes, which in turn generate arguments, which then reshape both rules and conduct." Where norms or mandates are ambiguous or imprecise, both *what* the norm or mandate is and *how* it is applied in practice will be subject to a new phase of political contestation at the domestic level. Insofar as a new challenge emerges in which the relevance of the regime to that area is normatively ambiguous, it is the sets of incentives at the domestic and international levels that determine whether or not regime stretching takes place.

What emerges inductively is that stretching or nonstretching in the context of normative ambiguity depends on whether elites at the national level are rewarded or punished for regime stretching by domestic and international incentive mechanisms. In other words, the book offers an interest-based account for the conditions under which international regimes adapt at implementation, an account in which the most relevant actor interests are domestic political elites within government. While some international relations scholars have recognized the important role that interests play in whether and how states adopt and comply with norms at the international level (Hurd 2005, 2007; Krasner 1999; Risse-Kappen, Ropp, and Sikkink 1999), the role of interests in playing this role in norm implementation at the domestic level has generally been marginalized in favor of explanations that privilege "logics of appropriateness" over interests (Acharya 2004; Wiener 2009, 2010). In doing so, the existing literature has bracketed off the political nature of how international norms and international organizations are contested and renegotiated at implementation on the basis of domestic interests.

Table 3 illustrates positive (+), negative (-), and neutral (0) incentives on national elites for stretching, incentives that emerge from the international system and from domestic politics. The table is not intended to represent a rigorous coding of the sets of incentives on host state ruling elites so much as to provide a simplified abstraction of the qualitative empirical data outlined below. The zeros generally denote some kind of canceling-out process whereby both positive and negative incentives exist in countervailing directions. The table illustrates that there is a correlation between the overall net incentives for stretching and the presence or absence of regime stretching.

TABLE 3 International and domestic incentives on government elites to engage in regime stretching or not

HOST STATE	ANGOLA	BOTSWANA	SOUTH AFRICA	YEMEN	TANZANIA	KENYA
Reward (+) / Punishment (-) by International System	Diamond mining investment (-)	Limited external criticism (0)	International reputation (+) Bilateral relationship with Zimbabwe (-)	Pressure to protect (+) EU pressure to manage migration (-)	Financial support (+)	Financial support (+)
Reward (+) / Punishment (-) by Domestic Politics	Reducing UNITA support base (-)	Xenophobia (-)	Civil society activism (+) Rising xenophobia (-)	Integrated Somali diaspora (+) Rising xenophobia (-)	Tolerance (0)	Tolerance (0)
Overall Net Incentive	Negative (-)	Negative (-)	Neutral (0)	Neutral (0)	Positive (+)	Positive (+)

The cases not only highlight how international and national incentives shape how the norm of who is a refugee is implemented but also imply that whether UNHCR's own mandate has stretched or not has followed sequentially from the interests of the national elites in stretching or not stretching. That is, the international organization's own role has been correlated with the prior decision of national elites on whether to stretch the underlying norm, and thus the international organization's own role in stretching (or not) appears to have been epiphenomenal. The only exception has been insofar as UNHCR has—at the margins—been able to influence the government's own cost-benefit calculus by shaping the incentives for regime stretching (e.g., financial support).

Kenya

Kenya has achieved significant financial and diplomatic gains from hosting refugees. Given its porous border and the difficulty of forcibly excluding Somalis, its inclusive approach has enabled it to delegate responsibility directly to UNHCR, minimizing the costs of hosting. In such a context prima facie recognition has been cheaper and more efficient than individualized screening (Albert 2010). The international community has absorbed the costs of maintaining the refugee camps, and the refugees have been mainly confined to a particular area of the country. Moreover, refugee hosting gives Kenya a bargaining tool vis-à-vis the international community. For example, in its bilateral relationship with Denmark, it has used refugee hosting to attract additional development assistance.[29]

Domestically, there has been a mixed response to hosting Somalis. There is some xenophobia toward the Somali populations, and historically there have been fears of secession. However, Somalis have been generally tolerated. Those in camps are geographically confined, while those in Nairobi contribute heavily to the economy: Somalis run one of the city's biggest market districts, in the Eastleigh area. Only as numbers have increased dramatically with the 2011 famine and drought have domestic politicians begun to seriously challenge the country's openness to Somali refugees.

For most of the period since 1991, there has therefore been a net incentive for regime stretching and for maintaining a broadly inclusive approach. Consequently, UNHCR has also been able to be inclusive in its assistance and use of prima facie because of the response of the government. UNHCR appears to have had some influence in the original development of the Kenyan legislation that led to the country being only state in Africa to recognize Somalis as prima facie under the OAU convention. Arguably, however, UNHCR was able to do so only because incentives existed for Kenya to adopt that approach. Hence, sequentially, the government's interest in stretching the norm seems a precondition for the organization to also stretch the scope of its work.

Tanzania

At an international level, Tanzania has historically derived significant financial and diplomatic gains from its inclusive refugee policies. This has gradually changed over time. It was once one of the most generous refugee hosting states in Africa. However, democratization and structural adjustment beginning in the late 1980s made elected governments more accountable to their own citizens and created pressure—especially at local and regional levels—to reduce pressure on local resources (Betts and Milner 2006). The central government in Dar-es-Salaam has maintained a strong interest in upholding good relations with the donor community, recognizing the links between refugee hosting and overseas development assistance and diplomatic status. Despite pressure from regional and district commissioners to repatriate refugees, the central government has therefore followed UNHCR advice and refrained from invoking the cessation clause for the Congolese left in the country after the Congo Wars.

Domestically, there has also not been significant xenophobia directed toward the Congolese, who are generally tolerated by Tanzanians. In the Kigoma region, the Nyarugusu camp does not exert significant pressure on the local host population, and the presence of other Congolese immigrants as fisherman and traders along Lake Tanganyika is generally tolerated.[30] This is in contrast to Burundians, who were often seen as a potential security threat due to the spillover of conflict and violence to the Burundian refugee camps.[31]

Overall, then, there has been a net incentive to not forcibly repatriate the Congolese from South Kivu despite improved circumstances within South Kivu. This has allowed a degree of regime stretching to take place to protect de facto survival migrants, who might otherwise have been returned to South Kivu. UNHCR's role has followed this logic. Insofar as the Tanzanian government has not exerted significant pressure to return the Congolese, UNHCR's country representation also been able to stretch to maintain the Nyarugusu camp. A UNHCR staff member admitted in interview that the organization hoped to maintain the camp because "otherwise we would be effectively packing up the [country] operation."[32]

Yemen

The international incentives on Yemen to engage in regime stretching have also pulled in both directions. On the one hand, there has been international pressure, notably from UNHCR, not to return people to Somalia. On the other hand, there has been growing pressure from the European Union, the United Kingdom, Denmark, and the Netherlands to limit the onward movement of Somali migrants and asylum seekers to Europe and to control Somali mixed migration "in the region of origin."[33] This shift has contributed to a change in the policy of the government, reducing incentives for regime stretching over time. At the same time, the EU has established a Mixed Migration Task Force to triage Somalis crossing the Gulf of Aden, separating "refugees" from "nonrefugees."[34]

Similarly, domestic incentives have gradually shifted from a position of tolerance and inclusivity toward growing hostility. There has historically been a sizable and well-integrated Somali diaspora, which has had a significant role in the national economy and in sustaining economic and social ties with Somalia. This has been in stark contrast to the far less tolerant response to the Ethiopian population. However, there has gradually been a shift toward xenophobia, competition for resources, and concern with terrorist links, leading the government to more closely control who is on its territory.

At both the international and domestic levels, then, there have traditionally been incentives for stretching. But over time, countervailing pressures have emerged in both directions. Consequently, there has been a gradual move from regime stretching toward an intermediate and less coherent response. UNHCR's own position has followed this trend. It has traditionally been part of an inclusive response, but as the position of the government has changed, so too UNHCR has moved toward a more triage-based approach, becoming, for example, an active partner in the Mixed Migration Task Force.

South Africa

The international incentives on South Africa have pulled in both a positive and a negative direction. In terms of incentives for nonstretching, the main one has been the bilateral relationship with Zimbabwe. The personal relationship between Thabo Mbeki and Robert Mugabe for a long time stymied South African criticism of Zimbabwe, and that has continued even with the election of Jacob Zuma in 2009.[35] The government acknowledges that its response to Zimbabwean survival migrants has been shaped significantly by the Department of Foreign Affairs, which does not want its grant of status to Zimbabweans to be interpreted as condemnation of the Mugabe regime.[36] For example, when in March 2009 South Africa was considering some kind of temporary visa exemption status for all Zimbabweans in South Africa, it first discussed the issue with the Zimbabwean government at a meeting in Victoria Falls.[37] On the other hand, countervailing international pressure has tempered the impact of the bilateral relationship.

In particular, the government has been susceptible to the international criticism it has received from a range of human rights organizations for its treatment of the Zimbabweans on its territory.

There has been a similar two-directional pull at the level of domestic incentives. On the one hand, there has been rising xenophobia within South Africa. In May 2008, for example, Zimbabweans were among those targeted in severe xenophobic violence in the townships. Against the backdrop of economic recession, there has been increasing political pressure to move beyond Pan-African open borders and toward increasing deportation for illegal immigrants (Landau and Misago 2009). On the other hand, this shift has been partly offset by a consistent condemnation of xenophobia by a vibrant civil society that upholds and litigates for the rights of immigrants.

At both the international and domestic levels, then, there have been countervailing pressures in both directions. Hence the response has been an intermediate one. There has been some degree of tolerance of Zimbabweans but certainly not full stretching of the refugee norm to incorporate them. The result has been an ad hoc, incoherent, and somewhat schizophrenic policy response. UNHCR has followed this approach, being constrained in taking on a strong role but able to do so when ambiguities in government positions have opened up space for assistance. For example, UNHCR has been able to offer some assistance insofar as all Zimbabweans are asylum seekers up until the point at which refugee status determination takes place, after which UNHCR has not taken any responsibility for those who have been rejected and are liable to be deported.[38]

Botswana

The international incentives on Botswana with regard to Zimbabweans have been fairly neutral. It has not faced significant international pressure or incentives to stretch or not. Few arguments have been made to the government that it should recognize Zimbabweans. The international organizations in Gaborone, especially UNHCR and the UN resident coordinator, have not criticized the government position, either privately or publicly.[39] Instead, they have been passive and accepting of their own noninvolvement in the issue and have recognized the sovereign right of the government to detain and deport.

Meanwhile, there have been strong domestic incentives against regime stretching. The electorate strongly favors deportation, and there has been growing xenophobia toward the Zimbabweans. The numbers of Zimbabweans (40,000–100,000) have been high relative to the overall population (1.8 million), and Zimbabweans in Gaborone have been associated with crime and prostitution.[40] With pressure on the country's own resources and high HIV rates, the electorate has been reluctant to allocate rights to noncitizens. The country spends more on deportation than any other country in the region except South Africa.[41]

The incentives on the government have thus been neutral at the international level, but at the domestic level there have been strong incentives against regime stretching. UNHCR's own role has followed the government's decision on non-stretching. In interviews, UNHCR staff members argued that the organization's work has been constrained by the government position, and they claimed that they could not get involved unless invited to do so by the government.

Angola

The international incentives on Angola were strongly against regime stretching for Congolese migrants. From an international political economy perspective, the government had a strong incentive to remove Congolese from the diamond mining areas. After victory in the civil war in 2002, the Movimento Popular de Libertação de Angola (MPLA) government acquired control over the previously União Nacional para a Independência Total de Angola (UNITA)-controlled diamond mining areas of the Lundas (Marques and de Campos 2005; Pearce 2004). In attempting to develop the diamond industry as part of its national economic strategy, Angola privatized the mines, selling concessions to a range of multinational corporations, which had a strong interest in controlling and limiting diamond smuggling. When the deportations began in 2003, they were therefore conceived as an anti–diamond smuggling operation to ensure exclusive access to mines for corporations rather than artisanal immigrant labor (Médecins Sans Frontières 2007). Aside from this set of economic incentives, there was almost no countervailing pressure from the international community to condemn Angola's human rights violations, partly because the international community retained a vested interest in the diamond and oil industries.

In terms of domestic incentives, the timing of the main waves of deportations correlates closely with preparations for national and regional elections. The diamond mining areas are a UNITA stronghold, and the Congolese have traditionally supported UNITA, which had tolerated their presence in the Lundas before 2002. After the MPLA government took control of those areas in 2002, however, the government sought to systematically remove Congolese from the region to prevent them from registering to vote in the buildup to regional and national elections and thus bolstering UNITA's electoral support (Médecins Sans Frontières 2008, 39).

There have therefore been strong incentives—both national and international—against regime stretching, based primarily on the privatization of diamond mines and elections in the context of the post–civil war era. Furthermore, the role of UNHCR in Angola has followed the government's nonstretching of the norm. Having not been invited by the government to engage in responding to the presence of the Congolese, it has had no clear basis for involvement and has consequently played no role on the Angolan side of the border. And on the DRC side of the border, it has argued that responding to the needs of the expelled migrants falls outside its mandate.[42]

Alternative Explanations

Beyond process tracing to highlight the sets of incentives underlying regime stretching, it is important to reflect on alternative explanations. The most obvious alternative explanation is that variation across the six cases is explained by the population itself (i.e., the level and nature of threat faced by the population in the country of origin). This might be important, because there are significant differences in the circumstances of the Zimbabwean, Congolese, and Somali populations. However, responses to the same populations are located at different points on spectrum. The Congolese (albeit from different regions of the DRC) have been met by one case of nonstretching and one of stretching; the Zimbabweans with one of nonstretching and one intermediate; and the Somalis with one of stretching and one intermediate. This suggests that what might initially be the most intuitive default explanation provides an insufficient account of the variation in response.

Furthermore, although it might be suggested that the "incentives matter" story outlined above is in some ways obvious, it is far from banal, having significant theoretical implications for the main alternative explanations, which can be derived from constructivist international relations scholarship. In particular, it offers a robust engagement with arguably the three most significant contributions to constructivist international relations in the last ten years. The three alternative explanations for variation in regime stretching can be summarized as institutionalization, international organization power, and norm localization. The important point is not to refute these as irrelevant explanations but rather to note that they are insufficient without an additional focus on the role of elite interests at the national level.

Institutionalization

Finnemore and Sikkink (1998) develop a three-stage "norm lifecycle" model, in which norms emerge, cascade, and are internalized by states. From this model, one can derive a hypothesis about what might explain variation in regime stretching at the national level. The implicit expectation would be that variation in a norm at the national level would be explained by variation in institutionalization in the international norm. However, if one were to observe variation in states with the same levels of institutionalization of the same international regime but significantly different policies and practices in a given issue area, this would be a basis on which to reject institutionalization as an adequate explanation for variation in regime stretching.

All six host states have signed and ratified the same international treaty (the 1951 convention). All except Yemen and Botswana have also signed and ratified the same regional normative framework on refugees. They have broadly similar degrees of acceptance and socialization of the regime. Yet paradoxically, one nevertheless observes very different ways in which states with similar levels of institutionalization implement that regime. The only cases in which variation in institutionalization cannot be excluded as explanatory are Yemen and Botswana, because they have not signed and ratified the regional normative refugee framework for the African region (the OAU Refugee Convention).

In that sense, institutionalization cannot provide an adequate explanation for variation in regime stretching. This is not in any way to refute Finnemore and Sikkink's (1998) norm lifecycle model. Rather, it reinforces their argument that institutionalization can be seen as an international-level process. However, it adds to the model by highlighting that there is arguably a fourth stage to the norm lifecycle model—implementation—which begins with a new phase of political contestation at the domestic level.

International Organization Power

In their work on international organization (IO) pathology, Barnett and Finnemore (2004) argue that IOs have autonomous power and authority. One of their principal case studies is UNHCR. In this case study, they claim that IOs have authority based on their power to label. In other words, IOs have the power to define how a norm is implemented in practice. In their work on UNHCR, Barnett and Finnemore look at the norm of who is a refugee. They suggest that because UNHCR can determine who is a refugee in its refugee status determination procedures for Rohinga refugees in Burma, it has power, and thus this case illustrates that IOs in general can have autonomous power (2009, 73–120).

From this work, one could generate a possible explanation for variation in regime stretching: the autonomous role of IOs defines whether stretching takes place or not. This alternative explanation would be falsifiable on the basis of a simple counterfactual: in the absence of the IO, would the government's decision about regime stretching have been significantly different? Observing the absence of a significant difference would imply that the IO was largely epiphenomenal at the level of implementation.

Indeed, within the six cases, UNHCR's role appears to have followed the state's choice about who is a refugee. Sequentially, the preferences of government elites, rather than those of UNHCR, determine how the question of who is a refugee is defined. Contra Barnett and Finnemore (2004), IO autonomy appears limited at the level of implementation.[43] However, there is some nuance to this: an important distinction exists between IOs' role at implementation between (1) an endogenous role in preference formation (where it appears to have some influence) and (2) an autonomous influence on policy (where it appears to be more of an implementing partner than an independent political actor). In none of the cases has UNHCR been able to define a position in relation to stretching that contradicts the government elite's preferences. However, it has—as in Kenya and Tanzania—been able to play a marginal role in influencing the government elite's own cost-benefit calculus through, for example, financially supporting protection and assistance for additional groups.

Norm Localization

In his norm localization model, Amitav Acharya (2004) offers an account of the way in which norms do not remain fixed in their encounter with the national level but are themselves changed. Localization, for Acharya (2004, 245–246), is the active construction (through discourse, framing, grafting, and cultural selection) of foreign ideas by national actors, which results in the former developing significant congruence with local beliefs and practices. In that sense the theory offers an implicit alternative explanation for variation in regime stretching: variation in political culture.

This explanation competes with the book's central hypothesis that variation in regime stretching can be explained by variation in incentives on government elites, and raises the question whether variation in regime stretching can be understood in primarily ideational or interest-based terms. Falsifying the role of ideas and culture is challenging. Nevertheless, there are at least two ways in which such an explanation might be rejected in favor of an interest-based account. First, this would be the case if there was variation in regime stretching across countries (or different regions within a country) with broadly the same political and legal cultures. Second, it would also be the case if one observed temporal variation in regime stretching in a given country case study.

There are several reasons to see this explanation as insufficient. First, states with broadly the same political and legal cultures, with similar colonial heritage— such as Kenya, Tanzania, Botswana, and South Africa—have had radically different responses in terms of regime stretching. Second, there have been temporal changes in policy responses to survival migration in the South African,[44]

Angolan,[45] and Yemen[46] cases, in which culture has remained constant but incentives have changed over time. Third, there is a strong epistemological argument for rejecting a cultural or ideational argument—given the difficulty of falsifying ideas—when a more parsimonious, interest-based explanation is sufficient.

Why the Theory Matters for Practice

This chapter has set out a basic conceptual framework for understanding how international institutions adapt at implementation. The framework highlights how regime adaptation can be understood at three different levels: international bargaining, institutionalization, and implementation. While there is significant literature on adaptation at the first two levels, the third remains neglected. Yet implementation matters for both theory and policy. It tells us why it is that in a given regime, even states with broadly the same levels of institutionalization may have radically different practices. Drawing attention to this institutionalization-implementation gap is crucial for understanding how international institutions really work and the impacts they have on people's lives.

Through the concept of regime stretching, the chapter has developed a way for us to understand the conditions under which international institutions adapt (or not) at the level of implementation to address new challenges that were unforeseen by the creators of the original regime. The concept is especially useful in the context of understanding when and why the refugee regime has sometimes adapted to the challenge of survival migration but other times has not. The chapter has set out regime stretching as the main dependent variable for this book. Given that the same refugee regime has adapted differently to the challenge of survival migration in different national contexts, how can we explain this variation?

In looking at this variation, the chapter has proposed a straightforward explanation for variation in regime stretching across the cases. It has argued that politics matters. When norms and international organizations enter the domestic sphere, they face a new phase of political contestation in which they are adapted and changed. In areas in which law is ambiguous or imprecise, domestic political interests will shape how old institutions are implemented in practice. Where there are positive incentives on national elites in government to engage in regime stretching, it will take place; where there are negative incentives to engage in regime stretching, it will not take place. The role of the international organization, while not entirely passive, sequentially follows the decision by the government elites.

This argument matters for both policy and theory. On a practical level, it shows that how international institutions work and what they mean in practice is shaped by their interaction with domestic politics. More importantly, though, it points to the causal mechanisms (and levers) that international policymakers can use to shape how international institutions adapt at the national level—including in relation to new and emerging challenges. Even in the absence of formal renegotiation of the international institution, and even in the absence of new signatures or ratifications of institutions, there is much that international public policymakers can do to change what international institutions do in practice. On a theoretical level, it fundamentally changes our understanding of international institutions, demonstrating that rather than being static global entities that exist primarily in Geneva or New York, they can vary in their national manifestations, and that how they vary is often shaped by rational incentives on national government elites. The book now turns to the particular case studies of national and international responses to survival migration in order to substantiate this argument.

SOUTH AFRICA

The Ad Hoc Response to the Zimbabwean Influx

Since the start of the millennium, Zimbabwe has gone from being one of the most developed countries in Africa to one that is mired in economic and political crisis. After the government of Robert Mugabe initiated a wave of land invasions to transfer white-owned farms to its political supporters in 2000, the resulting international sanctions, capital flight, declining agricultural productivity, and hyperinflation conspired to plunge living standards to a level that ranks the country alongside the most fragile and failed states in the world. In addition to widespread political violence and the persecution of people associated with the political opposition, the economic situation has undermined the majority of the population's access to food, basic services, and livelihood opportunities. Simply in order to survive or to provide basic subsistence for their families, millions of people have been forced to migrate within or beyond the borders of Zimbabwe, with nearly one-quarter of the population going into exile in neighboring countries. The resulting movement has been described as "the largest migration event in the region's recent history" (Polzer, Kiwanuka, and Takabvirwa 2010, 30).

The largest proportion of Zimbabweans abroad have moved across the border into South Africa (Betts and Kaytaz 2009; Crush and Tevera 2010; Hammar, McGregor, and Landau 2010; Kiwanuka and Monson 2009; Médecins Sans Frontières 2009; Polzer 2008). Although there are no accurate statistics available, it is commonly suggested that around 1–1.5 million Zimbabweans crossed into South Africa between 2000 and 2012 (Crisp and Kiragu 2010; Polzer 2008;

Solidarity Peace Trust 2012), making it the largest mass influx anywhere in the world since the start of the twenty-first century. However, despite the fact that the Zimbabweans have left a desperate humanitarian situation in which their most fundamental human rights cannot be guaranteed, the overwhelming majority have not been recognized as refugees. Instead, both the government of South Africa and UNHCR have consistently argued that—with very few exceptions—the Zimbabweans could not be regarded as refugees given that most were not fleeing individualized persecution. In the words of one South African human rights advocate, "most have been escaping the economic consequences of the political situation" rather than political persecution per se.[1]

The result has been that despite fleeing a desperate human rights situation—and being in a situation very similar to that of refugees—most Zimbabweans in South Africa have lacked access to a formal status and to humanitarian services such as housing, food, and health care; and they have at times been liable to roundup, detention, and deportation by the government. The gray area into which most Zimbabweans have fallen—between refugees and voluntary economic migrants—has also created ambiguity about which international organizations should take responsibility for ensuring protection and humanitarian assistance for the population. The Zimbabwean situation therefore represents an archetypal case of survival migration and a profound illustration of the limits of the existing international refugee protection regime (Polzer 2008; Betts and Kaytaz 2009). As UNHCR has acknowledged, "Zimbabwean survival migrants who have left their own country because they cannot sustain themselves and their families at home fall into an important protection gap" (Crisp and Kiragu 2010, 21).

In the absence of legal standards or specialized institutions to address such a situation, the response of the South African government has been limited, slow, and ad hoc. In practice, the bureaucratically anomalous nature of the Zimbabwean situation as outside existing categories has meant that the only way Zimbabweans have been able to regularize their stay in the country is through the asylum system. The unique nature of the South African asylum system, which provides so-called asylum seeker permits to anyone who arrives in the country seeking asylum—and provides them with the right to remain in the country and to work and move freely pending an outcome to their asylum claim—has allowed Zimbabweans to stay in the country until their claim to refugee status is adjudicated. This same quirk of granting asylum seeker permits has in turn given UNHCR a mandate to play a limited role in relation to the Zimbabwean population. However, neither the government nor any international organization has consistently taken any responsibility for providing housing, food, or access to health care. Furthermore, although the government of South Africa made some proposals for the temporary protection of all Zimbabweans in the country, these were limited in nature and never fully implemented. As a result, many have been left in a desperate humanitarian situation because of falling between the cracks of existing protection standards, and those who have not obtained an asylum seeker permit or refugee status have often been subject to roundup, detention, and deportation.

This chapter is divided into four main areas. First, it explains the underlying causes of exodus within Zimbabwe, showing that they represent an archetypal case of survival migration. Second, it outlines the response of the government of South Africa and how it has evolved over time. Third, it documents the response of the international community and in particular UNHCR's role in relation to Zimbabwean survival migration. Fourth, it offers an explanation for the response of both South Africa and the international community. Overall, the chapter suggests that the response can be characterized as ad hoc at best. On the one hand, the asylum system has been able to partly adapt in order to cover some of the humanitarian needs. On the other hand, significant gaps have been left. It argues that this response can be explained by national politics. The set of domestic and international incentives on the government to support a proactive and inclusive response have been ambivalent; a human rights–focused civil society and international criticism for the government's handling of the influx are offset by growing xenophobia within the country and a reluctance to recognize Zimbabweans in a way that might damage the country's bilateral relationship with the migrants' country of origin. Meanwhile, UNHCR's own role, it is argued, has been fairly passive, coinciding with and following the ambivalent response of the government, meaning that the refugee regime has adapted to the new challenge but only to a very limited extent and within the parameters of the government's own interests.

The Causes of the Exodus

The range of proximate motives for Zimbabweans moving to South Africa during the first decade of the twenty-first century is diverse and complex. Tara Polzer (2008, 4) highlights how the motives—both across people and even within the same person—straddle a range of conventional categories, including refugees, humanitarian migrants, economic migrants, traders, shoppers, borderland residents, transit migrants, and unaccompanied minors. Yet despite the diversity and complexity of these mixed migratory movements, the underlying cause of most of the movement has been the desire of individuals and families to develop survival strategies in the context of a politically and economically collapsing state, in which the complex interaction of state fragility, livelihoods failure, and agricultural decline have left the majority of the population destitute and without access to subsistence, employment, or health-care services within the country.

The modern history of Zimbabwe is highly politicized, and there is no single, objective historical account. Zimbabwe was previously a British colony called Southern Rhodesia. In 1965, fearing a handover to black majority rule, the white settlers' government proclaimed a Unilateral Declaration of Independence (UDI) under the leadership of Ian Smith. This led to the continuation of a liberation war by the black majority until the British government, the white Zimbabwean government, and the Zimbabwe African National Union (ZANU) met in London at Lancaster House to agree on the terms of Zimbabwean transfer to black majority rule under the presidency of Robert Mugabe.[2]

At Lancaster House an agreement was struck in December 1979 whereby the British government would support independence and provide financial assistance in exchange for postponement by the new Zimbabwean leadership of significant land reform for ten years, allowing white settlers to retain their farms. This postponement was informally extended in 1990, and it continued until New Labour came to power in the United Kingdom in 1997 and repudiated the agreement and discontinued the transfer of money.[3]

With the discontinuation of financial assistance, there were greatly diminished incentives for ZANU to desist from land reform. Under mounting pressure from war veterans and tribal leaders, the government of Zimbabwe began a process of land reform in 2000. In February 2000, it implemented its Fast Track Land Reform Programme (FTLRP). The ensuing "land reform," or *jambanja* (chaos), displaced hundreds of thousands of white commercial farmers and black farmworkers (Hammar, McGregor, and Landau 2010, 272; Kinsey 2010, 340). The reforms led to land invasions and the seizure of farms by people with little experience in large-scale food production. The ensuing agricultural collapse, exacerbated by drought, began to transform a country previously dubbed "the breadbasket of Africa" into the "basket case of Africa."[4]

As the Zimbabwe African National Union–Patriotic Front (ZANU-PF) government was increasingly challenged by the opposition Movement for Democratic Change (MDC), reports of violence, torture, and intimidation grew. The intelligence services, the police, armed mobs, and the youth wing of ZANU-PF have all been implicated in widespread human rights abuses (Human Rights Watch 2008, 2009a). During the early 2000s, the government led a series of "operations" in urban areas to assert its authority over areas that were strongholds of MDC support. In Operation Murambatsvina (Clean Up Filth), for example, it carried out demolitions that destroyed some 700,000 people's homes or livelihoods, contributing further to displacement inside and outside the country (Hammar, McGregor, and Landau 2010, 270; Musoni 2010, 301).

With accusations of human rights abuses and electoral malpractice, economic sanctions were imposed on the country by the Commonwealth, the EU, and the United States.[5] This in turn contributed to the withdrawal of multinational corporations and foreign direct investment from the country (UN Conference on Trade and Development 2008). The combination of sanctions, capital flight, land invasions, and drought led to a massive decline in agricultural productivity and economic collapse. Hyperinflation ran to millions of percent per year so that the Zimbabwean dollar was rendered worthless, and only the U.S. dollar and the South African rand represented viable sources of currency with which to purchase food. The majority of Zimbabweans lacked access to foreign currency and therefore were unable to purchase basic subsistence. Along with mass livelihood collapse and food shortages, which left 5 million dependent on food aid, disease was widespread; HIV/AIDS in particular decimated families unable to obtain antiretroviral drugs (ARVs) and often deprived families of their heads of household (Human Rights Watch 2009a).

In this context of economic and political transformation, people have adapted their survival strategies (Musoni 2010; Mawowa and Matongo 2010; Kinsey 2010). Jeremy Jones (2010), for example, has explained the emergence of a *kukiya-kiya* economy based on "getting by" within an increasingly informal political economy. A key aspect of this adaptation strategy has been migration, with people and families either choosing to leave the country in order to survive or sending particular family members abroad temporarily to engage in circular migration and send remittances back to relatives in Zimbabwe.

With almost total collapse of the formal economy, the situation reached its nadir in mid-2008. The inconclusive March 2008 elections and one-man runoff elections in June 2008 were marked by increases in state-instigated violence, the hyperinflation level reached its peak, and the country suffered the worst cholera outbreak in Africa in more than fifteen years. The exodus to South Africa reached its high point, the number of Zimbabwean asylum seekers arriving in the country representing a staggering one-quarter of the world's total number of asylum seekers for that year (Polzer 2008, 6; Hammar, McGregor, and Landau 2010, 265; Médecins Sans Frontières 2009). After South Africa brokered talks between Robert Mugabe and opposition MDC leader Morgan Tsvangirai, a Government of National Unity was proclaimed in February 2009. Meanwhile, the U.S. dollar was adopted as the country's official currency. These changes led to some improvements in the economic situation as inflation rates dropped and more goods began to appear in stores. However, despite this, those with no access to U.S. dollars are still unable to buy goods, and drought and food insecurity have continued, leading to ongoing displacement and outward migration (Crisp and Kiragu 2010; Solidarity Peace Trust 2012).

Testimonies taken from Zimbabweans in South Africa reinforce the sense that the majority of the migrants have left because of economic and social rights deprivations that in many cases violate their right to life. A thirty-three-year-old man in Musina said, "We are not here because we want to be. We are here because we were suffering in Zimbabwe. The masses are hungry—they are running from their own country" (Médecins Sans Frontières 2009, 7). And a twenty-eight-year-old man in Musina commented, "Everything was tough. You couldn't use the money to buy even a loaf of bread. That is what pushed me to leave the country. Everything was deteriorating—there was no water. It was about eight years without running water. You could get it for about two hours a day—you had to get it about around midnight" (Médecins Sans Frontières 2009, 7).

There is a lack of reliable data on the numbers and changing patterns of cross-border displacement. This is partly because of the clandestine nature of much of the movement and partly because of the political desire of both Zimbabwe and South Africa to keep the numbers low so as not to embarrass or discredit the Zimbabwean government (Crush and Tevera 2010; Polzer 2008). The politically contested nature of the figures is revealed in how the government of Zimbabwe vehemently disputes existing estimates; in the words of the Zimbabwean ambassador to South Africa: "The figures are thrown left, centre, and right, depending on what one wants to achieve. . . . Those who are negative will give you a frightening figure. Those who are objective will give you a far lesser figure."[6] One South African NGO has claimed that estimates of the number of Zimbabweans in South Africa in 2007 ranged between 1 and 9 million (Consortium of Refugees and Migrants in South Africa 2008, 17). The South African Department of Home Affairs (DHA) has frequently quoted a figure of around 2 million, based on numbers coming through the asylum system.[7] Most academics, though, suggest a number closer to 1–1.5 million entering South Africa during the entire period (Polzer, Kiwanuka, and Takabvirwa 2010). The only official statistics available come from asylum numbers; new applications were 45,000 for 2007, 250,000 for 2008, and 150,000 for 2009. However, in practice, many Zimbabweans have chosen to remain outside formal channels, which offer few economic and social benefits. Once inside South Africa, Zimbabweans have dispersed to major urban centers, townships, smaller provincial towns (such as Polokwane, Nelspruit, Bloemfontein, and Port Elizabeth), or rural villages, depending on their own combination of motives and networks (Polzer 2008, 4).

The Response of the South African Government

The response of the South African government can be characterized as ad hoc, at best. There has been a lack of formal institutional framework for addressing a group of people who fall between the extremes of refugees and voluntary economic migrants, and there have been limited legal or bureaucratic structures to deal with survival migration. The only two formal channels available for irregular immigrants to regularize their stay in post-apartheid South Africa—asylum and work permits—were of limited relevance given that so few were ultimately eligible for these statuses. Furthermore, there has been little political will to develop a fully coherent response to the Zimbabwean situation. For much of the period, Zimbabweans were vulnerable to arrest, detention, and deportation, and generally received limited material support.

Nevertheless, despite these limitations, and the absence of a coherent and focused response to the influx, a form of incremental adaptation has taken place. Existing legislation and institutions have been adapted to provide some minimum, albeit patchy and inconsistent, forms of protection. Two forms of adaptation have taken place at implementation. First, asylum legislation has been implemented (through so-called asylum seeker permits) in such a way that allowed Zimbabweans to at least obtain access to territory and the right to work, pending assessment of their asylum claim. Given the backlog in refugee status determination procedures, this has often allowed access to territory for a significant period. Second, there has been a gradual shift in the political response toward finding alternative ways to enable Zimbabweans to avoid being returned to their country of origin, mainly by drawing on and reinterpreting existing legislation. This section documents the evolving nature of the South African government's response during the period of influx in three main areas—access to status, treatment at the border, and access to material support—and examines what each has meant in practice for Zimbabweans.

Access to Status

The main laws in post-apartheid South Africa relevant to cross-border mobility are the Immigration Act and the Refugee Act. However, the Zimbabwean influx did not fall squarely in the purview of either of these laws because the overwhelming majority of Zimbabweans were not eligible for either work permits or refugee status. Despite this situation, there was a failure to produce alternative migration legislation to make provision for large-scale mixed migration (Polzer 2008). The application of the existing legal framework to the address the situation of the Zimbabweans is best understood as divided into two phases, pre- and post-April 2009. Until April 2009, the main policy toward Zimbabweans was "arrest, detain, and deport" for all those outside formal asylum or labor migration channels. After April 2009, there were some attempts to adapt policy and the application of existing legislation.

However, even before April 2009, the unique features of the South African asylum system provided the main route through which most Zimbabweans were able to acquire at least some form of legal status. As we have seen, within South Africa, anyone who wishes to seek asylum can claim an asylum seeker permit (under Section 22 of the Refugee Act), which confers on asylum seekers the right to work and freedom of movement until such time as their refugee status determination (RSD) procedure takes place and the state judges them to be a refugee or not. These permits are available at the main government Refugee Reception Offices (RROs) in Johannesburg, Pretoria, Port Elizabeth, Durban, and Cape Town (with an additional one in Musina from June 2008 until February 2009 and at Marabastad near Pretoria beginning in April 2009). The Refugee Act does not specify a time limitation for the permits, which vary between one and six months and are renewable. Given the backlog in RSD, many Zimbabweans have, in practice, been able to hold asylum seeker permits for a significant period of time. This unique feature of the South African asylum system has been the principal way in which existing legislation has offered some form of at least temporary legal status to many of the Zimbabweans. In the words of UNHCR, "the easiest (and in most instances the only) way for Zimbabweans to remain legally in South Africa and to work there is to submit an application for refugee status" (Crisp and Kiragu 2010).

However, UNHCR has described the reliance on the asylum system as "seriously dysfunctional" (Crisp and Kiragu 2010). Not only has it placed enormous strain on the asylum system itself, but it has also left significant protection gaps for the Zimbabweans. Especially until April 2009, this reliance on the asylum system left many Zimbabweans liable to arrest, detention, and deportation. Indeed, there were reasons why many people would be stopped by police and detained before obtaining an asylum seeker permit. First, people were often stopped in transit to the limited number of RROs. Although the Department of Home Affairs can and has at times issued an asylum seeker an asylum transit permit under Section 23 of the Immigration Act, which is intended to enable an asylum seeker to travel from a port of entry to a Refugee Reception Office to apply for asylum, this kind of permit has been issued for only limited periods (in Musina after February 2009).

Second, getting entry to the RROs has not always been straightforward. For example, in early 2009, the Johannesburg Refugee Reception Office located at Crown Mines, near Soweto, which has the capacity to deal with up to 700 cases per day, was receiving more than 2,000 people per day, and in 2008 the number peaked at around 3,000 per day. Those wishing to seek asylum, or to acquire an asylum seeker permit, are met on a "first come, first served" basis each morning, with those beyond the first 700 being turned away and having to wait until the next day to try to make it to the front of the line.[8] In this situation, bribery and corruption became a means of access to the building.[9] Those awaiting access to the facility often camp on vacant land near the reception center, which is housed in an industrial park. Without the valid asylum seeker permits the Zimbabweans are attempting to obtain from the reception center, they face police harassment and the risk of being rounded up, detained, and deported (Vigneswaran et al. 2010).

Furthermore, once RSD was complete, the Zimbabweans were no longer able to receive asylum seeker permits unless recognized as refugees and were liable for arrest, detention, and deportation. The refugee recognition rate for Zimbabweans has been extremely low. In the first decade of the 2000s, the Department of Home Affairs had an informal practice of rejecting all Zimbabwean applications (Polzer, Kiwanuka, and Takabvirwa 2010). Even at the peak of the crisis in 2008 and 2009, the refugee recognition rate was only around 10 percent of Zimbabweans, and refugee status was made available only to people individually persecuted because of direct political links to the opposition MDC.[10] The majority of Zimbabwean claims were regarded as "manifestly unfounded." Furthermore, significant concerns were raised about the poor quality of the process, which has generally involved rapid and illogical decision making (Amit 2010) and was described even by South African government officials as "a joke" (Crisp and Kiragu 2010, 17).

Yet once outside this system, Zimbabweans have been at risk of deportation—especially because many police officers have used their discretion in detaining illegal immigrants as a means to extort bribes (Vigneswaran et al. 2010). According to the Department of Home Affairs' own statistics, around 150,000 people were deported each year between 2001 and 2003, increasing to 175,000 in 2004, 200,000 in 2005, 250,000 in 2006, and 300,000 in 2007 and 2008 (Vigneswaran et al. 2010, 466; Crisp and Kiragu 2010). It has been suggested that a sizable majority of people recorded in these government statistics are Zimbabweans (Polzer 2008, 8).

Around the time of the peak outflow in 2008, the government came under increasing international scrutiny and pressure relating to its treatment of Zimbabweans. A range of policy options were discussed regarding how existing legislation could be applied to provide formal status. Two options were widely debated. One was the possibility of applying the broader refugee definition contained in the OAU Refugee Convention and covering events "seriously disturbing public order" in the migrant's home country (Polzer 2008). Indeed, South Africa's Refugee Act incorporates both the 1951 and OAU conventions. However, both UNHCR and the government resisted this option on the grounds that this clause in the OAU convention "lacks doctrinal clarity" (Crisp and Kiragu 2010). Beyond that, a more serious suggestion was made, based on recognition that Section 31(2)(b) of the Immigration Act allows the Home Affairs Minister to "grant a foreigner or a category of foreigners the rights of permanent residence for a specified or unspecified period when there are special circumstances." Refugee rights advocates—and UNHCR—began lobbying the government to grant Zimbabweans temporary residence permits under Section 31(2)(b).

Emerging from this discussion, and the recognition of the inadequacies of the response up until that point, several policy proposals were made in April and May 2009. First, in April, Home Affairs Minister Mosiviwe Mapisa-Nqakula announced a moratorium on deportations and a temporary "special dispensation permit" for all Zimbabweans under Section 31(2)(b) of the Immigration Act. Second, in May, the government announced a three-month visa waiver for all Zimbabweans in line with the provisions of the Southern African Development Community (SADC) Protocol on the Free Movement of Persons. Third, an additional RRO outside Pretoria, reserved for use by people coming from other SADC countries, was established to take pressure off the other RROs.

However, all these policy proposals had limitations. First, the permit system was not implemented, and Mapisa-Nqakula left office two weeks after making the announcement (Crisp and Kiragu 2010). Furthermore, although deportations were formally stopped, there were reports that the South African Police Services (SAPS) continued to deport in the aftermath of the announcement (Médecins Sans Frontières 2009). Second, the three-month visa waiver applied only to Zimbabweans with travel documents, and in practice, obtaining a passport in Zimbabwe is difficult and can cost more than eight hundred dollars. Third, although the new RRO was opened at Marabastad, the backlog of RSD decisions remained at around 400,000 and most Zimbabweans in the country continued to lack formal status (Tshisela 2010).

Even these limitations aside, the lull in South Africa's restrictive response proved short-lived. The moratorium on the deportation of Zimbabweans ran only from May 2009 until October 2011. During that period, the government implemented the Zimbabwean Dispensation Project (ZDP), which provided a short window (September 2010–December 2010) during which Zimbabweans without status could attempt to obtain either asylum seeker permits or temporary work, business, or study permits for up to four years. By the time applications submitted during the window were processed in August 2011, it was revealed that just 275,000 of the estimated 1–1.5m illegal Zimbabweans had applied. One of the biggest weaknesses was that use of the system had required applicants to have a Zimbabwean passport, which are often expensive and difficult to obtain. In the words of CoRMSA, "the entire process was held to ransom by the Zimbabwean authorities' ability to make passports available" (Consortium of Refugees and Migrants in South Africa 2011).

In October 2011, Home Affairs Minister Nkosazana Dlamini-Zuma proclaimed that "those who have failed to take advantage of this [ZDP] process will in due course face the full consequence of South Africa's immigration laws" (IRIN 2011a). The number of documented deportations at the Beitbridge border crossing was 7,755 between October and December 2011 and 7,177 between January and March 2012 (Solidarity Peace Trust 2012). The brief moratorium for Zimbabweans was effectively over.

Treatment at the Border

The main crossing point into South Africa is at Beitbridge, Zimbabwe, which borders the Limpopo province of South Africa. It is a difficult and dangerous journey that involves crossing the Limpopo River, an electrified razor wire fence, and the threat of crocodiles and other wild animals. One of the biggest threats is posed by so-called *magumagumas*—gangs that prey on border crossers, subjecting them to assault, theft, rape, and extortion. Migrants often use smugglers known as *malaishas*, but the smugglers frequently work in collusion with the *magumagumas* (Crisp and Kiragu 2010; Médecins Sans Frontières 2009; Araia 2009; International Organization for Migration 2010). Without exception, all those we interviewed had been robbed on the Zimbabwean side of the border, and there was anecdotal evidence of murder and torture.[11] Many people there arrived without money, identity documentation, or their mobile phones, and sometimes even without their clothes.[12]

On the other side of the border is the town of Musina, South Africa, with a population of around 30,000 people, which has been the first stopping point for many of the Zimbabweans. New arrivals have often been in need of assistance in the aftermath of the abuse they have been subjected to at the border. However, the government's provision of assistance at the border has been very limited, being restricted to the role of the police and the Department of Home Affairs (DHA).

The police have run a facility known as the SMG, a military base used as a detention facility. In a surreal game of cat and mouse, the police have frequently held and deported Zimbabweans if they catch them before they are able to make contact with Department of Home Affairs staff to enter the asylum system

(Crisp and Kiragu 2010). On the day we were present, for example, the police had rounded up and detained several Zimbabweans, including several heavily pregnant women. The police denied us access to the detention facilities, and it was left to UNHCR to negotiate their release. Up until April 2009, there were repeated allegations of cruel, inhuman, and degrading treatment at the SMG.

The role of the DHA in Musina has varied over time and can be considered in different phases. Before 2008, there was no DHA presence in Musina. From June 2008 until February 2009, during the peak influx after the election runoff in Zimbabwe, DHA opened an RRO at the Musina showgrounds in the center of the town. Zimbabweans previously in hiding arrived at the showgrounds to seek asylum and collect their asylum seeker permits. As a result, many thousands congregated, and the showgrounds became a de facto refugee camp. But with extremely limited security or material assistance, conditions deteriorated, and the site became squalid, disease-ridden, and violent (Human Rights Watch 2009a).

In February 2009, DHA closed the Musina RRO and the police cleared the showgrounds, forcing the Zimbabweans present to flee to Johannesburg. There the majority sought shelter in the Central Methodist Church (Médecins Sans Frontières 2009). Beginning in February 2009, DHA stopped providing asylum seeker permits in Musina and instead provided only short-term asylum transit permits to enable Zimbabweans to travel to one of the country's other RROs. Generally, they were allowed to remain in Musina only up to three days. Local churches in Musina provided land and buildings to serve as transit shelters, one for men, one for women and children, and one for unaccompanied minors.

The transit shelter for men was a small, basic plot of land, with open tents, four portable toilets, and a single drinking water tank, a camp that one of the Zimbabwean volunteers informed us sometimes hosts up to a thousand people at a time. Every day the South African Red Cross (SARC) provided only a single evening meal, delivering enough maize meal for around three pots of "pap." Furthermore, the shelter was located next to a large housing area for the local population, and some of the Zimbabwean migrants claimed that they were afraid to leave the perimeter of the shelter after dark because, in the words of one, "the local people will kill us if we do."[13] Yet there was no security presence or means of guaranteeing the safety of those staying in the exposed shelters. The women's transit center was a building situated immediately next to a nightclub where loud music was played for much of the night.

A range of international organizations and NGOs gradually formed an ad hoc but functional coalition to address basic protection needs at the Musina transit shelter centers. Between them, UNHCR, Médecins Sans Frontières (MSF),

International Organization for Migration (IOM), Save the Children UK, UNICEF, Lawyers for Human Rights, Musina Legal Advice, and the South African Red Cross had by March 2009 been able to provide basic advice and assistance to the Zimbabweans at the border, but with little support from the government and largely in spite of rather than because of guidance from the headquarters or regional offices of the major international organizations (Betts and Kaytaz 2009). From there, the Jesuit Refugee Service has provided train tickets to enable Zimbabweans to reach the RROs in Pretoria, Johannesburg, Cape Town, Durban, and Port Elizabeth (Crisp and Kiragu 2010, 16).

These limited reception structures remained relatively constant during the moratorium period of April 2009 to October 2011, and Zimbabweans were able to either claim asylum seeker permits or enter on ninety-day visas at the Musina border crossing. However, by 2011 the government had moved to gradually introduce a new set of restrictions at the border. In March 2011, it passed the Immigration Amendment Bill. Among a range of measures, it reduced the period of time that asylum seekers have to travel to an RRO to file a formal application from fourteen days to five days and created a provision to enable officials to pre-screen asylum seekers at the border post, refusing access to those whose claims are regarded as "manifestly unfounded based on the country they have come through or their transit through a 'safe third country'" (Consortium of Refugees and Migrants in South Africa 2011; IRIN 2011a). In addition, steps have been taken to close down the urban RROs and to gradually relocate all refugee reception services to border areas to enable more efficient processing, detention, and deportation (Amnesty International 2011).

Material Assistance

South Africa's "self-settlement policy" for refugees and asylum seekers has meant that, unlike in many countries, migrants have freedom of movement and the right to work, but they have very limited access to basic humanitarian services such as housing, food, and health care (Betts and Kaytaz 2009; Polzer 2008, 3). The Zimbabweans have been dispersed throughout the country, and some have found work in rural areas. However, the majority live in urban areas, with the largest number of urban Zimbabweans probably in Johannesburg, where they make up around 13 percent of the entire population, followed by other cities such as Durban, Cape Town, and Pretoria.

In Johannesburg, the downtown Central Methodist Church has been the most visible and highly publicized manifestation of the Zimbabwean exodus. Starting in May 2008, it has been occupied by Zimbabwean migrants, hosted by Bishop Paul Verryn. In April 2009, there were around 3,400 Zimbabweans living inside and outside the church. With no material assistance from government or the international community, they have formed a functioning community under challenging circumstances.[14] The church provides daily services, Bible study, a dance group, and adult education, and has worked to ensure access to a local school for children.[15]

Nevertheless, conditions in the church are dire and illustrate the desperate situation of the urban Zimbabweans. Inside the church it is difficult to stroll around corridors and rooms without stepping over or treading on sleeping bodies strewn across the floor. The building is overcrowded and has extremely poor sanitation. Young mothers, pregnant women, and small children were sleeping on the floor. We also found 102 unaccompanied minors as young as seven years old sleeping on the floor in a room of about 10 meters by 10 meters, with supervision from just one MSF volunteer. Meanwhile, a small, cramped upstairs room with foam mattresses was the only space for seriously ill Zimbabweans, looked after by Zimbabwean volunteers and suffering from illnesses including HIV/AIDS, cholera, and tuberculosis.

Beyond the Central Methodist Church, the majority of Zimbabweans are fairly hidden from public view. In Johannesburg, many stay in urban, crime-ridden ghettos such as Hillbrow, Yeoville, and Windsor, which have a reputation for gun crime, prostitution, and drugs. An MSF survey looked at 62 buildings in these inner city areas where 50,000–60,000 people, mainly migrants, live. They found appalling conditions, including high rates of respiratory and dermatological illnesses that specifically relate to poor living conditions. Lynne Wilkinson, deputy head of mission for MSF, said: "Many of the people living in these buildings have been displaced by political violence, instability and economic crisis in their own countries—they have been forced to migrate to South Africa to survive, similar to people seeking refuge in formal refugee camps around the world. We need to start recognizing that the majority of the building inhabitants have nowhere else to go and are forced by circumstance to live in these appalling conditions" (Mail and Guardian 2010).

In theory, the South African Constitution guarantees noncitizens access to the same basic services as nationals, including access to health care. However, in practice, Zimbabweans have faced discrimination from public service providers. UNHCR has reported that "despite the generous provisions of the South African Constitution, practical access to public services such as education and health is often very difficult for foreign nationals" (Crisp and Kiragu 2010). A report by MSF (2009) highlights how foreigners are frequently discriminated against in access to health care: people seriously ill with HIV/AIDS and malaria, even victims of rape and serious assault, have been turned away from emergency rooms because they are foreign.

The Response of the International Community

The protection of Zimbabweans in South Africa has fallen between the cracks of different international organizations' mandates. UNHCR's role in relation to the Zimbabweans in South Africa has, by its own admission, "been a subtle and arguably ambiguous one" (Crisp and Kiragu 2010). It has consistently regarded most Zimbabweans as not being refugees. Only the quirk of the South African asylum system—of granting asylum seeker permits to all who request them—has categorized Zimbabweans as people who fall within the purview of UNHCR's mandate. In the words of one staff member, "in South Africa, an involvement with refugees and asylum seekers inevitably means an involvement with migrants because such large numbers of migrants have entered the asylum system" (Crisp and Kiragu 2010, 21). This asylum seeker link to UNHCR's mandate has meant that UNHCR has played a practical role in trying to ensure and oversee access to the asylum system at the border and at RROs. However, due to its limited staff and presence at both locations, its significance in relation to this role has been called into question; one DHA staff member described UNHCR as "largely invisible."[16]

Furthermore, UNHCR has provided very little material assistance to the Zimbabweans. Its community services role for urban refugees has been limited. Even in the case of the Central Methodist Church—arguably the most visible example of Zimbabwean sanctuary during the crisis—no UNHCR staff member even entered the building until February 2009 and that was only to do a registration exercise with DHA. Rather than work to provide assistance, UNHCR has generally seen Zimbabweans in the asylum system as a problem. In the words of the organization's regional representative at the peak of the crisis:

> South Africa—we have a big problem here, primarily because you have only the asylum route as a way for people to regularize their stay. Of course, under the Immigration Act, there are possibilities for people to obtain different permits, work permits and student permits. But for whatever reason, people are not resorting to that. So people just use the asylum system and become asylum seekers. . . . After the xenophobic attacks, many undocumented people sought to regularize their stay through asylum. The easiest way to stay is to go the asylum route. But this needs to be revisited. You cannot allow each and everyone to take the asylum route because you are penalizing the genuine cases, and then this whole system becomes unmanageable.[17]

Consequently, UNHCR began to advocate for alternative responses to the crisis that would take responsibility outside the asylum and refugee framework. In UNHCR's own words: "In advocating for a moratorium on the deportation of

Zimbabweans, however, UNHCR has unusually asked for the principle of non-refoulement to be applied to a non-refugee group" (Crisp and Kiragu 2010, 21). On the one hand, this can be read as an attempt to ensure a more coherent and sustainable response to the problem. On the other hand, it can also been seen as an attempt to take the issue outside UNHCR's mandate.

According to UNHCR, other members of the UN Country Team were "relatively inactive" because "they perceive it as a 'UNHCR problem,'" and "irregular migrants constitute a grey zone in the UN system" (Crisp and Kiragu 2010). The Office of the High Commissioner for Human Rights (OHCHR) is the UN's human rights agency but has had very little presence in the country and has remained relatively quiet on the issue of the treatment of the Zimbabweans. The Office for the Coordination of Humanitarian Affairs (OCHA), as the main humanitarian actor, became involved with situation of immigrants including Zimbabweans during the xenophobic violence in May 2008 but subsequently played no role because it did not regard the situation as a humanitarian crisis. Meanwhile, IOM, although a specialized migration organization, has been able to get involved only insofar as it has specific projects with earmarked budget lines to engage with the situation. Given the absence of such funding, it has played almost no protection function in relation to the Zimbabweans.[18] The South African Red Cross has attempted to provide material support and basic humanitarian assistance, but its budget is extremely limited and staff members have acknowledged that they are overstretched and that the amount of food they have supplied has been insufficient.[19] This was starkly illustrated by the fact that they were able to provide only one meal per day to Zimbabweans staying in the church shelters in Musina; on the day we were present, the shelters received no delivery at all.

In the absence of coherent action by the major international organizations, it was left to NGOs or the initiative of specific agency employees on the ground to try to fill the gaps on an ad hoc basis. In particular, MSF-Belgium covered gaps in health-care access, as well as other forms of urban assistance. In 2007, it opened two projects to respond to the health needs of Zimbabweans: a mobile clinic Musina and a fixed MSF clinic at the Central Methodist Church, both of which provided primary health care, referrals to hospitals, and other humanitarian assistance. It also recorded and published testimonies from Zimbabweans and provided other services such as support to unaccompanied minors (Médecins Sans Frontières 2009).

Meanwhile, in both Musina and urban areas, it has been an ad hoc coalition of staff from international organizations and NGOs—often working in spite of rather than because of coherent instructions from their headquarters or regional offices—that has ensured at least some basic forms of coordinated assistance. The coalition of organizations working to offer legal advice and assistance in Musina, for example, has gradually evolved, based largely on the goodwill and adaptation of individual employees as much as formal organizational mandates (Betts and Kaytaz 2009). In summary, the Zimbabwean issue has been treated by the international community like a "humanitarian hot potato," with key actors in the UN system consistently trying to pass protection responsibility on to other actors.

Explaining the National Response

South Africa's response can be characterized as ad hoc. In comparison with the other case studies in the book, it represents an intermediate response to the new challenges of survival migration. On the one hand, its national asylum system partly stretched to cover the situation of the Zimbabweans: the asylum system was able to adapt somewhat through making asylum seeker permits available to all, and starting in April 2009, the government began at least to consider alternative ways to protect the Zimbabweans. On the other hand, adaptation was not a serious priority for the government, and serious political engagement with the issue was late and involved limited adaptation to the situation, leaving significant gaps in protection. The question is, why?

Following the conceptual framework outlined earlier in the book, this section identifies the sets of incentives on the government to adapt and stretch the notion of who is a refugee. It examines the domestic and international incentives on government elites and, in both cases, finds countervailing tendencies. In one direction, there was pressure from civil society and the international community to respect the human rights of Zimbabweans and not deport them. In the other direction, though, domestic pressure created by increasing xenophobia and international limitations created by the desire of the government to maintain a strong bilateral relationship with Zimbabwe curtailed serious political engagement with the problem.

Domestic

Domestic public opinion has created an ambivalent set of incentives for the government's engagement with the Zimbabwean influx. On the one hand, post-apartheid South Africa has attempted to uphold a commitment to respecting the rights of migrants, based on a form of Pan-African cosmopolitanism. This has its roots in the apartheid history of the country and the transnational solidarity that emerged between black South Africans and the citizens and governments of neighboring states that frequently offered sanctuary and political support to South African exiles. The idea had one of its most vocal expressions in former president Thabo Mbeki's famous "South Africa for Africans" speech in the late 1990s, and strikes a chord with cultural notions of *ubuntu*, which implies an Africa for Africans. In migration policy, the implications of this idea are that there are normative restrictions on the extent to which regional migration policy can be developed in a purely exclusionary and narrowly self-interested way. The idea can be found in the policy justifications of decision makers in almost all branches of the South African government that work on migration:

> During Apartheid days, many South Africans were in exile. They were accommodated by neighboring states. There is a need to reciprocate. It made us look at migrants in a very different way. (Director, Immigration Policy, Department of Home Affairs)[20]

> When Mbeki was head of state, he had to make everyone toe the line. He said: number one, we have to give respect to Africa; number two, we have to give help; we have to have an African renaissance, and he got everyone to toe the line. In foreign affairs, this was clear; in Rwanda, we had peacekeeping forces; in West Africa, we had problems and we had to go to Ivory Coast, to Liberia; he was asked by the Economic Community of West African States [ECOWAS] region to go and talk to Taylor and persuade him to leave. So that period of Mbeki—and I don't think the new administration is going to change that policy—was to make everyone toe the line. That is why up to now the policy is when people come here, South Africa will not build refugee camps; the policy of South Africa is to let people stay within the communities so that they can share whatever we have. That still stands, and I don't think it will change. . . . During the era of apartheid, we were isolated; we never linked with anyone. We were just like a frog in a little pond; we never got out. Now we have to learn to live with other people, and you cannot live with other people unless you allow other people to live with you. (Executive manager, International Relations, Africa Desk, Department of Labour)[21]

> South Africa's interests are African interests. The thrust of our foreign policy is to say "a better Africa, a better world." We cannot be an island of prosperity in a sea of poverty and underdevelopment and insecurity. That is why our first priority is that we prioritize Africa. Whatever Africa experiences negatively affects us. The first priority is the African agenda. (Director, Humanitarian Affairs, Department of Foreign Affairs)[22]

Indeed, post-apartheid South Africa has a constitution that reflects this view, explicitly enshrining the rights of migrants to many of the same fundamental sets of rights available to citizens. Furthermore, the country has developed a vibrant civil society and an active human rights community that has consistently litigated on behalf of the rights of migrants (Crisp and Kiragu 2010). The NGO Lawyers for Human Rights, for example, has fought numerous cases on behalf of Zimbabwean migrants, creating a judicial constraint on the restrictive policies that the government can adopt.[23]

On the other hand, this ideological and judicial barrier to total exclusion has been counterbalanced by a set of disincentives to expand the rights of Zimbabweans. With 27 percent unemployment in the country in 2010 and increasing competition for jobs and resources, there has been a shift in public attitudes toward a more communitarian sense of South Africa for South Africans. In the words of one young, white South African: "There is no real future for whites in South Africa. . . . What I am asking for is an equal chance. . . . If there is going to be a revolution in this country, it is going to come from our side. . . . Immigrants compete down wages and so they are resented by the blacks, who are already preventing whites from getting jobs."[24]

Indeed, the massive growth in xenophobia was especially particularly evident in May 2008, when large-scale xenophobic violence was perpetrated by South Africans against immigrants predominantly from other sub-Saharan African states. More than sixty foreigners were killed and more than 100,000 displaced, contributing to a shift in the terms of the immigration debate (Landau and Misago 2009). Against this backdrop, it has been difficult for politicians to argue for an expansion of migrant rights. The regional representative for UNHCR articulated the dilemma faced by the country:

> By definition, if you start looking at an issue, you will adopt a more restrictive policy. South Africa is like any other country. It cannot afford to let everyone and anyone in. . . . I ask myself if we are playing with fire here. When we look at the xenophobic violence last year, it shows a total disconnect between the way the government sees things and the policies it articulates and the population's concerns especially in relation to immigration. When it comes to people moving, you cannot ignore it. . . . It poses fundamental questions for the post-'94 South Africa, which was a pro-Africa agenda. They will keep telling you their foreign policy is essentially a pro-Africa policy. There is a little bit of a contradiction there between, on the one hand, saying that, and, on the other hand, controlling immigration. But on the other hand, you still have to deport people.[25]

Given these countervailing pressures, it is unsurprising that there was little decisive response by the government and that its approach was characterized by ad hoc "muddle through." The government lacked the leadership or clarity of vision required to make addressing the Zimbabwean influx a major legislative priority in a country in which many other issues, such as housing, public service delivery, unemployment, income inequality, and HIV/AIDS, were competing for political priority (Crisp and Kiragu 2010, 19). Moreover, coherently addressing the issue would have required significant coordination among multiple government departments, including Labour, Home Affairs, Foreign Affairs, Health, Education, and Social Development (Crisp and Kiragu 2010; Polzer 2008, 10).

International

Incentives have pulled in opposite directions at the international level as well, which likewise helps to explain the muddle-through nature of the government's response. On the one hand, as a liberal democratic state, South Africa has been greatly concerned to maintain its international reputation and be seen as a benevolent hegemon in the region. Consequently, it has been sensitive to international criticism over how it has handled the Zimbabwean exodus, for which it has been subject to widespread condemnation by human rights NGOs (Human Rights Watch 2008, 2009a), international organizations (Médecins Sans Frontières 2009; Crisp and Kiragu 2010), academics (Betts and Kaytaz 2009), and the media. Polzer (2008, 16–17) highlights why South Africa has not been able to ignore this criticism: "There has been increasing international media and civil society attention to South Africa's response to Zimbabweans in the country. The focus has been on abuses which Zimbabweans experience in trying to access the asylum system and during deportation. As with South Africa's treatment of African foreigners more generally and the xenophobic attacks in townships throughout South Africa, this issue is significantly denting South Africa's international reputation as a rights-respecting African leader." It is arguably these reputational concerns that led the government to at least begin to develop some kind of policy framework to address the influx in April 2009.

On the other hand, South Africa's regional priorities have served as a political barrier against an inclusive approach toward the Zimbabweans. The South African government has been trying to maintain a strong bilateral relationship with Zimbabwe and to play a regional role in mediating between ZANU-PF and the MDC in the establishment and consolidation of the country's power-sharing agreement. South Africa's approach in mediating the SADC-facilitated Global Political Agreement has been characterized by a silent diplomacy that attempts to avoid overt condemnation of Mugabe or the Zimbabwean regime (Vale 2003). This position has made the South African government reluctant to explicitly identify the Zimbabwean migrants as fleeing a desperate humanitarian or human rights situation in a manner that might alienate Zimbabwe. In Polzer's words (2008, 16), "South Africa's role, as mandated by SADC, in mediating between the Zimbabwean political parties has strongly coloured debates on potential responses towards Zimbabweans in South Africa."

Furthermore, during the Mbeki regime in particular, the president's personal relationship with Mugabe placed a strong constraint on the degree to which the country could be seen to be criticizing Mugabe, either directly or through recognizing fleeing Zimbabweans as victims of a failed and human rights–abusing state. For example, at the Zimbabwean embassy in Pretoria, the office of the Zimbabwean ambassador to South Africa was adorned with photographs of Mugabe and Mbeki embracing each other, and even of the ambassador and Mbeki socializing together. This camaraderie is characteristic of the unity between the heads of state in the SADC countries who were of the generation that fought liberation struggles against white colonial rule. As Hammar, McGregor, and Landau (2010, 269) put it: "Mbeki's protracted support for ZANU-PF revealed the importance of solidarity among a cohort of liberation leaders." Yet even with the election of Jacob Zuma as South African president, little seems to have changed in South Africa's approach toward Zimbabwe.

To illustrate how the bilateral relationship has served as a constraint on migration policy toward the Zimbabweans, we can turn to April 2009, when South Africa posited its policy reforms. Indeed, before South Africa announced the proposal for an immigration exemption permit for all Zimbabweans and the suspension of deportations, it first consulted the Zimbabwean government. According to the senior staff members in the Department of Home Affairs, a meeting was held at Victoria Falls in March 2009 in which the Ministry of Foreign Affairs, together with staff from the Department of Home Affairs, discussed its ideas for suspending deportations with Zimbabwean officials and sought their approval before announcing the changes.

Explaining the International Response

The response of the international community to the Zimbabwean exodus has been timid. Generally, international organizations—including UNHCR—have sought to pass the buck and avoid adopting the influx as "their" issue, principally because of the absence of designated staff or financial resources to address such a situation. The Zimbabweans have been within UNHCR's existing mandate insofar as they are holders of asylum seeker permits. However, the organization has tried to reduce its role by seeking alternative channels, outside the refugee regime, through which to address the influx. Interviews with UNHCR staff members in the Regional Office highlighted their despair at the pressure created on the organization and their personal workloads in the context of the influx. They have argued that the majority of Zimbabweans are not refugees; they have avoided invoking the OAU Refugee Convention in way that might have brought the Zimbabweans within the refugee regime; and they have advocated for special immigration exemption status as a way to alleviate pressure on the asylum system.

In advocating in this way, UNHCR has consistently maintained the same position as the South African government. In its own justification of its role—in its internal evaluation, for example—it consistently highlights the coincidence of interests with the government: "Like South Africa itself, UNHCR considers the majority of Zimbabweans not to be refugees," and "UNHCR and the South African government had a common interest in avoiding a situation in which a mixed migration scenario is turned into a refugee problem" (Crisp and Kiragu 2010, 21, 24). On the one hand, one could suggest that moving toward an alternative mechanism for addressing the influx was eminently sensible. On the other hand, UNHCR's advocacy position enabled it both to minimize its own responsibility for the situation and to avoid overtly contradicting the government. Médecins Sans Frontières (2009, 9), for example, raised concerns about the motives underlying UNHCR's advocacy of an immigration exemption permit: "The 12-month permit will be issued under the Immigration Act [rather than the Refugee Act]. This may allow the UNHCR to abdicate its international protection responsibility. This potentially means that there is no one responsible or accountable for addressing the needs of Zimbabweans in relation to shelter, for example." As well as its capacity constraints, UNHCR has, like South Africa, a strong disincentive to be seen as directly or indirectly critical of the government of Zimbabwe. The organization has effectively been compromised in its position to advocate for Zimbabwean rights in South Africa by needing to preserve diplomatic ties with Zimbabwe and protection space inside the country for other groups of refugees, not least the Congolese refugees in the Tongogara refugee camp.[26]

The coincidence of interest between UNHCR's advocacy position and the government's own position raises the question whether UNHCR had any significant autonomous influence over the direction of either its role or the wider policy developments toward the Zimbabweans. UNHCR has argued that it played an autonomous role in shaping the development of the April 2009 proposals: "UNHCR's Pretoria office has played an important role in advocating on behalf of effective refugee protection and migration management strategies in South Africa. Those efforts appeared to have come to fruition in April 2009, when Home Affairs Mosiviwe Mapisa-Nqakula announced a major change in the government's existing policy on mixed and irregular migration" (Crisp and

Kiragu 2010, 22). However, the fact that the proposals for immigration exemption permits were not fully implemented reinforces the sense that UNHCR's influence over policy has been extremely limited and that UNHCR has been more of a follower than a leader of South Africa's policy toward the Zimbabweans. In other words, UNHCR's own mandate has "stretched" to address survival migration only insofar as the government's own policy has been prepared to adapt and frame UNHCR's role and involvement. The sense of weakness felt by UNHCR is reinforced by the fact that in UNHCR's own evaluation, one staff member likened his job to "constantly banging your head against a brick wall" (Crisp and Kiragu 2010, 22).

Conclusion

The Zimbabwean influx represents an archetypal case of survival migration. People have been displaced by a complex variety of factors and have had mixed motives for migrating. However, underpinning most people's decision to leave has been their inability to maintain the most basic conditions of life for themselves and their families in their country of origin. Yet because the majority have fled the interaction of state fragility, food insecurity, and the absence of livelihood opportunities—rather than political persecution per se—most have fallen outside the definition of a refugee.

The South African response has been at best ad hoc, representing an intermediate response in comparison with the other cases addressed in this book. This domestic refugee regime has been more adaptive than in Botswana and Angola but less so than in Tanzania and Kenya. For much of the period, Zimbabweans have been liable to arrest, detention, and deportation. Yet there have been two ways in which the refugee regime has partly stretched to mitigate this. First, the quirk in the asylum system that enables anyone who wishes to do so to acquire an asylum seeker permit pending refugee status determination has given hundreds of thousands of Zimbabweans the temporary right to remain on the territory, move freely, and work. Second, in April 2009 the government temporarily suspended deportations and even proposed some form of temporary protection, although the implementation of these proposals was patchy. However, throughout the period, there was no adaptation of the refugee regime to provide anything like adequate humanitarian assistance, food, and housing to those who needed it. Meanwhile, the international response similarly stretched only partly. UNHCR reluctantly covered part of the protection gap for Zimbabweans to the extent that South Africa's own policy framework brought Zimbabweans within the asylum system. However, its role was confined to oversight and legal advice within the asylum system rather than more substantial humanitarian assistance.

The limited regime stretching that took place can be explained by South Africa's concern to uphold respect for human rights and limit international criticism. On the other hand, the domestic constraint created by increasing xenophobia and the international constraint posed by South Africa's desire to maintain a close bilateral relationship with Zimbabwe placed limits on any adaptation of the regime. Both of these factors created strong disincentives for politicians to assume the kind of leadership role that would have been required for a more coherent adaptation to the new circumstances. The international community's timid role can be explained by the fact that actors such as UNHCR sought to limit their involvement (and resource commitments) as much as possible, while also avoiding confrontation with the South African and Zimbabwean governments. The outcome was a passive and halfhearted adaptation that left hundreds of thousands of Zimbabwean survival migrants in desperate conditions.

BOTSWANA
The Division of Zimbabweans into Refugees and Migrants

South Africa has not been the only state affected by the Zimbabwean influx, although it remains the most high profile of the receiving countries. Zimbabwean survival migrants have dispersed throughout southern Africa, including to Botswana, Zambia, Mozambique, Malawi, and Namibia. Second to South Africa, Botswana has been the primary destination. Although far smaller than the movement to South Africa, the number of people crossing the border has been significant relative to Botswana's overall population. At the height of the crisis in 2008, it is estimated that some 1 million individuals crossed the border, and between 40,000 and 100,000 Zimbabweans were believed to have been resident in a country with an overall population under 2 million.[1]

Botswana has been recognized as having "the most exclusionary policy towards Zimbabweans" in the region (Kiwanuka and Monson 2009). In contrast to South Africa, where Zimbabweans have at least had access to territory and a brief period of moratorium against deportation, Botswana has drawn a sharp dichotomy between refugees and economic migrants. Those entering the asylum system have been detained in Francistown pending refugee status determination and then encamped in the Dukwi Refugee Camp if successfully recognized. Those who have not entered the asylum system or who have fallen outside the 1951 convention definition of a refugee have received no assistance and have faced the risk of roundup, arrest, and deportation—despite the virtual collapse of the Zimbabwean state (Betts and Kaytaz 2009).

The international response has replicated the government's approach of starkly distinguishing between refugees and economic migrants. UNHCR and the other UN agencies have provided assistance to the relatively small number of Zimbabwean refugees in the asylum system. UNHCR—with support from the UN Development Programme (UNDP), UNICEF, and the World Food Programme (WFP)—has focused on fulfilling this core aspect of its mandate, working to ensure that Botswana complies with its basic refugee obligations. However, the entire UN system has refrained from any protection, assistance, or advocacy in relation to the much larger group of vulnerable Zimbabwean migrants outside the asylum system.

This dichotomy has had significant human consequences for the many desperate Zimbabweans outside the asylum system. Eager to earn money to remit to family back home rather than be trapped in detention or the refugee camp, most have bypassed the asylum system. Yet by being present illegally, they have risked exploitation and have been forced to live in poverty. Those with HIV/AIDS have been deprived of access to ARVs and basic health care. Meanwhile, children, including unaccompanied minors, have lacked access to education.

The contrast with South Africa's response, and the attendant human rights implications, raises the question why the refugee regime has so manifestly failed to stretch to address the needs of the Zimbabweans. This chapter argues that the dichotomy can again be explained by the particular configuration of domestic and international incentives on the Botswana government elite. At the domestic level, there have been strong and growing popular pressures to limit Zimbabwean immigration, as an increasingly xenophobic population has become concerned about resource competition, jobs, crime, and security. The relatively weak civil society has meant a lack of sustained advocacy in favor of expanded protection for the Zimbabweans. At the international level, UNHCR and other international institutions have exerted very little influence over the government. Because Botswana is a "middle-income country," the UN system there has been small, with limited capacity or influence, and Botswana has had a degree of economic and political autonomy far greater than many other sub-Saharan African states.

Zimbabweans in Botswana

There is a long history of cross-border movements between Zimbabwe and Botswana, including by shoppers, informal cross-border traders, and skilled and unskilled migrants. However, the levels of movement increased rapidly in the first decade of the 2000s, reaching a peak immediately after the 2008 Zimbabwean elections. In contrast to South Africa, Botswana's president was quick to condemn the election results and the influence of Robert Mugabe, leading many Zimbabweans to regard Botswana as a sympathetic safe haven.

While the preferred route for many Zimbabweans has been to travel to South Africa, Botswana has offered a more accessible alternative. The border is near Bulawayo, is easy to access, and avoids the pitfalls of the crocodiles of the Limpopo River, the lions of the Krueger National Park, and the *magumagumas* (bandits) lining the South African border. Despite Botswana's three-hundred-mile-long electrified fence, entry at the Rwamakwegbana border crossing, which separates Plumtree, Zimbabwe, from Francistown, Botswana, is relatively straightforward.

Those entering Botswana have a slightly different profile from those entering South Africa, reflecting their different journeys. Whereas the nature of the route to South Africa necessitates longer-term migration, the patterns of mobility to Botswana have frequently been more short-term. They includes significant temporary, circular migration. People come to find piece jobs in agriculture, construction, and the service sector, for example, leaving their families and dependents behind with the aim of sending money back across the border. As Mary Ratau of the local NGO Ditshwanelo explains, "They are not here for purposes of wanting a long time or permanent stay. They are just coming to make a few pulas and then go back. But the law cannot accommodate this. Because they are very rigid and there is a maximum period of stay. After which you have to acquire a residence permit; otherwise you are breaking the law."[2]

Yet although many come as circular migrants, the strategy remains based on desperation. Ratau explains: "The majority come because the situation is dire and Botswana is closer to Zimbabwe. . . . It is survival migration."[3] They come because of the absence of livelihood opportunities in Zimbabwe and with the hope of remitting some basic income to support their families.[4] Kiwanuka and Monson (2009, 25) confirm this underlying motivation: "Migration emerged for many as the only solution to an economic situation that has depleted access to an increasing number of basic human rights, in many cases threatening the very survival of migrants and their families." Although there are many categories of migration—people leave for a range of proximate reasons, including persecution, economic deprivation, and labor migration—"all these categories of mobility occur against a backdrop of economic—and arguably state—collapse, and may thus be considered a form of forced rather than voluntary migration."

The precise number of Zimbabwean immigrants to have crossed into Botswana is hard to estimate accurately because so much of this migration has been informal. The government immigration office has recorded the number of people crossing into Botswana, and the International Organization for Migration (IOM) has begun to record the numbers of people being deported back to the Zimbabwean side. The available statistics suggest that at the height of the crisis more than a million people per year crossed from Zimbabwe to Botswana in 2008 and 2009. This figure, though, includes many people who came temporarily or "recycled" back and forth over the border. Anecdotal evidence suggests that in early 2009 there were likely around 40,000–100,000 undocumented Zimbabweans in Botswana, in addition to just under 1,000 Zimbabwean refugees.[5] Although this number is much smaller than in South Africa, it is nevertheless significant for a country with a population of around 1.9 million.

On arrival at the country's eastern border, Zimbabweans who are identified by the authorities are transferred to the detention center at Francistown for refugee status determination.[6] Routine detention began in 2002. All asylum seekers are detained, and the determination process is slow and can take more than a year. If accepted, refugees are passed to the nearby Dukwi Refugee Camp, where—with the exception of those who are granted work visas—they are forced to reside. Botswana's recognition rate for Zimbabwean refugees has been high, especially for those fleeing postelection economic and political collapse in 2008. Yet most Zimbabweans remain outside the asylum system, deterred by the long wait and the conditions in the Francistown detention center and the Dukwi camp.

The number of Zimbabwean refugees in the country has remained constant between 2009 and 2012 at around 900, out of a total national refugee population of around 3,800.[7] Instead, the overwhelming majority bypass the asylum system entirely and either cross the border illegally or use temporary visitor permits issued at the border. This places them outside both the national and international institutional response, rendering them largely invisible to the UN agencies in the country.

The majority of "illegal" Zimbabweans have resided in Gaborone and Francistown, while others have been in minor towns such as Lobatse and Selibe-Phikwe and villages close to agricultural areas such as Malepolole and Muchudi (Monson and Kiwanuka 2009, 31). They have been forced to live in poor areas and shantytowns. One of the main concentrations is in an area of Gaborone called Old Phakalane, which has gradually become known as Little Harare. There Zimbabweans line the streets, take residence in derelict or semi-complete housing structures, and either beg or line up each morning for piecework.

Outside formal channels, and without sources of assistance, the illegal Zimbabweans have been vulnerable to exploitation and abuse. High demand for unskilled labor on farms and in domestic work has created opportunities for exploitation. Women have been especially vulnerable, Ratau explains: "For women, they are selling commodities, small goods just to earn a living. Or they do piecework as domestic workers. But they are very abused because they do not have papers. Whoever employs them will not pay them at the end of the month or will benefit from them sexually, and they do not really have recourse because they cannot go to the police."[8] Both male and female prostitutes, sometimes underage, are common, with Zimbabweans offering unprotected sex for as little as 30 South African rand—around US$3.[9]

Although there are no significant reports of large-scale xenophobic violence, the Batswana have sometimes been hostile to Zimbabwean immigrants because of their perceived association with crime and HIV, and there have been occasional reports of attacks. Furthermore, many basic public services have been entirely unavailable to Zimbabweans. Health care—including ARVs—is unavailable to undocumented migrants.[10] This issue was raised in a report to the Committee on the Elimination of Racial Discrimination in 2006, which found existing practices to be discriminatory. However, in talks the government has opposed access to ARVs on the basis that people need to be on ARVs for life and it is "better not to start"; the government also fears that offering health benefits to Zimbabweans would "open up the floodgates."[11]

The absence of material assistance to Zimbabweans has also meant that there are no programs for undocumented children.[12] There are no reliable figures for the numbers of unaccompanied minors (UAMs) and children among the Zimbabwean populations. However, extrapolating from the proportion of Zimbabwean refugees who are under age fifteen would suggest that, based on the most conservative estimate of 40,000 undocumented Zimbabweans, there are around 3,000 undocumented Zimbabwean children, who have no access to protection or services such as education and health care.[13] The Botswana Council of Churches and the Botswana Red Cross have offered some support to the Zimbabweans, especially UAMs, but it has remained limited.

The Response of the Government

The Botswana government's approach to immigration has been dominated by a focus on internal security and economic nationalism under President Ian Khama. Since the 1990s, the state has been regarded as an economic success story, and has implemented austerity measures under structural adjustment programs to emerge with one of the highest economic growth rates and most stable democracies in sub-Saharan Africa. Yet, as a small state, with a former military president and facing the economic challenge of an HIV/AIDS epidemic, it has focused increasingly on national security.

This logic of national security has shaped the state's overall response to immigration. In 2003, it built an electric fence three hundred miles long and two meters high along the border with Zimbabwe, ostensibly to stop the spread of foot-and-mouth disease among livestock, giving it the strongest border capacity in the region.[14] In 2005, the government reviewed its immigration policy to increase deterrence, adding penalties for illegal migration and harboring migrants, and introducing a US$40 fine for unlawful entry. Those who are present illegally or are not recognized as refugees are liable to be detained and deported.

This approach is reflected in the national response to the Zimbabwean influx. Those conforming to the 1951 refugee definition have been allowed to remain but are confined to camps. Those not recognized as refugees have received no assistance or protection and have been liable to roundup, detention, and deportation. In contrast to South Africa, there has not even been a national debate on forms of protection or assistance to Zimbabweans who do not fit the refugee definition, even at the height of the crisis across the border. In that sense, the response reflects the limitations of the global refugee regime at the national level. Botswana's national refugee legislation is one of the oldest on the continent. The 1967 Refugee Recognition and Control Act predates the 1969 OAU convention, and the government entered reservations on the elements of the 1951 convention relating to freedom of movement and the right to work. Consequently, asylum seekers are required to remain in detention in Francistown during their RSD process. If they receive recognition, they are entitled to live in the refugee camp but can apply for a work permit if and when they find work.[15]

The recognition rate for Zimbabweans is high, and almost all who have applied were accepted after the 2008 Zimbabwean elections.[16] Once recognized, the refugees are compelled to stay in the camp, and the government even considered building a fence around the camp in 2009 before eventually dropping the proposal. The government is able to impose this policy of zero freedom of movement because at the time it developed its national refugee legislation in 1967, it entered reservations in acceding to the 1951 convention on refugees' rights to freedom of movement and employment. Many refugees abandon the Dukwi camp, but those who do so without a work permit break the law and forfeit their access to assistance.

Beyond the asylum system, the government operates an even more draconian approach to irregular migrants. Aside from South Africa and Namibia, it is the only country in the region that regularly deported large numbers of Zimbabwean nationals throughout the crisis, an average of 5,000 per month in 2008 and 2009 (Monson and Kiwanuka 2009). Botswana puts more money into deportation than any country in the region except South Africa, spending around 2 million pula (approximately US$285,000) per month.[17]

In order to carry out deportations, the police conducts sporadic raids, especially around Gaborone, detaining people and then transporting them back to the Rwamakwegbana border post in large trucks, where they are handed over to IOM and offered reintegration packages at the Plumtree border post on the Zimbabwean side. Using biometrics and iris scanning, IOM now routinely records data on those being sent back.[18] Since establishing its Plumtree Reception and Support Centre in 2008, it has documented and assisted more than 150,000 forcibly returned people.[19]

The International Response

International organizations have had little strategy in response to Zimbabwean survival migration to Botswana. Alice Mogwe of Ditshwanelo said of the response of UN agencies: "I'm not sure how effective they are. They are very governmental and so there are restrictions on them in terms of what they can and cannot do."[20] Across all the main UN agencies present in the country, there has been no mechanism or advocacy strategy whatsoever to promote protection or assistance for Zimbabweans outside the asylum system.

UNHCR's effort has been confined to working within the asylum system, sitting in on refugee status determination, and training government immigration officers involved in the asylum process. It has also run a variety of programs for refugees on livelihoods, water, education, and HIV/AIDS, and provided basic provisions such as food, paraffin, soap, and a "settling-in" package for refugees. However, at the height of the Zimbabwean influx, UNHCR's position on the majority of the Zimbabwean migrants was, "For now, we are not involved; I don't think we have given any thought to what the agency might do."[21] UNHCR nevertheless acknowledged the scale of the problem:

> There are lots of protection gaps, especially for vulnerable women and children. Sometimes they have no roof; it is very difficult to get employment. There is exploitation. Often they are not even paid. And they have no legal papers. There are unaccompanied minors. There is nobody to help them, and they fend for themselves. . . . It's very difficult to even follow up. They are everywhere. There is no way to capture their information. They are very difficult to discover, and I don't think we have the capacity to follow up. They are everywhere, and Botswana is huge.[22]

UNHCR has had no mandate to work with the undocumented migrants, and most of its programs focus on the Dukwi camp and Francistown detention center. The UNHCR representative engaged in dialogue with the immigration minister, asking for deportations to be suspended after the March 2008 elections. However, the position of the government was that there is a procedure for Zimbabweans in need of protection in place: the asylum system. It argued that there are cases in which illegal migrants, after being apprehended, have nevertheless been allowed to make a successful claim for asylum.[23]

Meanwhile, UNICEF's work on child protection for refugees follows that of UNHCR, focusing on assistance in the Dukwi camp. As UNICEF's deputy representative argued, "When people become refugees, a number of things kick in automatically. But for these undocumented, perhaps economic, migrants, it is not clear that we have any clear policies, structures, and guidelines on how to work on this as UNICEF."[24] He noted that the ambiguous data on the undocumented migrants and Botswana's position as a middle-income country have exacerbated the difficulty of programming or developing budget lines for the needs of undocumented migrant children.

The institutional response has been rendered even more inadequate by the absence of active NGOs in this field. The one NGO that is widely acknowledged to play an influential role in the human rights field, Ditshwanelo, admits that, given its limited capacity, this area is simply not a priority.[25] In the absence of an international institutional response, churches and the Botswana Red Cross have offered basic assistance to unaccompanied minors, and are among the few organizations able to provide any degree of support to Zimbabweans outside the asylum framework.

Consequently, the needs of Zimbabweans who fall outside the 1951 convention are generally overlooked. The government and the main UN agencies are confined to working within the dichotomous framework of refugees/economic migrants, which renders the realities of the Zimbabwean exodus all but invisible. While all the UN agencies in the country acknowledge the issue and the protection gaps that exist, they are unable to address these problems because of the inadequacies of the national and international institutional framework.

Explaining the Responses

The question, then, is why the dichotomous approach exists. Why, despite many Zimbabweans facing similar underlying human rights deprivations, has there been such a stark distinction between how "refugees" have been treated in contrast to those outside the asylum system? Once again, the answer can be found in the way in which politics has shaped the role of international law. In particular, elite interests in government have been crucial to defining the scope of protection for people displaced across borders.

From the government perspective, there has been a basic compliance with the refugee regime. Its 1967 Refugee Act is one of the oldest in Africa, and the government of Botswana has done the minimum to comply with its domestic and international legal obligations under the act. UNHCR claims, "The Botswana government is very difficult." The minister of justice, whose primary concern is internal security, is responsible for refugees. According to UNHCR, though, he never comes to UNHCR's annual Executive Committee meetings. Even the Botswana permanent mission to the UN in Geneva attends only the first day of the annual meeting.[26]

According to UNHCR, Botswana nevertheless perceives itself to "need to be seen to toe the line" simply because, having institutionalized the 1951 convention into domestic law, it finds that compliance represents a relatively efficient way to procure international legitimacy.[27] The annual presence of the minister of justice at the Human Rights Council—in contrast to UNHCR's Executive Committee— highlights the extent to which it values recognition as a state that is seen to broadly respect core human rights instruments.

Yet beyond these basic commitments, there has been almost no civil society pressure to extend protection or assistance for the Zimbabweans more broadly. The Law Department of the University of Botswana provides refugee law training for the government. However, in general, there is limited civil society or NGO capacity to work on refugee issues, let alone the protection of vulnerable irregu- lar migrants. Aside from the Botswana Red Cross, UNHCR has even had dif- ficulty finding an implementing partner in the country. The main human rights NGO in the country, Ditshwanelo, has strategically chosen to avoid focusing too much on the issue of the Zimbabweans. Its director, Alice Mogwe, explained why the organization focuses on refugees but is not actively involved in promoting the rights of Zimbabweans outside the asylum system: "Strategically, it does not work. The approach of all our work is a strategic approach. There's no point in shouting a message at people who won't hear it. . . . It's not that we are cushy- cushy with the government, but we need to find a way of engaging with them."[28]

Increasing levels of xenophobia have been directed against immigrants, not least the Zimbabwean population (Lefko-Everett 2004; Lesetedi and Modie- Moroka 2007; Campbell and Oucho 2003). As early as 2003, Campbell and Oucho surveyed changing attitudes to immigration and refugee policy in Bo- tswana and indicated a turn toward xenophobia (2003, 29). Their report high- lights a growing belief in the negative effects of immigration on jobs and crime, and a correlation between immigration control and economic growth (2003, 22). They argue that anti-immigration sentiment in Botswana is on a par with that of the other wealthier migrant-receiving countries in the region: 94 percent support deportation of illegal immigrants, compared with 90 percent in South Africa and 97 percent in Namibia (2003, 23).

At the community level, this has translated into not only anti-Zimbabwean sentiment but also even Batswana vigilante groups, engaging in rare but vio- lent attacks on Zimbabweans. Early in the influx, Rodrick Mukumbira (2003), a Zimbabwean journalist, described witnessing one such attack at a Gaborone bus station, where a gang of three hundred shouted, "We want to kill the Zimba- bweans!" and attacked Zimbabwean immigrants. Unsurprisingly, this translates into a strong electoral incentive for politicians to respond firmly to Zimbabwean immigration.

Rather than such incidents being isolated, one member of UNHCR staff suggested that there is "xenophobia at the highest level," and not just directed toward Zimbabweans. For example, in 2009, six hundred to seven hundred Somalis doing business and self-reliant in Francistown were systematically rounded up and sent to the Dukwi camp. The UNHCR staff member noted that part of the motivation was that the president himself does not like the Somalis, having served as an OAU soldier in Mogadishu in 1992–93.[29] One Batswana who was working for one of the main UN organizations in Gaborone, and has a family member who is a senior official in the government, told me: "The Zimbabweans are a real problem. We really just need to send them back; they cause crime and have no right to be here."[30]

The international community in general and UNHCR in particular have had little choice but to be guided by the national response. One of the main constraints has been capacity. Because Botswana is defined as an "upper middle income country" UN presence and capacity in Gaborone is restricted. As the head of the UN country team, UNDP's Kwin-Sandy Lwin, explained, "There are four main agencies: UNDP, UNFPA [United Nations Population Fund], UNICEF, and WHO. UNHCR is so small that it isn't even counted as one. FAO is a one-person show. UNAIDS doesn't have an agency mandate. With that level of country presence, we have very limited capacity."[31]

The UN agencies held a joint workshop on emergency preparedness and contingency planning in case of a severe humanitarian emergency, but that has been the extent of the response that limited capacity and the nature of UN work in middle-income country have allowed. The UN country team worked on an interagency basis to lay out three contingency scenarios in the aftermath of the 2008 Zimbabwean elections: "mass influx," "xenophobia," and "trickle." The plans were developed to support the government in the event of either a massive humanitarian emergency and influx or the kind of xenophobic violence witnessed in South Africa in May 2008. Yet in relation the third scenario, the decision was taken that this lay outside the scope of the UN system's mandate because the government had not invited an external role: "This focus on disaster and emergency preparedness looked at scenarios of displacement before the election and during the post-election. It is different to a trickle of people who have to leave the country to earn a living and to remit their salaries. Unless a government were to ask us, we don't have a mandate on the trickle-out issue. As far as the government is concerned, they are illegal immigrants."[32]

Indeed, within UNHCR there was a strong emphasis on not wanting to rock the boat in terms of the relationship with the government. A UNHCR staff member explained: "We have a very good relationship with the government; we can't do anything without the government. . . . The government is very sensitive on security; we have to be diplomatic. UNHCR is here because of the government. . . . We are here to give technical support."[33] Because Botswana is a middle-income country, UNHCR had even considered closing its Botswana office until the out-break of the Zimbabwe crisis.[34]

The political constraints on UNHCR's work in the country have been severe. For example, in 2009, when the government systematically rounded up Soma-lis and forced them to reside in the camps, then-representative Roy Hermann engaged in talks with the government to find a constructive solution. When I was there in 2009, UNHCR used this as an example of how it is able to critically engage with the government: "We are able to criticize the government. . . . Even if the government will not change its policy, we still talk about it, for example, the government rounding up Somalis and saying Somalis should only reside in the camp. Our representative is talking to the government about it. If they are left in the camp, there is no durable solution for them. They have been out trading, and if they are in the camp, what can they do there? The government will ignore us, but we are still talking to them."[35] Just a few weeks later, however, the government expelled Hermann from the country, accusing him of supporting lawyers from the University of Botswana who were litigating for the rights of the Somalis.[36]

UNHCR—faced with capacity and political constraints—has simply adopted the line that the government should "respect its obligations" in relation to the 1951 convention, and has refrained from bringing up the situation of Zimba-bwean survival migrants. The overall UN position has been that the most con-structive way to engage with the Zimbabwean issue is for the government to work collaboratively with IOM to improve the conditions of immigration man-agement: "There is a serious institutional gap as we are now, but if IOM were to come, that would address the gap." However, IOM does not have an office in Gaborone, and its role has largely been limited to the transit center it has set up at Plumtree to facilitate returns.[37]

Conclusion

Zimbabweans crossing into Botswana have fled the same underlying conditions of political and economic collapse as those who have crossed into South Africa. The economic consequences of the political situation, in addition to generalized violence, have led to flight across the western border. Nearly all those leaving, whether permanently or temporarily, have fled human rights deprivations re-sulting from state failure. They have been seeking a means of survival. Yet within Botswana the national and international institutional response has been stark. Refugees, recognized on the basis of individualized persecution, have received protection. Other survival migrants, fleeing for reasons other than persecution, have had no access to protection or assistance. Instead, they have faced roundup, detention, and deportation.

This harsh response contrasts with some of the other cases in the book. In Botswana, neither the national nor the international refugee regime has stretched to protect people who lie beyond its boundaries. Although responses to the Zimbabweans in South Africa have been weak and ad hoc, there was at least some leeway in the regime for Zimbabweans to get access to territory and to receive certain forms of protection. South Africa also had a temporary moratorium on the deportation of Zimbabweans, and some NGOs were present to fill the most egregious protection gaps. In Botswana, almost nothing has been done to address protection and assistance needs or to limit deportations.

Why has the response been so extreme? Institutionally, there has been no legal basis on which to recognize Zimbabweans outside the 1951 Refugee Convention. Politically, there have been strong incentives on the government against stretching the national refugee regime to protect the majority of the Zimbabweans. At the domestic level, widespread xenophobia and anti-immigration sentiment have been significant electoral incentives impelling expulsion, and unlike in South Africa, civil society has been extremely weak in campaigning for the rights of the Zimbabweans. At the international level, there have been few incentives on Botswana to stretch the boundaries of the national protection regime. The government has sought to "check the boxes" of compliance with international refugee law. However, because Botswana is a middle-income country, the UN system as a whole has had very little means of influence.

UNHCR and the international community's responses have largely followed the national position. Reliant on the invitation of Botswana to operate in the country, and aware of its limited capacity and leverage, UNHCR has strategically opted to remain quiet on the treatment of the Zimbabweans. While privately recognizing the significant protection gaps, it perceived itself to be organizationally constrained. The expulsion of UNHCR's national representative in 2009 illustrates the extent to which the UNHCR-Botswana relationship is led by the government. Other UN agencies have similarly abdicated responsibility for advocating for the rights of Zimbabwean survival migrants. Botswana therefore represents one of most extreme examples of national and international institutional failure to adapt to survival migration. For those fleeing fragility, the arbitrary distinction between persecution and deprivation has determined access to rights.

ANGOLA
The Expulsion of the Congolese

Between 2003 and 2009, the government of Angola (GoA) rounded up, detained, and deported between 300,000 and 400,000 Congolese from the diamond mining areas on its territory. While the use of deportation by states is not unusual, the scale of the expulsions, the methods used to deport, and the vulnerabilities of many of those deported sets this case apart from most state practices of deportation. The range of human rights violations that took place in the process of deportation include the systematic use of gang rape, sexual violence, beatings, unhygienic body cavity searches, mutilation, extended periods of detention, and women and children being forced to walk up to 200 kilometers to the border, often without food or water. Furthermore, the atrocities can be attributed directly to the state and were carried out by the Angolan Armed Forces (FAA) and the police. Yet, considering the scale of the human rights violations involved, the case of the Angolans' deportations remains relatively undocumented, receiving little attention from the media, academics, or international organizations.

The expelled Congolese were predominantly from two of the most fragile and underdeveloped provinces of the Democratic Republic of Congo (DRC): Bandundu and Western Kasai, where food insecurity, infant mortality, and malnutrition rates are high even by Congolese standards, and there is little infrastructure and few viable markets for food. Historically, there has been a long history of livelihoods migration connecting these provinces with the Lunda Norte region of Angola. The border is porous, and people have crossed freely between the regions for a long time. Movement across the border had traditionally been a survival strategy for many Congolese, becoming even more so with the virtual exhaustion of artisanal diamond mining in the two DRC provinces. In Lunda Norte, Congolese found opportunities to engage in artisanal diamond mining or to develop other economic activities in and around the mining areas.

This type of movement was tolerated for many years. It formed part of colonial and precolonial trading routes. During the Angolan civil war, União Nacional para a Independência Total de Angola (UNITA), now the opposition political party, continued to welcome Congolese migrant workers to work in the diamond mines. With the end of the civil war and the Movimento Popular de Libertação de Angola (MPLA) victory over UNITA in 2002, however, the situation changed, and the MPLA government sought to exert greater authority over the diamond mining areas. In the buildup to Angola's first legislative and presidential elections since 1992, the MPLA sought to remove the Congolese, who formed part of UNITA's traditional support base, in order, first, to prevent them from registering to vote, and second, to create the conditions to attract greater investment from international corporations engaged in diamond mining.

The repressive response of the Angolan government produced a host of protection and assistance needs. The protection needs of the Congolese migrants arose as a result of both the conditions in the country of origin and the conditions of reception in the host country. Although the Congolese migrants were not refugees, the lack of viable livelihood opportunities and the fragile nature of the state in much of Bandundu and Western Kasai highlight the necessity of migration as a survival strategy. Yet unlike the other cases of survival migration addressed in this book, the main protection needs stemmed from the migrants' treatment by the host country rather than just conditions in the country of origin. In order to uphold the human rights of these vulnerable irregular migrants, the international community should have been moved by the forced deportations to develop a strong and coordinated intervention.

Despite the scale of the human rights violations, the issue was almost entirely neglected by the international community, falling between the mandates of different international organizations. On the Angolan side, little access to the diamond mining areas was granted to international organizations and NGOs, making engagement and verification difficult; but there was limited and extremely delayed diplomatic condemnation of the deportation methods by other states or across the UN system. On the DRC side of the border, the response to the immediate health, food, water, sanitation, and shelter needs of the expelled was also minimal. In the UN system, the response was mainly limited to brief and sporadic interagency missions that focused on recording numbers or on channeling inadequate resources through local NGO partners. For most of the period, the only really engaged actors on the Congolese side of the border were Médecins

Sans Frontières (MSF), which worked outside the usual scope of its activities, and local NGO and faith-based organizations.

This chapter is divided into three main sections. It begins by providing background on who the Congolese migrants in Angola were and why they moved there. Next it examines the four main waves of deportations that took place between 2003 and 2009 and the response of the international community. Then it sets out an explanation for the Angolan response and its evolution over the period. It argues that the government's actions—and the degree of repression or restraint it showed at each stage—were related to the domestic and international incentives it had for tolerance or repression. The chapter concludes by assessing the case study's implications for both theory and practice.

Congolese Migration to Angola

The majority of the deported Congolese were originally from two of the country's eleven provinces: Bandundu and Western Kasai. These provinces are in the south of the country and border Angola's Lunda Norte region. In contrast to other provinces in the DRC, in which violent conflict has taken place, such as North Kivu and South Kivu in the east, or wealthier areas of mineral extraction such as Katanga, the southern provinces generally receive little attention. Nevertheless, the border areas of these provinces exhibit the characteristics of state fragility and have an infrastructure and environment that make it almost impossible for the majority of people to sustain viable livelihood strategies without resorting to either external assistance or migration.

The border areas of Western Kasai are among the most impoverished of the DRC. Food security is a particular problem, and the two Kasais, Western and Eastern, are "the most malnourished region of the DRC," according to government health statistics, with up to 50,000 deaths per year in Western Kasai as a result of malnutrition and 44 percent of children under age five suffering from chronic malnutrition and 16 percent from acute malnutrition (Butoke 2009). Low life expectancy means that 90 percent of women over fifty are widows. Low levels of agricultural production are exacerbated by poorly functioning transportation, which means that there is no organized interprovince food market to supplement local food production.

The economy of the border area of Western Kasai is divided between two territories. Luiza is mainly agro-pastoralist but has limited access to seeds and low crop productivity based on maize, beans, peanuts, soybeans, and cassava. Tshikapa has almost no agricultural land and its economy is based on diamond mining, but it has no organized extraction and the sources of diamonds accessible to artisanal extractors are virtually exhausted (Africa Inland Mission Canada and Butoke 2008). The population in both areas depends on external humanitarian assistance for basic levels of food security: FAO provides food support, UNICEF contributes to water and sanitation, and the local NGO, Butoke, offers a range of projects to facilitate increased food productivity. Butoke commented on the situation in Western Kasai: "The chronic malnutrition is not of a temporary nature, and is due rather to societal structural reasons, such as lack of child spacing, family instability, major dependence on diamond mining, roads that are impracticable for trucks, dysfunction of the market for produce, deforestation, difficult access to arable land, the depressed state of agricultural production" (Butoke 2009).

The border areas of Bandundu present similar challenges. As in Western Kasai, there is chronic food insecurity. The border area around the town of Kahemba is a mining zone in which artisanal diamond mining offers the main source of livelihood, albeit one that is gradually being exhausted. The area traditionally hosted large numbers of Angolan refugees and has low levels of agricultural production due to inefficient techniques, a lack of nutritional training, and poor land quality. Manioc is the only crop that can be grown indigenously without external intervention, and its production is far from self-sufficient, particularly since 80 percent of it is exported from Kahemba. A UN interagency mission to the area highlighted a range of problems: a lack of medical facilities, poor sanitation, acute malnutrition among 21 percent of the population, high levels of infant mortality, and the absence of functioning markets. Parents are often forced to leave their children with relatives in order to seek economic opportunity elsewhere, by either crossing into Angola or traveling within the DRC.[1]

Given these circumstances, it is unsurprising that many people cross the border to Angola in search of livelihood opportunities. The economy of the southern provinces depends almost entirely on transborder mobility. In the words of one MSF doctor who has worked in the region: "They have nothing; it's a survival strategy; they earn less than ten dollars a month. The motive [for moving] is hope and despair."[2] The overwhelming majority of the migrants were men who moved to Lunda Norte, either individually or with their families, to work in the diamond mining sector as artisanal diggers (*garimpeiros*). A smaller number of men were former soldiers who had fought with the rebel group UNITA. Among the minority of women who traveled independently, many were traders who often migrated long distances from other parts of the DRC to sell fried fish, clothes, or consumer products. Because prostitution is significant in the border area, reinforced by the diamond activity, there were also high numbers of prostitutes, both professional and occasional.[3] Aside from the female traders, who sometimes traveled from farther afield, the overwhelming majority of migrants were from the border areas of Western Kasai and Bandundu.

This type of cross-border movement is not new. As a UN report noted, "The populations on the two sides of the border are generally the same and exchanges have always taken place between the two neighbouring countries" (Office for the Coordination of Humanitarian Affairs 2007). The border area between Lunda Norte and the DRC was a part of old trading routes in both the colonial and precolonial eras. The Imbangala in Angola and the Pende in the Congo would regularly interact in order to trade cloth, slaves, and guns. It was only later, after Angolan independence in 1975, that the economic links became increasingly based on the development of a large-scale illicit diamond trade, connecting diggers, intermediaries, and sellers across the border.

Between 1975 and 1992, Angola had a socialist government that enabled relatively open access to the diamond mining areas for artisanal miners. However, civil war between the socialist MPLA and FNLA (National Liberation Front of Angola) and the Western-backed UNITA hampered investment in the mining industry. In 1992, a ceasefire was brokered between UNITA and the MPLA, leading to Angola's first national elections. With MPLA's victory in the elections, UNITA reverted to civil war, seizing de facto control of the diamond mining areas in Lunda Norte and Lunda Sul, effectively partitioning the country and its natural resources.

During this period, up until UNITA leader Jonas Savimbi's death in 2002, UNITA dominated the diamond mining areas of the Lundas, often drawing on Congolese labor to support its activities. As Filip de Boeck (2001, 554) shows, "UNITA's labour forces thus consisted primarily of Congolese." The Congolese were able to buy a permit issued by UNITA to cross the border into Angola, and camps were organized by UNITA for Congolese workers.

However, with UNITA's defeat and surrender in 2002, the MPLA government was able to assert authority over the diamond mining areas of the Lundas. It recognized that as the world's third-largest producer of diamonds, Angola had a significant opportunity for national development, and government elites had many opportunities for personal enrichment. The government immediately implemented the national diamond legislation that had been in existence since 1994 but was not implemented until 2002. The "Diamond Law" granted the "exclusive right to prospect, research, reconnoitre, exploit, handle and commercialize diamonds in all of Angola's national territory" to Endiama (the Empresa Nacional de Diamantes de Angola), giving a single national company control over the mines and the right to establish joint ventures with multinational companies to invest in extraction in certain areas as concessionaires. Endiama has brought in a range of international investors, including SPE of Portugal, De Beers, and Odebrecht of Brazil.

The territory of the Lundas became subject to increasingly strict rules governing freedom of movement, residency, and economic activity. Even for nationals, conditions were difficult, and many people were displaced, deprived of their livelihoods, or subjected to human rights violations as space was cleared to ensure exclusivity of access to Endiama and its foreign partners. The military, the police, and the private security companies employed by many of the foreign firms began to implement stricter controls.[4] Human rights activist Rafael Marques (2011; Marques and Falcão de Campos 2005) has documented many of the consequences of these controls for the rights of Angolan nationals. As part of this effort, the government sought to remove Congolese migrant workers from the Lundas.

The Waves of Deportations

The waves of deportations began on December 23, 2003. Units of the army, police, and Serviço de Migração Estrangeiro (SME) swept through the *garimpeiro* camps in the diamond provinces, rounding up illegal immigrants from other African nations and sending them back to their countries of origin. Over the next six years, the GoA launched a series of such operations, resulting in successive waves of deportations, each with its own pattern and underlying political dynamics. It is possible to document the expulsion of at least 270,000 immigrants, and the Office for the Coordination of Humanitarian Affairs (OCHA) suggests it is likely to have been around 400,000. However, compiling accurate figures is extremely problematic. The figures recorded by Congolese border officials are significantly lower than estimates of other actors such as Caritas, the UN Organization Mission in the Democratic Republic of the Congo (MONUC), and local NGOs. One of the reasons for this undercount is that the DRC border officials allegedly demanded a fee of around $100 to allow nationals back into the country, creating an incentive for people to avoid official border posts (Office for the Coordination of Humanitarian Affairs 2007). Furthermore, most deported migrants rapidly left the border zone to return to their own villages, making verification of numbers difficult (Médecins Sans Frontières–Belgium 2008). On the other hand, OCHA (2007) also warns that these underestimates may be partly mitigated by the "revolving door" nature of migration, with some Congolese returning to Angola after expulsion and being deported more than once.

Four principal waves of expulsions can be identified. The launch of Operação Brilhante signaled the first wave of deportations, in December 2003 and April 2004, in which around 100,000 Congolese were forced back to Western Kasai and Bandundu. Some of the most serious human rights abuses took place during a second wave of around 33,000 deportations that began in July 2007 and continued until February 2008. Many of these abuses were rights violations documented by MSF, which took testimonies from expelled women in Western Kasai and Bandundu (Médecins Sans Frontières. A third, pre-election wave took place in the run-up to the national legislative elections in September 2008, in which an estimated 120,000 Congolese were returned between May and August 2008. This was the highest number of deportations in a given period but entailed slightly reduced levels of rights violations compared with the previous waves. In the fourth wave, the Bas-Congo episode, around 18,800 Congolese were deported mainly from the Cabinda province of Angola to Bas-Congo in the west of the DRC between August and October 2009. This case involved different areas of Angola and the DRC but is nevertheless an important part of the overall story because it was the first time that there was a significant political response from DRC, which reciprocally expelled Angolan refugees. Beyond these four episodes, however, the character of the deportations has shifted from acute waves to a chronic crisis of ongoing expulsions that continue to the present day.

Wave 1: Operação Brilhante

The GoA launched its new anti–diamond smuggling operation—Operação Brilhante (Operation Brilliant)—with a series of nighttime and dawn raids in the *garimpeiro* camps. Regarding many of the Congolese as potential UNITA supporters, and estimating that the country was losing $375 million annually from diamond smuggling, Angola began the operation on December 23, 2003, focusing on the predominantly Congolese camps in the Lunda Norte mining towns.[5] An NGO working on behalf of the Congolese diaspora in Angola claimed that between December 24 and 26, soldiers from FAA (the Angolan army) entered villages and camps "as if prepared for war" and forced the Congolese to leave the territory in Cafunfo (Association des Congolais de Lunda 2004).

The patterns of the raids were characteristic of those that would define the deportations over the ensuing six years. Soldiers, police, and immigration officials descended on the makeshift camps and villages of Congolese artisanal miners. They rounded up the Congolese, set their homes on fire, and took them to local prisons or military bases, where they were detained, often alongside their children and without food or water. They were then marched or transported to the border, where they crossed the River Tungila into the DRC. Along the way, however, many were subjected to significant and degrading human rights abuses. In particular, men and women were beaten in their homes, often in front of their children; some of the women were raped, possessions were stolen, and women were subjected to degrading and unhygienic vaginal and anal searches for diamonds.

Although the first organized roundups took place over Christmas 2003, it was not until April 2004 that the human consequences of Operação Brilhante were reported in the international media. Beginning in February, the GoA began a more systematic and larger-scale operation in and around the major Lunda Norte mining towns in the area of Cafunfo. MSF began to receive reports of people in distress crossing back into the DRC as early as February, and between April 2 and 4, it received news that more than 8,500 Congolese had crossed the border along the River Tungila into the DRC at three different entry points in Bandundu in desperate condition. At the same time, and based on announcements by the GoA, OCHA warned that between 80,000 and 100,000 Congolese would face expulsion. By April 20, some 67,000 had been registered at five crossings in Bandundu and W. Kasai (Médecins Sans Frontières 2004).

Interagency missions on the DRC side of the border, led by MSF-Belgium and OCHA during April, highlighted the immediate humanitarian challenge posed by the returns. Most of the new arrivals had been robbed of their possessions, there was no registration process in place for them, water and food were in short supply, and many had health needs resulting from fatigue, shock, and dehydration.[6] Human Rights Watch publicly denounced the GoA's methods of deportation, and the executive director of the group's Africa Division proclaimed on April 22, "The Angolan government must immediately stop its soldiers from carrying out brutal abuses against Congolese migrant workers" (Human Rights Watch 2004). As a result of the coverage provided by MSF-Belgium, OCHA, and Human Rights Watch, knowledge of the human consequences of the deportations reached the international media. On April 22, the BBC ran the headline "Congo miners 'tortured' in Angola," and Reuters documented the results of an OCHA-led interagency report: "The U.N. Office for the Coordination of Humanitarian Affairs continues to receive numerous reports of physical and psychological abuse of Congolese civilians reportedly perpetrated by Angolan security forces . . . reports of rape, cruel, inhuman and degrading treatment, theft of personal belongings, arbitrary detention and killings." OCHA said there was "an acute humanitarian crisis in the making. . . . These civilians, some of whom have never set foot in Congo, arrive traumatised from their ordeal and with little, if any, means to support themselves."[7]

In response to the publicity, the GoA insisted on its sovereign right to control entry and exit on its territory. On April 30, it published an editorial piece in the *Jornal de Angola* titled "Rights and Sovereignty," in which it stated that "the Angolan government reasserts its sovereign right to expel illegal immigrants from its territory," denouncing and dismissing criticism from NGOs such as MSF and expressing its intention to continue with the operation. MSF responded to this with a press release in which it argued: "The question is not what is being done, it is how it is being done."[8] Shortly afterward, the DRC authorities may have made a formal request to the GoA to suspend deportations until better conditions of return were ensured (Médecins Sans Frontières 2004). In late April, the GoA an-nounced a forty-five-day moratorium on deportations effective in mid-May, and beginning in the first week in May there was a huge decrease in the number of new arrivals at the border (Médecins Sans Frontières 2004).

An OCHA-led interagency mission in Angola between May 12 and 17, con-ducted in Lunda Norte and Lunda Sol to monitor Operação Brilhante, showed that the main operation was over. However, it also demonstrated that by that stage, according to the GoA's own police records, a total of 127,788 people had been deported (124,289 to the DRC and 3,499 to West Africa) between March 29 and April 27, 2004.[9] By the time of the moratorium, the Angolan govern-ment had largely achieved its aim, with minimal intervention or criticism from the international community. In reflecting on the international response, MSF highlighted the difficulty it had experienced in mobilizing partners, describing OCHA's engagement as "timid" because it coordinated interagency missions but made few interventions on the ground; UNHCR had participated in the inter-agency missions but argued that the situation was "outside its mandate" because the Congolese were in their country of origin and were not refugees. While the Red Cross had provided eight national staff members and UNICEF had loaned equipment to MSF, neither the humanitarian nor the diplomatic response had been proportionate to the extent of the protection needs.[10]

Wave 2: MSF and the *Temoignages*

The second period of deportations, although involving fewer people, was argu-ably the most serious in terms of the human rights violations carried out by the GoA. These abuses were well documented, mainly because the MSF systemati-cally recorded the testimonies (*temoignages*) of deported women. The first waves of expulsions were announced by the local NGO Butoke in February 2007 in Western Kasai, where 5,000 returning Congolese registered with Caritas in the diocese of Luiza. Yet despite these early indicators, response by the international community was slow, and it was not until the end of the year that there was any significant humanitarian response. Even this limited response emerged only as a result of unprecedented action—at the boundaries of its mandate—by MSF.

In response to successive calls from local NGOs, OCHA led an interagency mission from Kinshasa to Western Kasai between April 12 and 14 in which OCHA, UNHCR, MONUC, and Caritas divided up their information gather-ing into the sectors in which they held expertise (Office for the Coordination of Humanitarian Affairs 2007). The report of the mission noted that deportees were arriving in "deplorable conditions" and documented thirty-four cases of rape and sexual violence by Angolan military and police. However, the report also maintained that the situation was "not a humanitarian crisis," and stated that "the mission judges that the situation, although worrying, is stable: it is not a catastrophe or humanitarian crisis" (Office for the Coordination of Humanitarian Affairs 2007). Instead, it highlighted the need to work through local partners to ensure better food security, the protection of the most vulnerable groups, and access to health care, water, and sanitation; malnutrition was cited as the biggest problem. According to an internal document of one humanitarian organization, however, the OCHA-led mission had stayed for only four hours in Luiza and five hours in Tshikapa. The same organization would later argue that OCHA "should have sent a plea to the authorities in Kinshasa concerning the situation" and it questioned "the lack of transparency, responsibility and professionalism of different humanitarian actors [involved in that mission]."[11]

Deportation continued throughout the summer months with virtually no intervention from the international humanitarian or diplomatic community. On October 12, Dr. Cecile De Sweemer, a Butoke consultant based in Western Kasai, alerted MSF's Pool d'Urgence Congolais (PUC)—its emergency response team in Kinshasa—about a worrying situation. The NGO reported receiving a significant number of Congolese women who had suffered sexual violence during their expulsion from Angola.[12] In response, a PUC team of four to five people left Kinshasa on October 23, arriving in Western Kasai for a fifteen-day mission to analyze the health situation of the women in consultation with other organizations, to begin to record testimonies of the women, and to offer care for the victims of sexual violence.

MSF staff were shocked by the accounts of sexual violence that they heard in the testimonies of women deported from the Lunda Norte towns. The patterns in the testimonies were almost identical. The Congolese settlements in Lunda Norte were encircled at night by Angolan soldiers, who arrived in several trucks. The men would often try to flee the site, leaving the women alone with their children. The soldiers entered the houses in groups of at least five. They made the women lie on ground at gunpoint and then systematically gang-raped them in front of their children, saying in French the same comments: "Prostitute of Congo. Go home. Here is not your country. Pack up your things. We are raping you so that you will not come back." The women and children were then led away in handcuffs, and the villages were ransacked and set on fire.

On average the women spent three to seven days in detention, generally in military bases in Dundo or Nzaji, in overcrowded and unsanitary conditions, detained alongside their children and without access to food or water. In detention, they were often escorted outside at night, where they were gang-raped by their guards. They were either forced to walk 200 kilometers to the border— over a period of a few days to two weeks—or piled into overcrowded trucks and transported. During the journey, they passed a number of checkpoints, often being raped at each. As they approached the border, they were held again at a destination around three hours walk away from the border, where they were subjected to unsanitary body searches of the anus and vagina. In the words of one woman: "They performed anal and vaginal searches, one after the other without protection." Men were also subjected to brutal violence, including mutilation and summary execution. On arrival at the border, most had been robbed of all their possessions and found no assistance in terms of water, food, or access to medical care (Médecins Sans Frontières 2007).[13]

The reports that MSF sent back to Kinshasa and Brussels reveal that staff members who took the testimonies were themselves traumatized by the accounts they heard, with one staff member commenting that "the most difficult thing was the heaviness of the testimonies." Given the gap in action by other international actors, MSF decided it had to act. It sent a team to the border town of Kamako in Western Kasai, where it was to set up a main clinic and four mobile clinics across the region. It arrived on November 27 with a mandate to care for the deported women who had suffered sexual violence. However, within two days of beginning consultations in a tent on November 28, it was confronted by the people of the local community, who also wanted health care, and so the organization broadened its treatment to include the local population. Alongside its health-related work, MSF's press officer continued to record testimonies from the deported women.

MSF (2007) published the testimonies of one hundred women interviewed in Kamako. On December 5, it organized three simultaneous press conferences in Kinshasa, Brussels, and Johannesburg to publicize the findings of the testimonies. The testimonies provide harrowing accounts of abuse, detention, rapes, and beatings by Angolan military and police. One typical example is taken from a thirty-one-year-old woman, married with four children, who, having spent four years living and working in Maludi in Angola, was expelled in May 2007:

> At 7 pm, the soldiers came with a truck. There was a whole battalion. My husband ran away. Husbands flee because they do not want to see their wives being raped. And in general, they get beaten up even harder in front of their wives. Four soldiers came into my house. They began to beat me with sticks. They ordered me to lie down and then raped me, in the anus and the vagina, one after the other. I was taken to prison with the children. I was in there for four days. We were given nothing to eat or to drink. In the prison, there were eight men, four women and children. We defecated in the room. On the first three days, I was beaten and raped every day by four soldiers, always the same men. The other women were subjected to the same treatment. They threw insults

at us: "Look at their breast, look at their buttocks. You're going to leave everything here." We walked for 12 days and passed four checkpoints. At the first checkpoint, the whole group was beaten up and then they let us go. At the second checkpoint, we were also beaten up. A soldier forced me into his hut and raped me. The other women were subjected to the same treatment. The same thing happened at the third checkpoint. At the fourth checkpoint, I was raped by two soldiers on the side of the road—and so were the other women. At the two borders, there were no incidents. I re-entered Congo at Kassa Mai. Shortly after Kassa Mai, my five year old child died of exhaustion. His body was thrown in the bush. I did not have any medical examination because I could not pay for one. I have no news from my husband. I do not know if he is still alive. (Médecins Sans Frontières 2007)

On a medical level, the MSF intervention had limited effectiveness. Most of the women had suffered sexual violence more than 72 hours earlier than they presented to MSF. This meant that there was nothing that could be done much medically in terms of HIV prevention. The only real support that MSF could offer was treatment of other STDs and tetanus or hepatitis B shots. Given MSF's primary role as a provider of medical assistance, this made its role questionable and highly contested. Fabienne de Laval, now deputy director of MSF-Belgium, who was present at the time, argued:

I didn't agree with the project we did. We were nine months too late. The big deportation was July and August 2007. . . . Somebody had spoken to the women and heard about the horrors. But most of the facts were from six to nine months before . . . as everywhere in DRC, we were in an area where access to health care is nearly zero, and we were coming with a very vertical project on just rape, which in a community is not accepted because you are only treating three people, when there are hundreds of people dying of anemia, malaria. . . . People were trickling in, but it is nearly impossible to access them on a however-long borderline. It is very difficult to pinpoint entry points. It is impossible to get access to post-exposure prophylaxis for HIV because it takes you 24 hours to get to the next village. The medical intervention was not viable unless we had been there at the peak of deportation.[14]

The recognition that the main time period for viable intervention had elapsed led to a redefinition of the MSF mission to monitor the deportation situation after the December press conference, to offer some medical support to women suffered sexual violence, and to try to coordinate a wider response by other NGOs to address malnutrition and malaria. MSF met these aims by establishing a clinic at Kamako for women suffering sexual violence and four mobile clinics in surrounding villages, all of which also opened their services to people from the local community. However, overall, MSF was able to contribute very little in medical terms, and its mission closed on February 1, 2008.

Nevertheless, in its less conventional role as the only organization that documented and disseminated testimonies of the human rights violations, MSF made a significant impact, filling a gap that other organizations notably failed to address. Fabienne de Laval, in spite of her reservations about the overall mission, confirmed: "We did get *temoignage* of women who had really been violated in horrendous situations. . . . We highlighted the people on the Angolan side who were the abusers. We had a press conference in Congo, Johannesburg, and Brussels. For me, that was a positive outcome."[15] Indeed, there is evidence that the testimonies and subsequent press conference made a difference. The press conference coincided with the anniversary of the Universal Declaration of Human Rights (UDHR), and the MSF testimonies were raised in Luanda by the head of the Office of the High Commissioner for Human Rights (OHCHR) Angola Office at events to mark the anniversary.[16] On the very same day, the deputy chief of staff of the FAA, General Geraldo Sachipengo Nunda, publicly promised to investigate the allegations. General Nunda followed through on this commitment, calling for a change in the way in which future deportations would be conducted. As Helene Lorinquer, MSF-B's analysis and advocacy coordinator, observed: "One person took the lead for pushing change within the Angolan government, and two to three people within the military were sanctioned."[17] After December 11, there was reduction in the number of expulsions: their frequency was reduced, the number of people deported declined, those deported did not generally suffer invasive body searches, most were not incarcerated, they were brought in trucks rather than being forced to walk to the border, and levels of sexual violence were reduced (Médecins Sans Frontières 2008). MSF argued that this shift could be traced directly to its own role: "One can reasonably believe that the reduction in the expulsions, and the end of mistreatment, are linked to the impact of the activities of MSF (the press conference and the presence on the border over several weeks)." However, it also accurately foresaw that "it should not be excluded that new waves may begin [again] following the cessation of our activities or the approach of the Angolan elections" (Médecins Sans Frontières 2008).

Wave 3: Before the Elections

Deportation resumed again on a larger scale on May 25, 2008, in Operation Broad Wings.[18] Angola's first legislative elections since 1992 had been postponed on several occasions since 2007 and were finally fixed for September 2008, with presidential elections to follow at a later date. In the electoral buildup, the GoA launched a large-scale roundup and deportation operation to last between 45 and 90 days. Its intention was to remove people who might be UNITA supporters and who might register to vote. By the end of June, around 120,000 Congolese had been deported. However, compared with 2007, the pattern of the deportations had changed, involving less brutality and fewer widespread and flagrant rights violations.[19] Details of the deportations were revealed by two fact-finding missions in mid-2008, one by MSF in Bandundu and the other by the UN in Western Kasai.

On receiving reports of new arrivals in Bandundu, MSF sent a mission from the PUC in Kinshasa to Bandundu in order to take testimonies in June. It arrived in Kahungulu, near the border, and spent time in the nearby towns of Tembo, Kikwit, and Kahamba. It noted that even the official Direction Generale des Migrations (DGM) statistics of the government revealed that in the short period between May 26 and June 11, the military had deported 22,457 Congolese back to Bandundu (Médecins Sans Frontières 2008). However, based on the testimonies, it found that—compared with 2007—the pattern of deportations had changed. Although far from perfect from a human rights perspective, the shocking sexual violence recorded just six months earlier was no longer such a prominent feature.

The testimonies revealed a consistent story of the methods used in these deportations. The military arrived in the *garimpeiro* settlements at night, encircled the camps, and assembled all the Congolese in the middle of the camp. The soldiers then announced that the Congolese were to leave Angola immediately. The migrants were given a few minutes to gather essential belongings. The camps were then systematically set on fire, and helicopters were used to check that no one had escaped. The Congolese were then taken by truck or on foot to military bases, where they were detained for one to five days. In detention, they were sometimes given water and food—although not on a systematic basis. From there, they were transported (women in trucks, men often on foot) in stages toward the border post, stopping at checkpoints along the way. At the border, they crossed the River Tingila by boat and arrived at the border post of Kahungula, where the Congolese DGM, the Agence Nationale des Renseignements, the Service de Renseignments Militaire, and the police were all present to undertake a count by age and sex. On their arrival, nothing was organized or provided by the Congolese state, and most of the migrants arrived exhausted and without possessions. After resting in Kahungula, they left again at three in the morning in the direction of the town of Tembo or Kahemba with the aim of contacting their families to arrange to return to their place of origin by vehicle (Médecins Sans Frontières 2008).

While the human rights picture was still very imperfect, and body cavity searches were still practiced on a large scale, some positive changes can be identified in comparison to the earlier waves. This time, deportations were more organized, and the Angolan army rather than the police (which had played a part in the earlier waves and had been complicit in some of the atrocities) carried out the entire deportation process. There were reduced levels of sexual violence and rape. Although there were still isolated cases, these had become the exception rather than the rule: "Rapes were not practised in a systematic fashion or on a large scale. Reported cases of sexual violence were isolated." Unlike in the earlier waves, some food and water was provided in detention. Women were less often subjected to the long walk to the border (Médecins Sans Frontières 2008).[20] This changing pattern of deportation meant that in Bandundu the main need faced by the returning population were food assistance rather than treatment for women suffering the consequences of sexual violence.[21]

The picture in Western Kasai was similar to that in Bandundu. Between July 5 and 10, OCHA led a UN interagency mission to the territory of Luiza to evaluate the deportations. Its report described how people were arriving in waves of 100 to 150 and were in "a deplorable humanitarian state, deprived of their possessions." Less than half had access to drinkable water, they had lost all their belongings, and many had serious health needs. It further described how 90 percent of the women had been forced to undergo anal and vaginal searches for diamonds. However, despite highlighting these significant protection needs resulting from obvious human rights violations, the mission concurred with the MSF mission's assessment about the reduction in levels of sexual violence, reporting that only 1 out of 24 interviewed women had been raped in Angola. The UN report concluded that two basic interventions were required: a strategic plan for interagency division of responsibility to address immediate needs along the border, and an appeal by OCHA to the Congolese government to contact the Angolan government to ask for the human rights and humanitarian law violations to cease.[22] By the start of July, around 120,000 Congolese had been deported ruthlessly and efficiently by the Angolan army—but at least some of the worst excesses of the previous waves had been curbed.

Wave 4: The Bas-Congo Episode

The main waves of deportation in 2009 focused on a different part of the country, in what became referred to as Operation Crisis. Between August and October, the GoA expelled around 18,800 Congolese from the far northwest of the country, the overwhelming majority being deported from the isolated Cabinda province to the immediate west of the DRC. Aside from the different geographical setting, two other significant differences stand out. First, the expelled population were not recently arrived *garimpeiros*; there are no diamond mines in Cabinda. Rather, they were professionals, artisans, or traders who had been on Angolan territory for a long time. Second, even though the scale and severity of the human rights violations were arguably less serious, the episode received far greater international attention than the previous waves. The political response by the government of the DRC and by international organizations on both sides of the border was much greater than in 2004, 2007, or 2008. The episode, although different from the other cases, therefore serves to shed light on the relative neglect in the case of the earlier, more serious rights violations.

The province of Cabinda is separated from the rest of Angola by Congolese territory, but it is territorially and economically important to the GoA because of its natural resources. Because of the area's value, the GoA has been concerned about the activity of the separatist group Front for the Liberation of the Enclave of Cabinda (FLEC), which has become increasingly active and in which a number of Congolese have been implicated. With growing concern about Congolese connections to FLEC, an increasing climate of xenophobia in Cabinda, and preparation for Angolan presidential elections on the horizon, the GoA began to expel the Congolese population from Cabinda.[23] The Angolan army and police in Cabinda rounded up single men, women, and families and ordered them to leave the territory, forcing them across the border into the Bas-Congo province of the DRC. An OCHA-led interagency mission to Muanda and Tshela between October 8 and 12 revealed that while many of the deported migrants had quickly dispersed to their home communities, many others had needed support. Churches, schools, and host families offered shelter, and food, water, and shelter were provided by an interagency response that worked mainly through Caritas and the Red Cross (Office for the Coordination of Humanitarian Affairs 2009).

In contrast to the earlier waves, in which the government of the DRC had remained largely passive, Kinshasa this time responded strongly to the deportations. For the first time, it launched reciprocal expulsions, deporting Angolan refugees who had been resident in Bas-Congo since the Angolan civil war. Emboldened by the bilateral rapprochement between the DRC and Rwanda, Joseph Kabila, president of the DRC, felt able for the first time to respond in robust and unequivocal terms to Angola.[24] The order to expel the Angolan refugees came straight from the top, signed by the minister of the interior.[25] Beginning in September, some 39,000 Angolans were expelled. The DGM, together with the Congolese military and police, visited the most easily identifiable refugee settlements and gave the refugees 24 hours' notice to leave the country, after which they were driven back to the border in groups of thirty to fifty. On the other side of the border, the GoA's Ministry of Social Integration announced the arrival of the

39,000 expelled Angolans in Cabinda (2,000), Uige (7,800), and Zaire (28,000) provinces, where the Red Cross set up reception and transit facilities to provide food, shelter, clothing, water, health care, and sanitation (International Federation for the Red Cross and Red Crescent Societies 2009).

Although there were no major human rights abuses in transit, the Angolan government condemned the response as disproportionate, and the diplomatic tussle led to the suspension of flights between Luanda and Kinshasa. Eventually, after bilateral talks, a moratorium on the tit-for-tat expulsions was agreed on by the two countries in October. While the rights violations involved—including arbitrary detention and the *refoulement* of refugees—cannot in any way be condoned, what is interesting about the case is the attention it received, in contrast to the earlier neglect of the much larger-scale and systematic violations of human rights during the earlier waves. In the Bas-Congo case, the DRC condemned the GoA's actions in ways that brought an end to deportation, UNHCR became involved on a diplomatic and practical level because the DRC's response implicated "refugees" in the deportations,[26] and, in contrast to 2004, 2007, and 2008, there was relatively widespread media coverage, perhaps reflecting the greater proximity to Kinshasa.

From Waves to Chronic Crisis

The expulsions did not end after 2009, but their character changed. Rather than being connected to elections or political events in Angola, the expulsions became a more constant trickle of people back into the DRC. They became, in the words of one NGO worker returning from a mission in the region, "every day and every day at a different door,"[27] reflecting the creation of a more systemic apparatus of immigration control in Angola.[28] By 2011, a more coherent monitoring system had been set up, the United Nations system, and was implemented mainly through an Italian NGO called Comitato Internazionale per lo Sviluppo dei Popoli (CISP), allowing better data to be recorded on the patterns of forced return and the experiences of those expelled. People were documented at numerous borders posts in Western Kasai, Bandundu, and Bas-Congo. However, the overwhelming majority of deportees, and especially those who were victims of violence, were in Western Kasai, particularly the Kamako zone of Tshikapa.[29] In 2011, CISP registered 55,590 deportees in the three provinces, of which 3,770 were victims of sexual violence by the Angolan authorities. Between January and May 2012, the number expelled was 13,000.[30]

The patterns of expulsion, although more systematic and marginally less brutal than earlier episodes, remained consistently appalling. The Congolese would be arrested in Angola by men in uniform—described by victims as

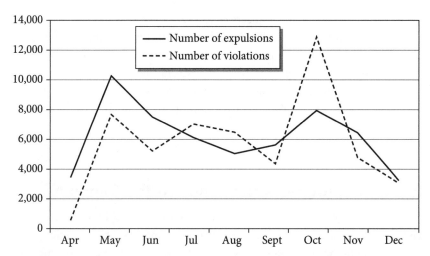

FIGURE 3. The number of recorded expulsions and documented cases of human rights violations (physical abuse, prolonged detention, sex and gender-based violence, theft of belongings) by month at border crossings in Bandundu, Western Kasai, and Bas-Congo for 2011. Source: CISP database.

"soldiers"—in villages, mines, or markets. Many would be subjected to violence or rape (although this behavior appears to have been less systematic than earlier) and taken to police stations or makeshift detention centers. One of the main detention facilities was a former prison near Dundu, where there have been strong and consistent rumors of people being held in a "hole in the ground" and where detention has lasted an average of three days to a week. Conditions of detention have continued to be characterized by the absence of food or medical care, sexual abuse, poor sanitation, and the lack of separate facilities for women and children. One nineteen-year-old woman, a mother of two, expelled twice, described her experience: "This prison is near Dundu and is called Cundueji. It's a big hole in the ground where the Angolans put the Congolese. Everyone is mixed there, women, men, children. . . . We had to do our business altogether there on the ground. They gave us a handful of rice in the mornings and nothing more. There were no medicines and many people fell ill. People died. I saw three bodies. The Angolans threw them in the river. I stayed two weeks in this place, and I was raped by six soldiers during my detention."[31]

Following detention, deportees are brought to the border in trucks and handed over to the Congolese border authorities. Compared with the start of the waves, levels of international organization and NGO presence at the border have increased. With money from UN Pooled Funding, a short-term system of monitoring and assistance was implemented in 2011. However, despite greater monitoring, an exploratory mission by MSF-Belgium in May 2012 highlighted the absence of adequate medical care or assistance and documented that people have been dying at the border. It recorded cases of torture, inhuman and degrading treatment—machete or bullet wounds, burns from boiling water, bayonet injuries—and sexual and gender-based violence, noting the ongoing inadequacy of response to these medical needs. Between January and May 2012 alone, the Red Cross buried ten people who died as a result of the untreated effects of deportation.[32]

Explaining Angola's Response to the Congolese

In the absence of clearly defined norms that set out states' obligations toward vulnerable irregular migrants, the Angolan government has had significant discretion in defining its response to the Congolese on its territory. In this case, almost all the incentive structures have leaned toward a repressive response. At the domestic level, the buildup to legislative and presidential elections gave the MPLA government a strong incentive to remove from its territory Congolese who had historically been close to UNITA. At the international level, the desire to create conditions that would attract inward investment in the diamond industry incentivized the harsh response toward the Congolese. While the overall trend during the period 2003–2009 created continuity in these incentives toward repression, changes in domestic and international incentives also help to explain shifts in the GoA's behavior over time.

Domestic

After independence in 1975, Angola was embroiled in a twenty-seven-year civil war. Peace talks between the MPLA and UNITA at the end of the Cold War led to national elections in 1992. In the legislative elections, the MPLA won 120 seats and UNITA 72 seats. The MPLA victory led to the resumption of civil conflict, and UNITA seized de facto control of the area in which it had its geographical support bases—predominantly the Lunda provinces to the northeast of the country—scuttling peace and giving UNITA control over most of the country's diamond mines. In February 2002, the leader of UNITA, Jonas Savimbi, was killed by the Angolan army, leading to a ceasefire agreement and the end of civil war.

For the first time, the MPLA controlled the entire territory of Angola. Yet 80 percent of the country lay outside its historical sphere of influence. During the conflict, the MPLA was primarily an urban-based movement, relying on its control of Luanda and the oil fields for its support. It had no historical support base in areas such as the Lundas in the periphery of the country. Through a combination of co-optation and coercion, the MPLA has sought to assert its authority across the country (Pearce 2005). It has bought out many former UNITA generals, acquiring their loyalties by, for example, giving them a stake in the diamond mining industry or the politics of the territories. In other cases, it has used violence as a means of demonstrating its authority (Marques 2011; Pearce 2004, 2005).

In taking control of the country, the MPLA agreed to work with the opposition parties—including UNITA—toward national elections, both legislative and presidential. However, on numerous occasions, the dates of these elections were postponed by the MPLA and President Eduardo Dos Santos. The first legislative elections held since 1992 were originally scheduled for 2007 and then postponed until September 2008, when the MPLA proclaimed itself to have won 81 percent of the vote and UNITA just 10 percent. Meanwhile, presidential elections had originally been suggested for 2009 but were repeatedly pushed back.

The most intense waves of deportations were in the buildup to the legislative elections, and the timing of the waves coincided with key moments in the election process. As part of the preparations for elections, a nationwide population census was carried out to establish entitlement to vote. One of the GoA's principal aims was to ensure that Congolese would not register to vote, given that they would be likely to vote for UNITA. In the colonial era, Lunda Norte had closer social and economic ties to the Congo than to Luanda, in which a strong Lunda-Chokwe identity connected the southern provinces and the Lundas (Pearce 2004). In the civil war, Savimbi had been a close ally of Mobutu, and both were strongly supported by the U.S. government in the struggle against the Soviet-backed MPLA (Pearce 2005). It was in this context that large numbers of young Congolese had not only been tolerated in the Lundas but actively recruited by UNITA as both soldiers and artisanal diamond miners. Consequently, in the aftermath of the civil conflict, the GoA continued to believe that Congolese living in Angola would inevitably be UNITA supporters, electorally if not militarily.

Each of the main waves of deportations links closely to aspects of the electoral cycle. The 2004 wave coincides with the MPLA's acquisition of control over the Lundas and recognition of the need to remove foreign UNITA supporters from the territory after an agreement was reached to work toward elections. The 2007 wave coincided with the setting of dates for legislative elections and the beginning of the census to register voters. The 2008 deportations took place in the buildup to the legislative elections of September. Although the Bas-Congo episode in 2009 follows a slightly different logic, it was partly motivated by a similar suspicion of a potential Congolese support base for the Cabinda secessionist group FLEC.

International

Between 1992 and 2002, the MPLA's control over the diamond areas was limited to Cafunfo, and the surrounding areas were controlled by UNITA. UNITA's exploitation of the alluvial and kimberlite mines had not been systematic or founded on international investment. Rather, it was based largely on artisanal methods, and a significant proportion of the diamonds were smuggled across the Congolese border to evade the international sanctions imposed on UNITA. With the end of the conflict, the GoA sought to privatize part of the diamond industry and to attract greater foreign investment. It created Endiama, a parastatal company to act as trustee for the nation's mineral rights. Endiama was empowered to develop joint ventures with foreign companies that could bring investment and technical expertise to the industry. Typically, a given mining project would involve Endiama, an Angolan national company, and a foreign company, all of which shared ownership of a mine.

The GoA strategy proved successful in hugely increasing production and revenue in the diamond sector. In the first five years after the civil war, production nearly doubled, from 5 million carats in 2002 to close to 9.5 million carats in 2006. Gross revenue from diamond sales also doubled, from US$638 million in 2002 to US$1.2 billion in 2006, while government income from diamonds tripled from US$45 million to US$165 million over that same period. A key part of this success came from creating conditions under which international companies were prepared to invest in the mining industry.

The GoA sought to ensure that concessionaire companies would enjoy exclusive rights to the mines, that firms would operate with security, and that diamond smuggling would be eradicated. A range of firms were attracted from around the world, but the most high-profile individual investor was the Israeli businessman Lev Leviev, who through his various business interests and his connections to the GoA established privileged rights to a significant proportion of the Angolan diamond industry. Many of these outside corporations not only demanded significant security but also employed private security firms, which have also been implicated in human rights violations toward nationals and migrant workers. Leviev and his business associates, for example, have been accused of encouraging an environment in which industry security is privileged over rights. It was in the context of creating attractive investment conditions that Operação Brilhante was conceived as an "anti-smuggling" operation.

However, while the political economy of diamond access privileged a repressive response, there was almost no countervailing pressure from the international community or neighboring states to encourage the GoA to develop and secure the diamond mines in a manner that was consistent with human rights. Western diplomatic partners and neighboring states were extremely slow and reluctant to criticize Angola's conduct. As a major oil-exporting country, Angola was partly insulated from international criticism. For example, even after news of the 2004 deportations had broken, the Bush administration still encouraged Dos Santos to stand for reelection and signed a deal for Chevron Texaco to extend its concessionary access to Angolan oil (Médecins Sans Frontières 2004).

Ricardo Soares de Oliveira (2011) highlights the reasons why Angola has been able to pursue a generally illiberal postconflict strategy that has remained relatively immune to criticism. He argues that the MPLA elite has stood apart from international criticism or influence because of the outright military victory of the MPLA, its economic autonomy, the coherent and pragmatic approach of the MPLA in managing international actors, the lack of a well-funded domestic liberal alternative, the interests of international actors and donors, and the lack of commitment by Western donors to their own purported liberal agendas.

Like that of the wider international community, the response from the DRC was almost nonexistent, even though its own citizens were the victims of the rights violations. MSF described the Kinshasa response as based on "a relative passivity" (Médecins Sans Frontières 2008). There were even claims that around 2007 and 2008, a prominent DRC minister argued that the Congolese in Angola "got what they deserved because of being illegals."[33] Part of the reason for the DRC's limited criticism of Angola was the asymmetrical power relationship between the two countries. There is a long history of Angolan military and diplomatic interference in the DRC, and even during the civil war the MPLA was important in bringing Laurent Kabila to power as Mobutu's successor in the DRC. Dos Santos was instrumental in enabling Joseph Kabila to succeed his father as president of the DRC in 2001, and since 1997, when Laurent Kabila came to power, Angolan soldiers have formed the basis of the presidential guard, being one of the main pillars of both presidents' ability to preserve some vestige of authority across the DRC. In the words of Felly Ntumba of OCHA, "Until 2009, the Kinshasa government was not very interested; there were discussions, but they mainly took place at the local level between the Western Kasai and local Angolan authorities. They trivialized things a bit; they did not take much responsibility; they took a laissez-faire approach, assuming and expecting that all the response will come from the international community."[34]

When the international response shifted and different sets of international incentives were created, Angola's behavior was at least partly tempered. In 2009, for example, the DRC government responded to the deportations from Cabinda to Bas-Congo with a stronger, more retaliatory approach, reciprocally deporting Angolan refugees. One of the reasons for this was that in 2009, an alliance between Kabila and Paul Kagame of Rwanda emboldened Kabila in his relationship with

Dos Santos, making him more prepared to stand up to a challenge. As a result, a moratorium was agreed to that rapidly ended the reciprocal deportations.[35] Similarly, during the 2007 and 2008 waves, international condemnation—for example, through the MSF testimonies and resulting press conferences—brought some change in the methods of deportation used by the GoA. While the deportations did not come to an end, the difference between the rights violations recorded in December 2007 and in May–June 2008 shows that an international reaction was instrumental in tempering the most serious violations.

Explaining the International Community's Response

In relation to the degree of human rights violations and humanitarian needs in the waves of deportations, the international community's response was extremely limited. On the Angolan side, there was little engagement by human rights or humanitarian actors, due in part to lack of access to the relevant provinces of Angola and also very little diplomatic engagement by states or the UN country team to facilitate greater access to the Lundas. On the DRC side of the border, a humanitarian response to address the protection needs of expelled migrants was stymied because the affected group fell between the mandates and designated priorities of the various humanitarian agencies.

The case of the Congolese expulsions therefore raises important questions about institutional responsibility for upholding the human rights of vulnerable migrants who are not refugees, and for responding to immediate humanitarian and protection needs, not only within the host country but also—in this case— within the country of origin after deportation. In spite of the obvious protection needs outlined above, UN agencies evaded responsibility and used a range of justifications linked to priorities, mandates, and resources to avoid filling an obvious and urgent protection gap. The result was that protection and assistance needs either were inadequately met or were filled by actors forced to stretch the their own mandates.

Throughout the main waves of deportations, OCHA was widely criticized for its limited engagement. Its role was largely confined to coordinating brief interagency visits to the southern provinces of the DRC and documenting DGM statistics at the border. It was also criticized by the NGOs involved for its inadequate and even "unprofessional" response. In interviews, OCHA staff members provided a range of justifications for their limited involvement. Three particular justifications were repeatedly provided. First, events must be seen in an African context: "You have to see it in African terms. . . . We haven't publicized it at the level that we are publicizing the situation in the Kivus. There are 20,000–30,000 rape cases reported in the DRC yearly"; and "You cannot expect the same degree of response as elsewhere in Africa. In the East, there are 500 rapes a week." Second, many of the deported people were undeserving of assistance because they were prostitutes. One said, "They are economic migrants without the right papers. Even though OCHA does not talk publicly about it, many of the migrants were prostitutes." Third, European states are also abusive of irregular migrants: "Is it that different from migration practices in Europe?" Consequently, "the decision was made by humanitarians in general that this was not such a big thing."[36]

Across the UN system, different actors engaged with the four main waves of deportations in the humanitarian "cluster" approach, participating in interagency missions to the border areas. However, most UN agencies found ways to limit their commitment to an area that fell between different mandates. UNHCR repeatedly argued that it had limited responsibility in relation to the expelled Congolese in Bandundu and Western Kasai, pointing out that the area was "outside the mandate," given that the deportees were (1) not refugees, (2) in their country of origin, and (3) the responsibility of the government of the DRC. Nevertheless, UNHCR became actively involved during the Bas-Congo episode. The fact that Angolan refugees were expelled invoked its refugee protection mandate. Consequently, even though UNHCR acknowledged that it was preparing for repatriation of the Angolan refugees anyway and, in contrast to the other earlier episodes, there was no systematic violence perpetrated against the Angolan refugees, the agency became actively engaged on both sides of the border. Other UN agencies such as UNICEF and FAO played a role in contributing to basic sanitation, water needs, and equipment, mainly through local NGO partners. The International Organization for Migration (IOM) did not play a role primarily because—despite expressing interest in becoming involved—it was not given funding by states to develop a project relating to the deportations. Its "projectized" organizational structure meant that without specific earmarked funding from its core donors, it could not become involved.

In the absence of significant UN engagement, the response during the four main waves came from what might be referred to as "networked protection actors": the International Committee of the Red Cross (ICRC), working through the national Red Cross; Caritas, working through its church network; and MSF, responding to information from its network of doctors and local medical practices. These kinds of networked actors were especially important in a country like the DRC, where it is difficult to get access or information relating to events in remote areas. The antenna structures of these networks allowed information and alerts and rapid response. In this context, MSF was the most engaged international actor during the waves of deportation to Bandundu and Western

Kasai. Despite its predominantly medical mandate, it found itself filling a significant part of the gap vacated by the international community. It chose to do so, largely on the basis of having a medical intervention, but then recognized that its presence, and what it witnessed, gave it a wider moral responsibility to provide protection and assistance, and also to document what it observed. Its relative flexibility as an organization gave it an adaptability that was not available for many of the UN actors in the DRC.

It was only by 2011 that a slightly more coherent international response began to emerge, some seven years after the initial waves. This shift was triggered by a visit made by Margot Wallstrom, the UN Special Rapporteur on Sexual Violence in Conflict, to the DRC and Angola in February and March 2011. Her visit to the region and subsequent comments[37] led to some immediate outcomes. The UN and the GoA made a joint communication, committing to prevent and punish sexual violence, and the GoA made a commitment to facilitate UN-IOM monitoring of detention and expulsions. A working group was also established in Kinshasa in order to better coordinate the activities of the UN system in responding to the issue. Perhaps most significant, though, a pot of $2.7 million from the UN Pooled Fund was disbursed to improve monitoring and assistance for those expelled.[38]

The pooled funding was divided between the Italian NGO CISP, Caritas, the World Health Organization (WHO), and the United Nations Population Fund (UNFPA) to achieve a set of short-term objectives. WHO temporarily provided drugs to local clinics in the relevant provinces; UNFPA provided training to local medical services and NGOs until December 2011; Caritas provided coordination of local church-based NGOs. Meanwhile, CISP used its $500,000 share of the funding to establish assistance and monitoring at the border posts, through a number of local implementing partners, in a project initially funded to run between March 2011 and August 2012.[39] However, even this post-2011 response has been inadequate to address either the underlying causes on the Angolan side or the humanitarian needs on the Congolese side. It has placed too much emphasis on recording numbers rather than providing assistance, its funding has been short-term, and it has continued to rely on local implementing partners that have limited capacity.[40] Meanwhile, the chief UN humanitarian organizations have continued to remain largely on the sidelines, with the exception of the working group set up in Kinshasa in 2011 and coordinated by OCHA.[41]

Conclusion

There has been a long history of livelihoods migration between the DRC and Angola. With the weakening of the economic infrastructure of the Congolese border regions, artisanal diamond mining has become less viable, food security has collapsed, and increasing numbers of people have moved across the border from Bandundu and Western Kasai to Lunda Norte. They are not refugees, but they have left one of the most fragile areas of an extremely fragile state, in which rates of malnutrition, disease, and infant mortality are high and livelihood opportunities are severely limited.

The Angolan response to the presence of Congolese on its territory has not been to provide asylum or sanctuary, or even to offer opportunities to engage in forms of regularized migration. Rather, it has been to round up and deport the Congolese in successive waves. The methods of deportation have been brutal, and at times the levels of violence and the systematic use of rape and sexual violence have bordered on constituting crimes against humanity.

The Angolan response can be explained by the MPLA's attempt to consolidate authority over the diamond mining regions in the northeast of the country. In preparing for elections, it has tried to remove Congolese, who it has regarded as a core part of UNITA's support base. Furthermore, it has tried to end artisanal diamond mining in order to encourage inward investment in the diamond industry and maximize government revenues (and associated kickbacks) from the mines.

Unlike in other situations in which vulnerable irregular migrants have crossed international borders, the international refugee regime has not stretched to address the situation of Congolese in Angola. The main reason why the Angolan government has not adapted refugee norms to address the situation of the Congolese or drawn on a human rights framework to offer forms of complementary protection to people outside a fragile state is that the MPLA has had a strong set of domestic and international incentives to engage in a repressive rather than a tolerant and inclusive response. Its electoral and economic interests have been served better by repression than by tolerance. However, in the period of 2003–2009, the incremental shifts that took place in increasing or reducing the levels of brutality used in deportation, and the numbers deported, can be attributed to shifts in these domestic and international incentive structures. At the domestic level, the main waves have coincided with the cycles of electoral politics. At the international level, the levels and duration of brutality have been shaped by the degree of international passivity or condemnation. For example, the MSF testimonies and subsequent press conferences in December 2007 led to a commitment by individuals in the Angolan army to change aspects of the practices of deportation.

The international response to the deportations was woefully inadequate. In relation to the extent of the atrocities, there was very limited diplomatic condemnation of the deportations, partly because many Western states had core economic interests in maintaining a close diplomatic relationship with the GoA, given the country's natural resources and strategic location. Similarly, the asymmetric power relationship between the DRC and Angola circumscribed the extent to which Kabila's government was prepared to stand up for the rights of its own citizens and openly condemn the actions of the GoA. The humanitarian response was equally limited. International agencies and NGOs had virtually no access to the diamond mining areas in Angola. On the DRC side of the border, actors failed to take responsibility because the situation fell between traditional agency mandates. UNHCR argued that it fell outside its refugee protection. OCHA argued that it was not a priority. IOM could not get funding to engage with the issue. OHCHR had little voice or presence in the DRC. Other UN actors worked mainly through local NGO partners. This left MSF as the main actor to fill the gap in a way that pushed the boundaries of its own mandate. Over time, its own advocacy led the way for increased monitoring and assistance by the international community after 2011.

That such atrocities can take place on such a scale with so little action not only highlights a major gap in the international protection regime. It also shows how the changing dynamics of migration and forced migration cannot be adequately understood through a neat division between "refugee" and "voluntary economic migrant," nor even between "host state" and "country of origin." Rather, at different stages of mobility, irregular migrants face vulnerabilities that result from conditions in both the country of origin and the host country. In order to address these issues, we must do some urgent rethinking about how international institutions respond to the human rights of vulnerable irregular migrants.

TANZANIA

The Paradoxical Response to Congolese from South Kivu

This chapter tells the story of survival migration from the Congolese province of South Kivu to the Kigoma region of Tanzania.[1] South Kivu was a focal point of the two Congo Wars (1996–1997 and 1998–2003), during which the spillover of Tutsi-Hutu violence from the Rwandan genocide was manipulated by a range of state and nonstate actors for economic and political gain (Lemarchand 2004, 62; Vlassenroot 2002, 501). The Congo Wars led to massive human displacement, including the outflow of refugees (Lischer 2007, 151). Around 150,000 Congolese refugees crossed Lake Tanganyika to the Kigoma region, where many have been living in designated camps.

Since 2003, the war in South Kivu has been officially over,[2] and pockets of stability have developed in the province, especially in the coastal areas along the lake. Some refugees have even returned from Tanzania. However, the province has been characterized by fragility and the absence of clear state authority. The infrastructure is almost nonexistent, rates of malnutrition and child mortality are among the highest in the world, and there are few sustainable livelihood opportunities available.[3] There have been episodes of sporadic violence—including by armed nonstate actors—and rape and sexual violence are endemic. During this period, Congolese from South Kivu have continued to cross Lake Tanganyika in large numbers (ADEPAE and SVH 2011, 14).

During and immediately after the Congo Wars, all Congolese arriving in Kigoma were recognized on a prima facie basis and, once registered, taken to the Lugufu or Nyarugusu refugee camps. Over time, however, this response has changed (Rutinwa 2005, 7). Under increasing pressure from local and regional authorities to alleviate the perceived burden on host populations, Tanzania set itself the goal of becoming "refugee free" (ADEPAE and SVH 2011, 15). Congolese arriving in Kigoma have encountered an array of obstacles, frequently facing roundup, detention, and deportation at the hands of local immigration officials.

Despite the precarious human rights situation in South Kivu (Office of the High Commissioner for Human Rights 2012), Congolese have been classified primarily as economic migrants, and increasingly denied access to protection. The argument—reiterated by officials at all levels of government and by representatives of the international community—has been that there is no longer grounds within international refugee law for most Congolese from South Kivu to seek asylum in Tanzania.

There has nevertheless been an interesting paradox within the position of the Tanzanian government. On the one hand, it has been argued that there are few grounds for newly arriving Congolese to receive refugee protection, and limited grounds for claiming that persecution or generalized violence are present in South Kivu. It is no longer seen as a refugee-producing region. On the other hand, both the Tanzanian government and UNHCR are refraining from implementing the cessation clause for Congolese in the camps or from engaging in "promoted repatriation." Their justification for this is not that returning Congolese will face persecution or conflict but that state fragility in the region would make it inhumane to return them.

Tanzania has de facto become a protector of survival migrants. The Tanzanian refugee regime has partly stretched to protect Congolese survival migrants who no longer face persecution or generalized violence, albeit only those who are already present rather than new arrivals. Given Tanzania's implementation of the cessation clause and its repatriation of Burundian refugees since 2009, it could have chosen to act differently with respect to the Congolese (Rutinwa 2005, 15). How can we explain this paradox? Why is it that the Tanzanian government has been putting up barriers to new Congolese arrivals while refraining from returning those who arrived in the late 1990s? Why has it recognized the need not to return already-present Congolese but deports newly arriving Congolese even when the situation to which they will be returned is identical?

This chapter outlines and explains that paradox. Showing that Congolese from South Kivu can be conceived of as survival migrants even beyond the Congo Wars, it argues that there has been an arbitrary distinction between the nonreturn of the camp refugees and the frequent deportation of those who have arrived subsequently.

The chapter finds its explanation for the paradox in the distinction between local and national politics within Tanzania, and the different relationships of UNHCR and the international community to each of these levels of politics.

National politics—subject to a particular set of domestic and international incentives—has defined the politics of return for the camp-based Congolese. In contrast to other populations such as the Burundians, the national government has not been faced with immediate electoral incentives or pressure from the country of origin to return the Congolese but instead has had international incentives to refrain from forced return. Meanwhile, local politics—subject to a very different set of domestic incentives and largely insulated from international influence—has defined a far less inclusive response to new arrivals.

From Refugee Flight to Survival Migration

There has been a long history of Congolese migration across Lake Tanganyika, which has an average width of only 50 kilometers. For many years, Congolese have moved across the lake for commercial reasons, selling produce or seeking employment and livelihood opportunities in the Kigoma region. Large numbers of Congolese fishermen have settled along the Tanzanian shore of the lake, integrating with the local population.[4] Today the Tanzanian side of the shore is lined with Congolese fishing communities that have been present for several generations. The Congolese community has generally been accepted by the local population, which has sometimes shared an ethnic background such as Nyamwezi or Sukuma that transcends state boundaries.

Since the late 1990s, however, the profile and scale of arrivals across the lake have changed dramatically. Most obviously, a large population of Congolese refugees fled the two Congo Wars in South Kivu between 1996 and 2003. The movements that took place during the wars were classic refugee movements, based mainly on flight from persecution and conflict. Both conflicts had their origins in the 1994 sudden influx of Hutus into the DRC in the aftermath of the Rwandan genocide. The exodus of Hutus associated with the previous regime exacerbated a range of political conflicts, based partly on Hutu-Tutsi divisions in North and South Kivu. In South Kivu, the Banyamulenge (ethnic Tutsi indigenous to South Kivu) suffered particular persecution as a result of the political manipulation of Hutu-Tutsi differences (Lemarchand 2004, 62).

The First Congo War (September 1996–May 1997) can be traced to the consequences of the Rwandan genocide. In 1996, the Hutus in exile—backed by DRC president Mobutu—carried out a series of cross-border raids against Rwanda. In response, the new Rwandan government supported a rebellion by the AFDL (Alliance des Forces Démocratiques pour la Libération du Congo-Zaire), mainly consisting of Tutsi Banyamulenge from South Kivu and headed by ethnic Congolese Laurent Kabila for reasons of legitimacy (Akokpari 1998, 216). With support from Rwanda and backed by most countries in the region, Kabila managed to reach Kinshasa, where he overthrew Mobutu in May 1997 (Lemarchand 2004, 62; Emizet 2000, 168). The conflict led to massive population displacement in the eastern DRC, notably in South Kivu (Talley, Spiegel, and Girgis 2001, 412). Many fled to Tanzania, where they were offered assistance in the Lugufu refugee camp, established in February 1997 for an initial 32,000 refugees. Of this group, a significant proportion were persecuted Banyamulenge, mainly from the Uvira and Fizi districts or from Bukavu across Lake Tanganyika (Office of the High Commissioner for Human Rights 2010, 72–79). More than 10,000 of these refugees repatriated to South Kivu in September 1997, once conditions improved, leaving 10,500 behind in Lugufu.

The Second Congo War (August 1998–June 2003) was triggered by then president Laurent Kabila, who recognized that he had become too dependent on Rwanda and then chose to distance himself from Kigali, expelling the Banyamulenge from the government and initiating an anti-Tutsi campaign across the region (Lemarchand 2004, 62). In response, Rwanda and Uganda launched another proxy rebel movement, the RCD (Rassemblement Congolais pour la Démocratie). However, this time, without the clear common enemy of Mobuto and an obvious Rwandan-Ugandan invasion, most other states of the region sided with Kabila. The assistance to the government by Angolan and Zimbabwean troops proved to be decisive for the course of the war, which soon became static. On the local level, the Congolese army (FAC) joined forces with the Hutu *génocidaires* (FDLR) and local militias (Mai-Mai) to fight against the Rwandans (RPF) and the RCD. There were significant massacres and human rights atrocities on both sides (Office of the High Commissioner for Human Rights 2010, 177–178). Much of the worst fighting in South Kivu took place in the Fizi region between pro-government Mai-Mai groups and RCD rebels. A significant number of civilians were displaced, and many fled to Tanzania beginning in January 1999. Around 55,000 had arrived in Lugufu by June 1999, with 1,000 per day coming in at the peak of the influx (Talley, Spiegel, and Girgis 2001, 413).

The Lusaka Peace Agreement in July 1999 led to a commitment by the primary states to end the war. However, implementation was stalled by foreign armies that continued to benefit from mineral wealth extraction and the ongoing role of transnational rebel groups. In December 2002, a peace agreement among the main rebel groups led to an interim power-sharing arrangement and a commitment to hold national elections within two years (Whitaker 2003, 216). By the time the Second Congo War came to an end, there were around 150,000 Congolese in the Lugufu I and II camps and the Nyarugusu camp in Kigoma. Interviews in the camps reveal that nearly everyone still in the camps a decade later had arrived in either 1997 or 1999 and had fled the Fizi district, particularly the areas around Uvira and Baraka, where fighting had been most intense.[5]

The war in the DRC officially ended on June 30, 2003. Until that point, the causes of flight are relatively clear-cut and broadly fit the 1951 convention and its 1967 protocol's definition of a refugee. After 2003, however, those who have left have done so for a variety of reasons linked to state fragility rather than persecution or generalized violence. They more closely fit the category of survival migrants than refugees. This is partly because of the conceptual gap in the refugee definition, discussed earlier, but also due to the perception of violence in DRC. As Séverine Autesserre describes, the country was officially declared a postconflict country during the transition, a designation that ignored the ongoing violence at the local level that often maintained the terror of the war years (Autesserre 2006, 3; 2010, 65–83). Fixed on the postconflict framework, international actors wanted to move on with the peace agenda, which meant repatriation of the refugees and preparation for national elections (Autesserre 2010, 100). A Tripartite Agreement on Repatriation was concluded between the DRC, Tanzania, and UNHCR in 2003, and in 2005, returns were initiated from Kigoma to Uvira and Fizi, coordinated by UNHCR in Bukavu. Despite occasional pauses in repatriation during periods of escalation of violence and insecurity, the start of repatriation was an acknowledgment that those leaving South Kivu, for the most part, no longer fell within the refugee definition.

Even with the war officially over and repatriation under way, instability and fragility continued in South Kivu. High levels of malnutrition and disease meant that civilians continued to die every day. Poverty rates in the Kivus are higher than national averages, school attendance rates for primary schools are low, maternal and infant mortality rates are high, and there are inadequate health services (1 doctor per 27,700 inhabitants across South Kivu) (Jacquemot 2010, 7). With a weak state and the absence of security, there were continued reports of massacres, cannibalism, rapes, looting, extortion, and other serious violations of human rights committed by various armed groups (Autesserre 2006, 2). Rwanda continued to carry out hit-and-run operations in the border regions, maintaining its presence in the Kivus. Meanwhile, the FDLR (Democratic Forces for the Liberation of Rwanda)—based on the remnants on Hutu refugees who arrived in 1994—continued to operate out of South Kivu, contributing to instability and sporadic attacks on civilians (Rafti 2006, 7). South Kivu, with its varied forest landscape, its natural resources of gold, cassiterite, and coltan deposits, and the absence of central state control, provided a safe haven where the FDLR could operate embedded among the civilian population (Rafti 2006, 12).

The FDLR, the Armed Forces of the Democratic Republic of Congo (FARDC), and the Mai-Mai militia created by the local population have been a source of sporadic human rights violations, occasionally seizing land, occupying property, setting up roadblocks to extort money, or plundering mineral wealth (Jacquemot 2010, 6; Fanning 2010, 37). All armed groups including the national army have regularly engaged in extreme violence against civilians in remote areas of South Kivu such as the Kahuzi Biega Park (Rafti 2006, 15; Stearns 2011). One of the most extreme features has been widespread sexual violence. According to a report by the Harvard Humanitarian Initiative (2010, 39), there has been a "normalization of rape among the civilian population" in South Kivu. Local health center data suggest that an average of forty women per day are raped in South Kivu,[6] and there is almost total impunity regarding that crime.[7] A culture of blurred lines of consent has been emerging in which women are seen as the property of the husband's family or become property of the community if the husband dies or leaves (Rodriguez 2010; IRIN 2011; Holmes 2010, 4).

At certain times there have also been spikes in more generalized violence. In 2009, for example, repatriations were suspended during a joint Congolese-Rwandan military mission against the FDLR. This surprising cooperation was based on a secret agreement between President Joseph Kabila of the DRC and President Paul Kagame of Rwanda, the arrest of Laurent Nkunda, leader of the rebel group National Congress for the Defense of the People (CNDP), on January 22, 2009, and subsequent integration of the CNDP into the national army. This led to the so-called Kimia II mission, in which both countries, together with the UN peacekeeping force MONUC, chose to aggressively pursue the FDLR. A scattered FDLR withdrew farther into the bush, exacerbating violence along its way.

Consequently, even though the war ended in 2003 and repatriations began in 2005, South Kivu has been extremely fragile and insecure for the civilian populations. While South Kivu's coastline along Lake Tanganyika—around the towns of Uvira and Fizi, for example—has been relatively secure over the last decade, just 100 kilometers farther inland, the province has had an almost total vacuum of political authority. There are almost no roads or infrastructure, very limited livelihood opportunities outside the rebel-controlled mining areas, and an environment of impunity.[8] It has been characterized by extreme state fragility.

In this context of insecurity, people have continued to cross Lake Tanganyika, many of them fleeing basic rights deprivations within South Kivu. Most have taken informal routes, and so they have not entered the asylum system or led to an increase in refugee numbers.[9] In the words of one UNHCR employee, "the Congolese don't take the formal routes. They are not claiming asylum.... Since I have arrived in Kigoma, only six to seven families have sought asylum, but there are others coming.... We know that people are crossing the lake all the time."[10] They have come with a variety of motives. As noted by the UNHCR representative, "there have been several kinds of movement, from those looking for security, to Congolese fishermen who have settled on the coast of the lake."[11] They have adopted a variety of strategies in Kigoma. Because of the response of the Tanzanian government—of mainly rounding up, detaining, and deporting new arrivals—many have bypassed the asylum system and instead integrated among the Congolese fishing communities present along the lake[12] or even secretly embedded themselves with relatives in the refugee camps without registering.[13]

With the change in circumstances in South Kivu, the view taken of the refugees in the camps has also changed. By 2009, all the Congolese in the camps were incorporated in the Nyarugusu refugee camp. And while they are recognized to have originally fled conflict in the late 1990s, there is a widely held assumption that they are now mainly outside their country of origin for a set of reasons that fall outside the refugee definition—notably because of disorder and violence and the absence of infrastructure. As the head of the UNHCR Field Office in Kigoma stated: "Many are staying on for economic reasons because their subsistence is provided. They are sending their children for education, health care, jobs, food, which would not be possible in the DRC."[14]

It seems clear that the circumstances in South Kivu have changed since the first decade of the 2000s such that people have not primarily faced threats that fall within the refugee regime. However, there has been an acknowledgment that even for refugees recognized in the 1990s, the new circumstances of fragility and lack of economic opportunity are themselves serious threats that might require some kind of protection. The head of the Kasulu Field Office articulated this clearly: "The reasons why they left may not exist anymore but the general situation—e.g., health and education—and the constant fear makes me agree that those that stay, have to stay."[15] This statement represents an acknowledgment that while the refugees may have left persecution and conflict in the late 1990s, today the main threats to rights in South Kivu are of a different nature—yet might justify ongoing protection. Interviews with refugees similarly confirm this view of the change in reasons for remaining outside South Kivu. Mandeleo, a refugee in his late twenties in Nyarugusu, said: "I cannot go home. There is violence and conflict. But the main reason is that there is no food there; I cannot grow anything. There is no commercial activity or work. So I will take UNHCR advice, and UNHCR says it is still not safe to go back. Life in the camps is hard, but there are no options. I have been here since 1997. I'd like to go back, but it is not possible."[16]

Tanzania's Response

Reflecting the changing causes of movement outlined above, Tanzania's response to Congolese migrants from South Kivu can be thought of as a reaction to two phases of migration: flight from the Congo Wars until 2003, and flight from fragility since 2003.

During the first phase, in the context of the Congo Wars, Tanzania recognized Congolese refugees on a prima facie basis, based on its national asylum legislation. The Tanzanian Refugee Act (1998) set out a refugee definition drawn from both the 1951 convention and the OAU convention. Including the OAU convention meant that, in addition to victims of persecution, four further categories of persons could be recognized as refugees: victims of external aggression, occupation, foreign domination, and generalized instability. The act had been introduced partly as a restrictive move, signaling an end to Tanzania's earlier open-door policy (Kamanga 2005, 104), but its scope at least allowed all the Congolese fleeing in the late 1990s to receive prima facie recognition.

The response to people who arrived from South Kivu during this first phase was therefore to treat them as refugees. On December 31, 1998, the Lugufu refugee camp was created for a population of approximately 10,500. By end of June 1999, the camp, designed to accommodate 40,000 refugees, far surpassed its maximum capacity with population of 55,279 (Talley, Spiegel, and Girgis 2001, 413). Most refugees came from villages in the Fizi district that were in close proximity to the shoreline of Lake Tanganyika; they crossed into Tanzania via private boats at a cost of US$10 (Talley, Spiegel, and Girgis 2001, 413). Once in Tanzania, they were transported by truck from Kigoma to Lugufu by aid organizations including UNHCR, and on arrival at the camp, they were screened and received food aid (Talley, Spiegel, and Girgis 2001, 413). Lugufu was expanded to two camps, and a third Congolese refugee camp, Nyarugusu, was opened later. In 2009, all the Congolese refugees were consolidated into Nyarugusu.

During the second phase—when flight was based on state fragility rather than conflict per se—the response changed dramatically. According to the official process, newly arriving Congolese remained eligible for prima facie refugee recognition under the 1998 Refugee Act, subject to screening by an ad hoc committee at the local level acting under the auspices of the regional commissioner, drawing on criteria defined in the capital by the National Eligibility Commission. However, in practice, there has been an erosion of prima facie recognition in general and for the Congolese in particular (Rutinwa 2005, 5, 22). Indeed, the composition of screening panels at the local level has varied; UNHCR has not even warranted observer status in some districts, and the Congolese have effectively been subject to procedures verging on individualized status determination (Rutinwa 2005, 25).

The view at the regional level has been that Congolese are no longer welcome. The sentiment is that they are not genuine refugees and should therefore not be permitted to burden local communities. The representative of the Department of Refugee Affairs in Kigoma suggested that after the influxes during Congo Wars there has been "nothing since" other than illegal immigration. Commenting on the ad hoc committee interviews at the local level, he said, "We reject them if they have socioeconomic reasons; any other reasons aside from persecution. . . . Anyone who stayed in the villages would be considered an illegal immigrant."[17] Indeed, UNHCR staff confirmed that "new arrivals is not a popular thing to talk about" with the local and regional authorities.[18]

Both the regional commissioner for Kigoma and the district commissioners[19] have attempted to place significant restrictions on Congolese immigration and to use their authority to make access and use of the asylum system virtually impossible. A range of barriers were put in place that impede access to refugee status determination procedures for Congolese. These begin almost as soon as Congolese arrive in the port of Kigoma. Police and border control officers representing the Immigration Office try to identify and arrest illegal immigrants on arrival. Using informants, they also try to identify Congolese in the local community, although many of the long-standing settlements of Congolese fishermen along the lake are left alone.[20] Meanwhile, refugee status determination procedures are frequently suspended as the ad hoc committees at the regional level are intermittently halted under pressure from the regional commissioner.

On a visit to the Kigoma Immigration Office, officers proudly pointed out fifteen Congolese men, handcuffed and detained, seated on the ground in a small area behind the reception desk, all brought in during the previous two days. The immigration officers boasted of the large number they arrest on a regular basis, explaining how they are intercepted at the lake and then arrested and deported. No precise figures were available, but more than one thousand had been arrested and deported in 2009 alone. The deputy immigration officer explained that they sometimes refer Congolese to UNHCR and, where possible, refer to the ad hoc committee, but only when there is a clear case of persecution.[21]

UNHCR confirmed that they suspect that many Congolese fleeing instability in South Kivu are deported without access to asylum procedures, and that this often happens without the involvement of the anti-immigration regional commissioner. The head of the Kasulu Sub-Office said that in 2009 only around fifty new asylum seekers had been brought to UNHCR's attention, stating that, "I'm sure that there are other people not able to reach the camp."[22] Other staff confirmed that there is without doubt *refoulement* resulting from the deportations.[23] While I was conducting an interview at the UNHCR Kigoma Office, a phone call interrupted to say that two Congolese families hiding in a guest house had been arrested by the authorities, and the authorities wanted to deport them without the possibility of access to asylum procedures.[24] Local NGOs have documented cases of alleged *refoulement*.[25]

Yet the Tanzanian response toward Congolese has in some ways been para-doxical. While new arrivals have generally been unwelcome and subject to depor-tation, Tanzania has broadly respected the rights of those Congolese refugees in camps. Sporadic periods of repatriation have taken place to Uvira and Fizi, but these have been—in UNHCR's language—"facilitated" rather than "promoted" returns. In other words, there has been no element of compulsion or coercion for those who have not wanted to return. In contrast to the Burundian refugees, the cessation clause has not been invoked for the Congolese from South Kivu. International refugee law allows for the cessation clause, by which refugee status can be withdrawn when fundamental changes have taken place in the refugees' country of origin (Whitaker 2002, 336).

Yet this has not been applied in relation to the Congolese in the Nyarugusu refugee camp, who arrived during the two Congolese Wars. How can we explain this paradox? Why is it that Tanzania has on the one hand imposed obstacles on newly arriving Congolese asylum seekers while on the other hand recognized that it would be inappropriate to impose the cessation clause for those who are already in Tanzanian refugee camps?

The International Response

The international community's response has to a large extent mirrored that of the Tanzanian government. UNHCR has been in Kigoma since 1984. Until then, refugees were just accepted and integrated and UNHCR was not needed.[26] With greater strain placed on the region, an initiative called the International Confer-ences on Refugees in Africa (ICARA I and ICARA II) led to UNHCR involvement in Kigoma to register refugees. However, it was with the successive mass influxes from Rwanda, Burundi, and the DRC in the 1990s that UNHCR took on a more significant assistance and camp management role.

UNHCR's main role in Kigoma during the Congo Wars was to ensure that Tanzania's borders remained open while it worked to establish camps, first the Lugufu camps and later Nyarugusu. It expanded the Kigoma Sub-Office and opened the Kasulua Field Office. It provided screening, registration, initial food assistance, and transportation to the camps. UNHCR received significant co-operation from the Tanzanian government. Most of the Rwandans had gone home—with the support of UNHCR—and that facilitated a relationship of trust between UNHCR and the government. The 1998 Refugee Act had also just been passed, and the Congolese influx gave the government and UNHCR an opportu-nity to show that it could be applied in practice (Talley, Spiegel, and Girgis 2001).

By the end of the war, there were 152,284 Congolese refugees registered in three camps in Tanzania. UNHCR was under pressure from a Tanzanian government anxious to reduce the presence of refugees in its territory. With the security situation improved in parts of South Kivu, there were eight hundred spontaneous returns every week during August 2005. On September 12, 2005, UNHCR brokered a tripartite voluntary return agreement with the DRC and Tanzania, and beginning on October 15, the UNHCR began repatriation, using the First World War German boat *Liemba* to transport refugees back across to the relatively more secure Uvira and Fizi. In total, UNHCR has helped 66,000 refugees to return since 2005 (Rwegayura 2011).

The return operation was gradual and has been repeatedly interrupted by outbreaks of violence on the other side of the lake. Significantly, UNHCR opted to engage only in what it calls "facilitated" rather than "promoted" return. In the words of one UNHCR staff member, the distinction is about the degree of voluntarism involved: "This is just information that we give you . . . rather than we are really pushing you."[27] And even facilitated return was limited to certain areas of the country: "Facilitated return can only take place to those areas which are safe and accessible to humanitarian actors."[28]

Over time, UNHCR faced increasing pressure to facilitate return. In 2009, Tanzania agreed with UNHCR to naturalize the 1972 Burundian caseload while declaring a cessation and returning all subsequent Burundian refugees. With the Tanzanian aspiration to be refugee-free by 2010, UNHCR placed greater emphasis on facilitating return, and offered a growing set of incentives and initiatives to encourage it.

In engaging in facilitated return, UNHCR has provided refugees with information, on paper and through radio in the camps. It has offered a "return package" that includes "support items"—a choice of a bicycle, a mattress, or a chair. It has also advised refugees on safe and nonsafe areas and established "go and see" programs to Baraka, Fizi Town, and Uvira Town, allowing refugees to return for a visit and make an assessment. "Come and talk" programs have also been used to enable some who have returned to come back and explain their experiences. The organization has arranged transfer from the port of Kigoma to Baraka and to two transit centers in South Kivu, where returnees have received food, household items, and transport home.[29] In 2009, UNHCR also cooperated with the government to close down the Lugufu camps and consolidated all the remaining Congolese in the Nyarugusu camp.

Meanwhile, UNHCR has been extremely constrained—and often muted—in its response to Tanzania's deportation of new Congolese arrivals. While it has engaged in quiet advocacy at the local level, it has been limited in its ability to influence arrests and deportations by local police and immigration staff. Occasionally, it has been able to intervene to ensure that some of the people at risk of *refoulement* have had access to the asylum system.[30] However, its degree of influence has been limited, partly because of a poor relationship with the regional authorities and partly because UNHCR has generally recognized many of the arriving Congolese as economic migrants and hence outside its mandate.[31]

Where UNHCR has—somewhat paradoxically—drawn the line is in refusing to engage in promoted returns or to invoke the cessation clause for Congolese refugees. In contrast to its implicit recognition that new arrivals are not entitled to protection, UNHCR has continued to insist that the Congolese cannot be "strongly encouraged" to go back to South Kivu, not because of a risk of persecution or conflict but simply because of the generalized situation of fragility and the absence of infrastructure and livelihood opportunities to make return viable.[32]

Explaining the Tanzanian Response

The challenge, then, is to explain the paradox of Tanzania's response to survival migration. Why has it continued to tolerate the presence of old arrivals while seeking to deny access to new arrivals from South Kivu? The answer can partly be found in the shift over time in Tanzania's refugee policy from an open door to an aspiration to be refugee free. Yet even as the country as a whole has moved toward a less tolerant asylum policy, there has been an important nuance. At the national level, where policies relating to return of the camp populations are largely decided, a different set of incentives has been present than at the local level, where policies relating to immigration and deportation of new arrivals are implemented. In other words, a gap between national and local politics lies behind the apparent paradox.

Since independence in 1961, Tanzania had an open-door policy under President Julius Nyerere (Chaulia 2003, 147; Rutinwa 1996, 295). Informed by Nyerere's belief in Pan-African socialism, Tanzania allowed spontaneous, self-settled, rural refugees fleeing the colonial liberation struggles and the Cold War proxy conflicts to seek refuge on its territory. It hosted up to 400,000 refugees at a time in twenty settlements from a dozen countries, notably protecting Burundian refugees fleeing in 1972 and Rwandans during the influxes of 1959, 1964, and 1972 (Chaulia 2003, 147; Rutinwa 1996, 291; Gasarasi 1990, 89). Those who sought asylum received it.

After Nyerere's departure as president in 1985, a gradual shift took place in Tanzanian asylum policy. Under pressure from international financial institutions, the country adopted structural adjustment programs and underwent democratization (Chaulia 2003, 147; Whitaker 2002, 339). With these changes, resource competition between citizens and noncitizens became a new feature of political debate, and anti-asylum rhetoric a source of political gain (Milner 2009). Consequently, the newly elected president, Benjamin Mkapa, made "the refugee issue" a part of his political rhetoric in 1995 despite the explicit position of Mwalimu Nyerere (Landau 2004).

The mass influx in the aftermath of the Rwandan genocide marked a key turning point in Tanzanian asylum policy. Between April and May 1995, 500,000 to 700,000 Rwandans arrived, making Benaco camp in Ngara the second-largest city in Tanzania (Rutinwa 1996, 295; Landau 2004, 36). The influx led to pressure on the environment and social services, and created insecurity and instability, for which the government received little or no international support (Rutinwa 1996; Whitaker 2002; Landau 2003, 2004; Milner 2009; Waters 1999). In December 1996, Mkapa issued an ultimatum to half a million Rwandan refugees to leave by end of the month (Whitaker 2002, 328).

Between 1993 and 1998, almost 1.3 million people from Burundi, Rwanda, and DRC sought refuge in western Tanzania (Whitaker 2002, 339) right at the time of the transition to a multiparty system. That experience led to a dramatic shift in Tanzania's refugee policy (Milner 2009). The 1998 Refugee Act introduced a clear refugee definition and a bureaucratic framework in which to clearly distinguish refugees from nonrefugees (Rutinwa 2005, 10). Building on the act, the government created the 2003 National Refugee Policy. It promoted repatriation as "the best solution to the refugee problem" and even proposed "safe zones" for refugees inside their own countries, starting with Burundi, and citing the approach of the international community in northern Iraq and Bosnia as its inspiration. The policy shift also introduced encampment, requiring the majority of refugees to reside in designated areas, which they are not allowed to leave without a permit. The government set itself the aspiration of being refugee-free by 2010. As a result, it has, for example, implemented the cessation clause for Burundian refugees alongside naturalizing the 1972 caseload, while attempting to strengthen border control to limit illegal immigration. In Bonaventure Rutinwa's words: "Tanzania is aspiring to be refugee-free by the end of 2010. Because of this background, you observe a change in the posture, especially on the border. The position is, 'Go back, because we are going to be refugee-free next year.'"[33]

Although the overall trend has been a shift from openness to exclusion, there has been significant moderation in the policy's application, which is largely explained by core-periphery relations in the Tanzanian state (Milner 2009). While the government in Dar es Salaam, in particular the Ministry of Home Affairs, has responsibility for the overarching framework of asylum and immigration policy, in practice much of its implementation is defined at the local level. Regional entities, such as like Kigoma, are governed by the Regional Administration Act (1997), which makes regional commissioners and district commissioners the principal representatives of the national government in both immigration and asylum policy. For example, even within the Kigoma region, there is variation in how different district commissioners set up extra-statutory ad hoc committees to do RSD-like screening for Burundian and Congolese refugees, notwithstanding the fact that the official position of the Ministry of Home Affairs in the capital is prima facie recognition (Rutinwa 2005, 11).

UNHCR staff members consistently point out that one of the biggest obstacles to their work in Kigoma is the role of the regional commissioner.[34] As we have seen, the regional commissioner possesses a high degree of autonomy and makes decisions that de facto go against national refugee politics. Kigoma's regional commissioners vary, but during my fieldwork, the retired colonel in the position was widely cited for his anti-refugee and immigration stance, consistently claiming that refugees are better off than many nationals and insisting that there is commercial activity on the other side of the lake and so there is no justification for Congolese from South Kivu to be in Tanzania.[35]

Consequently, while UNHCR can maintain a clear and principled agreement with the Ministry of Home Affairs to not immediately invoke the cessation clause for Congolese in the camps, it has far less ability to influence access to asylum for new arrivals at the regional level. Even when concessions are made in Dar es Salaam, this does not necessarily translate into change in Kigoma. In the words of one UNHCR staff member, "the relationship between the minister of home affairs and the regional commissioner is not too good . . . there is a power struggle."[36]

It is this division between national and local politics that explains the paradoxical response toward Congolese from South Kivu. On the one hand, the ministry has responsibility for the status of recognized refugees in the camps. It is the central government in Dar that ultimately decides whether the Congolese are subject to cessation or what type of repatriation is warranted. On the other hand, issues relating to new arrivals—immigration control, deportation, and access to asylum procedures—are largely beyond the control of the national government and subject to the oversight of the regional and district commissioners.

Government elites have been subject to different sets of incentives at the national and local levels. In Dar es Salaam, the government is largely insulated from the negative impacts of refugee hosting and the corresponding electoral pressures to repatriate or deport the Congolese, who are almost exclusively confined to the Kigoma region. While the central government is committed to making the country refugee-free, it recognizes the need to cooperate with UNHCR in order to achieve this goal in a way that is recognized as legitimate. Since repatriation is subject to a tripartite agreement between UNHCR, the DRC, and Tanzania, and because international funding is what makes repatriation logistically viable, the Ministry of Home Affairs has a strong incentive to take a more cautious and sustainable approach. After all, the situation in South Kivu is still volatile, and unilaterally repatriating the refugees against the explicit advice of UNHCR could jeopardize Tanzania's international reputation. Unilateral repatriation could both put the refugees at risk to new waves of violence and further destabilize the fragile status quo of local communities in eastern DRC (Autessere 2006, 15).

Importantly for the central government, there has also been steady funding earmarked for supporting the Congolese refugees.[37] European Commission humanitarian aid (ECHO) money is, for example, consistently directed through implementing partners to support the Congolese refugees in the Nyarugusu camp, and it remains a priority for European donors and Belgium in particular.[38] Hence concern for Tanzania's international reputation, insulation from domestic electoral pressures, and access to international funding mean that at the national level there are strong incentives against forcibly returning the camp-based Congolese refugees at a time when the situation in South Kivu remains volatile and unstable.

The incentives for regional and district politics differ considerably from those that influence policy in Dar es Salaam. The negative impacts of refugee influxes, such as inflation, the increased competition over resources, perceived insecurity, and degradation of the environment, manifest locally (Whitaker 2002, 355). While hosting refugees has also had positive impacts on employment opportunities, government revenues, and health, transport, education, and water services (Milner 2009), these benefits and their distribution vary with area and are often not to the advantage of the local population (Whitaker 2002, 345–349; Landau 2003, 25–29). Prejudices against refugees have been fostered by one-sided media depictions that stress the negative impact of the refugee presence (Rutinwa 2005, 15). Local politicians often play on these sentiments to gain popular support (Landau 2003, 35–36). In Kigoma, regional commissioners and district commissioners have generally sought to portray refugees as a burden in a way that partly reflects local attitudes toward the Congolese (Whitaker 2002, 349). Close to election times, regional and district commissioners have had strong incentives to negatively portray the Congolese, and there have been often documented clampdowns on immigrants and refugees found outside the camps around these times (US Department of State 2010). Regional authorities do not have the jurisdiction to repatriate the old arrivals, so they seek to push them to the margins of society and to reduce the likelihood that new arrivals will remain in Kigoma.

Furthermore, in contrast to the national level, there are few direct incentives for regional commissioners to cooperate with UNHCR. Unlike for the ministry, there are no direct financial or political channels of influence. Hence the regional commissioner has had a consistently confrontational relationship with the UNHCR office in Kigoma, having none of the same incentives as the central government to adopt a more tolerant or collaborative position.[39]

In summary, then, the seemingly arbitrary paradox of protecting people from South Kivu already in the camps while arresting and deporting new arrivals can be explained by the division of authority between national and local politics, and the different incentives that elites face at these different levels to protect or to return Congolese fleeing fragility in South Kivu.

Explaining the International Response

These same dynamics have also been influential in explaining a similar paradox in UNHCR's response to the Congolese from South Kivu. UNHCR has faced very different constraints at the local level than at the national level. Its ability to engage with and shape the policies of the Ministry of Home Affairs, through working with the Department of Refugee Affairs in Dar es Salaam, has been very different from its ability to work with the regional commissioner and immigration offices in Kigoma. In other words, UNHCR has confronted a different politics at different levels of government.

At the local level, UNHCR has had little influence. It has had to rely on forming a working relationship with the district and regional commissioners and with local immigration officers in order to get access to newly arriving Congolese before they are deported. Yet these regional authorities in Kigoma have had very little incentive to cooperate with UNHCR. Their interests de facto lead them to conflicting practices that they justify by their responsibilities to the local population and through portraying the issue as one of illegal immigration, which places it partly outside UNHCR's mandate.

To reduce the potential for *refoulement* at the Kigoma level, UNHCR has had to rely on more subtle forms of influence such as training and awareness raising. Bonaventure Rutinwa commented while working as a "mixed migration" adviser to UNHCR: "When you get to know the situation or deal with the refugee officers, immigration, everybody, to avoid these people getting pushed back to the DRC. . . . What we are trying to do is extensive programs of capacity building and training to raise awareness among border officials."[40]

At the national level, though, UNHCR has had a different relationship with the Ministry of Home Affairs. Even though successive ministers have taken a strong line on the burden imposed by generations of refugee hosting (Milner

2009), UNHCR has been able to exert significant influence over the direction of the ministry's refugee policies. In particular, international burden sharing has been greatly valued by the ministry, and while voluntary contributions channeled to UNHCR to support Tanzania's refugee programs have often been inadequate relative to the need, they have nevertheless given UNHCR leeway to influence the ministry. Moreover, despite being vocal on the security implications of long-term refugee hosting, the national government has been attuned to the need to maintain an image of legitimacy in the eyes of the international community.[41] Hence UNHCR has been able to exert relatively greater influence over broader issues relating to the cessation and repatriation of camp refugees, which are decided at the ministry level, than it has on issues relating to the treatment of new arrivals, which fall under the de facto authority of regional actors.[42]

Conclusion

The response to survival migration of Congolese from South Kivu to Tanzania can be characterized as a paradox. On the one hand, both the government and UNHCR have recognized the need to not force refugees who arrived in the late 1990s to go back to South Kivu. This position has been based not on a current risk of persecution or an ongoing civil conflict but on the recognition that the present state fragility would make cessation or promoted return inappropriate. On the other hand, however, the government has rounded up, detained, and deported many of the new arrivals from South Kivu, frequently depriving them of access to the asylum system.

This radically different treatment of new arrivals and old arrivals is arbitrary from a human rights perspective because, if returned, both sets of people would currently face the same conditions of state fragility and weak governance in South Kivu. Tanzania has become a de facto protector of survival migrants by not returning many from South Kivu, explicitly on the grounds of state fragility. However, this protection of survival migrants has not extended to people crossing Lake Tanganyika after 2003 as a result of exactly the same sets of threats and rights deprivations.

The reasons for this paradox are political. In particular, they lie in the distinction between national and local politics. The politics of refugee protection—and the influence of UNHCR—are not the same in Dar es Salaam as in Kigoma. The core-periphery structure of Tanzanian state governance has defined responses to the Congolese. National politics has had authority over the refugee camp populations. The Ministry of Home Affairs makes decisions on questions of repatriation and cessation for recognized refugees. In contrast, local politics in Kigoma has had authority over the implementation of immigration policies, thereby determining the day-to-day reality of what happens to newly arriving Congolese.

At the national level, the government has had strong incentives to cooperate with UNHCR and not insist on the return of the Congolese. Financially, it has received significant assistance from UNHCR. Furthermore, the central government has valued the legitimacy it derives from being seen to respect the rights of refugees. At the local level, though, the regional commissioner has had few incentives to refrain from *refoulement* of new arrivals. The impact of the Congolese is more acutely felt at the local level than in Dar es Salaam, and thus there have been electoral incentives to maintain a strong immigration policy but few incentives to cooperate with the international community.

The case highlights the way in which refugee protection is subject to different politics at different levels of government. It suggests that the extent to which the refugee regime stretches to protect groups such as the Congolese from South Kivu relies on incentives at those different levels. If the international community is to influence the practice of protection, it has to be aware of the factors that shape protection at the local as well as the national level.

KENYA
Humanitarian Containment and the Somalis

Since the collapse of Siad Barre's authoritarian regime in Somalia in 1991, civil conflict and interclan violence have led to state collapse, destroying the governance structures that characterize most functional nation-states. The formal institutions that usually guarantee property rights, ensure law and order, and enable markets to exist have given way to an anarchical territory in which constantly shifting distributions of power among rival groups undermine security.

Without a functioning state, people have lacked the most basic institutions to ensure their fundamental human rights. Faced with a lack of access to food, water, physical security, or a viable livelihood, with the exception of the autonomous areas of Somaliland and Puntland, Somalis have had no functioning state to offer recourse or protection. Instead, they have been left dependent on their own private networks. Where these have failed, millions of Somalis have been forced to leave their homes, either being displaced within the country or fleeing across international borders.

The movement of Somalis is an important case of survival migration, one that challenges the basis of the refugee regime. Cross-border displacement has been driven by a combination—and frequently the complex interaction—of persecution, conflict, and environmental factors. For some Somalis, the most immediate cause of cross-border movement may have been persecution, which would fall within the 1951 Refugee Convention. For others, it may have been generalized violence, as covered by the OAU Refugee Convention and applied selectively in the African context. For others still, it may have been environmental factors, which may fall outside the existing framework of international refugee law.

The complexity of cross-border movement, and its imperfect fit with the refugee regime, was most starkly illustrated by the effects of the famine and drought in the Horn of Africa in 2011, in which unprecedented numbers of people crossed from south-central Somalia into neighboring countries. From a human rights perspective, however, it is irrelevant whether the proximate cause is primarily persecution, conflict, or environment. What makes these factors matter is that weak governance in Somalia means that fundamental human rights deprivations—resulting from whatever cause—cannot be restituted in the state.

Given the range and complexity of factors underlying displacement, states have responded to displaced Somalis differently. Recognition rates for Somali refugees have varied greatly across states. In Europe, there has been different jurisprudence based on whether, for example, persecution by nonstate actors is included in the 1951 convention; the United Kingdom and Germany in particular have different interpretations of this. Furthermore, European states have differed in their interpretation of which areas of Somalia are safe for return within the EU refugee protection framework.[1] Nevertheless, the European Convention on Human Rights has ensured that sources of complementary protection in international human rights law have prevented many Somalis who fall outside the 1951 convention from being returned.[2] Within Africa, there has also been significant variation in response. Some states have applied the OAU convention to recognize Somalis fleeing generalized violence as refugees; most have not.

Kenya's response has been unique. In terms of defining the contours of who a refugee is, its policies have been almost unrivaled in their inclusivity. It has hosted hundreds of thousands of Somalis on its territory for more than two decades, irrespective of the individual circumstances that have led to flight. It has recognized refugees under both the 1951 convention and the OAU convention, and it has recognized people fleeing south-central Somalia on a prima facie basis rather than using individualized refugee status determination. It has assumed that if people come from those regions, then they are, by definition, in need of international protection and there is no need for individualized screening. Even Somalis fleeing primarily famine and drought have been admitted onto Kenyan territory and registered in the refugee camps, where they have been supported by UNHCR and the organizations that make up the refugee regime.

In that sense, Kenya's refugee regime appears to have stretched to include people who fall outside the dominant interpretation of who a refugee is. Yet there has been a trade-off. While the regime has stretched at the level of quantity of asylum, this has come at the price of the quality of asylum. Somali refugees—irrespective of the causes of their flight—have faced extremely restrictive conditions. Hundreds of thousands have been confined to the overcrowded Dadaab refugee camps in the arid and insecure North Eastern Province of the country. Kenya's de facto encampment policy toward refugees has created severe restrictions on their freedom of movement and access to livelihood opportunities, and most live in the camps in an intractable state of limbo. A minority of Somalis who have left the camps for the Eastleigh district in Nairobi generally live outside formal protection and assistance channels.

In terms of the argument of the book, this chapter shows how the Kenyan refugee regime has stretched to be inclusive of people at the margins of the international refugee regime fleeing fragile and failed states. The price of inclusivity, however, has been a reduction in the quality of asylum at the cost of depriving Somalis of their rights to freedom of movement and self-employment, and their access to basic necessities of life. Thus, paradoxically, the extension of the refugee regime has resulted in the failure to meet the basic rights guaranteed by the convention to refugees lawfully present. The reasons for both the inclusiveness of quantity and the limitations on quality, the chapter argues, can be found in the configuration of elite interests. It shows how a convergence of interests at the international and national level has conspired to create an implicit bargain of "humanitarian containment." On the one hand, the government has faced significant international incentives to admit Somalis onto its territory. On the other hand, it has faced both international and domestic incentives to contain the refugee population within a clearly designated physical and socioeconomic space. Over time, the result has been a trade-off between numbers and rights.

Somali Displacement as Survival Migration

Somalia is generally seen as the archetypal failed state (Murphy 2011; Patrick 2011; Shay 2008). The label of "failed state" can be misleading both because it assumes a normative ideal of a functioning state and because it risks ignoring the range of informal institutions and networks that continue to regulate social, economic, and political life within the country. Nevertheless, it captures the reality of a state in which weak governance means that there is no state willing or able to provide the most basic protection against fundamental human rights violations.

Since the collapse of Siad Barre's dictatorship in 1991, the south-central parts of the country have been characterized by the collapse of central government functions. In the absence of a strong central government in Mogadishu, clans, warlords, and religious groups have competed for power and authority, contributing to violence, persecution, and environmental disaster. Without an effective state, Somalis have relied on their own networks and informal institutions. When these have proved insufficient, the only option for many has been to flee, either within the country or across international borders. By 2011, it was estimated that around 25 percent of Somalia's 7.5 million population was either internally displaced or living outside the country as refugees.[3]

Patterns of Displacement from Somalia

The causes and cycles of displacement from Somalia can be divided into three broad phases (Lindley 2011; Menkhaus 2010a). First, between 1988 and 1995, Somalia entered a period of state collapse. Mohamed Siad Barre was president and dictator of the country from 1979 to 1991. His rule contributed to a period of stable government based on creating an elaborate patronage system that allowed him to manipulate Cold War interests to attract foreign aid that was used to buy the support of particular factions within Somalia's deep-rooted clan system. As sources of foreign aid began to wane, distrust with Barre's corrupt regime began to emerge, and he was toppled in 1991, leading to a full-scale civil war in which clans competed for control and authority. In particular, the warlord General Aidid competed with the supporters of Barre. The international community became involved, and the United States advocated UN intervention in order to support the deposed government of Barre, but eventual withdrew in 1995. As warlords competed for power and the basic functions of the state collapsed, large-scale internal and cross-border displacement took place.

In the second phase, between 1996 and 2005, the violence decreased. By 1996, Barre's supporters had been largely defeated, Aidid's forces had taken control of Mogadishu, and more stable patterns of clan-based territorial authority were emerging. In certain parts of the country, basic functions of government returned. In particular, Somaliland, which declared independence in 1991, created a stable and functioning government, and Puntland began to develop a viable regional administration. While south-central Somalia remained prone to violence and instability, the basic distribution of power between warlords was more or less stable and the international humanitarian community was able to operate in the country. By 2004, there was optimism that a UN-backed peace deal would bring an end to violence, and a transitional federal government (TFG) was negotiated based on an internationally backed coalition among prominent Somali warlords. During this period, there were only occasional periods of new displacement, and the main displacement challenge was how to manage the protracted refugee situation of Somalis living in camps and settlements throughout the region since the early 1990s.

In the third phase, between 2006 and 2011, serious conflict returned, marked by the rise of al-Shabaab. While the international community backed the TFG's installment in Mogadishu, a radical Islamic movement, the Islamic Courts Union (ICU), emerged to compete for authority in south-central Somalia. In June 2006, the ICU declared that it had defeated a U.S.-backed warlord coalition. In December 2006, the UN Security Council authorized the African Union to send soldiers in support of the government. In response, the African Union Mission in Somalia (AMISOM) was deployed to support the TFG, and Ethiopian soldiers invaded (Shay 2008). The conflict and Ethiopian invasion led to massive displacement. While the invasion achieved the defeat of the ICU, it triggered the growth and expansion of the ICU's military wing, al-Shabaab, which subsequently waged a jihadist war against the TFG, acquiring growing territorial authority and imposing sharia law across south-central Somalia and most of Mogadishu. Throughout the period, generalized violence and brutal persecution led to significant internal and cross-border displacement.

By 2011, al-Shabaab controlled most of south-central Somalia, and the TFG—protected by AMISOM—was limited to a small block of streets in Mogadishu, an airport, and a port. Until that point, generalized violence and persecution—classic drivers of displacement—were the most significant and obvious, yet not the only, sources of displacement. Without recourse to effective structures of government, and with humanitarian agencies and the UN having withdrawn from south-central Somalia in 2009, growing numbers of people were increasingly displaced by environmental factors and the absence of available livelihood opportunities.

In 2011, when rains failed for the second year running, there was a humanitarian crisis in the Horn of Africa, prompted by drought and hunger at famine levels in southern Somalia. Complete crop failure in southern Somalia and rising levels of malnutrition meant that in April the UN proclaimed a humanitarian emergency amid large-scale internal and cross-border displacement. By July, the UN formally declared famine in two regions of southern Somalia. By September, nearly half of Somalia's 7.5 million people were affected by drought, and the UN declared famine in six regions of southern Somalia. The UN estimated that drought and famine led to massive internal displacement and around 273,000 to cross international borders, particularly into Kenya and Ethiopia, between January and September 2011 alone. Facing acute malnutrition, having lost the cattle that sustain their pastoralist livelihoods, and with no recourse to a functioning state, many Somalis faced little choice but to flee.

The level of exodus reduced as the UN Food Security Nutrition Analysis Unit downgraded its "famine" designation for three Somali regions—Bakool, Bay, and Lower Shabelle—to an "emergency" phase following both a break in the region's deadly drought and an improvement in the UN's ability to deliver food assistance in the country. By November, the famine and drought were considered over, and UNHCR ended registrations at the Dadaab camps in Kenya for those fleeing famine and drought. By this point, the total number to have fled across borders into neighboring countries during the famine and drought was 289,349 (UN High Commissioner for Refugees 2011b).

Unpacking the Causes of Displacement

Across the patterns of displacement described above, the population of Somalis recognized as refugees has fluctuated. In 1994, the global Somali refugee population was just over 630,000, with more than 200,000 registered in Kenya. By 2004, with stabilization and repatriations, this had been reduced to nearly 390,000 globally and just over 150,000 in Kenya. Yet with increased insecurity and the emergence of drought and famine, the numbers escalated to an all-time peak of more than 1 million globally and more than 500,000 in Kenya by 2012.

Displacement has been driven by the interaction of persecution, conflict, and environmental change (Lindley 2011). The predominant drivers of displacement have shifted over time and across regions of Somalia. It would be intuitively tempting to suggest that the primary causes can be divided along the lines of the periods of displacement outlined above, with conflict and persecution being the dominant causes of displacement across most of the two decades of displacement, and famine and drought changing its nature to a more characteristic example of survival migration in 2011.

This conclusion, however, would be misrepresentative. Although the balance of the drivers of displacement has certainly evolved, and survival migration has

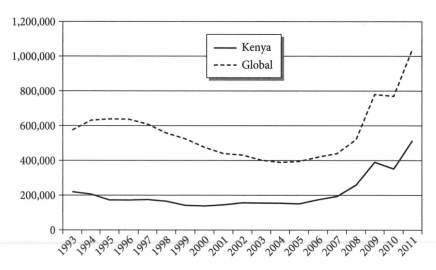

FIGURE 4. Numbers of registered Somali refugees in Kenya and globally, 1993–2011.

become extremely evident since 2011, the reality is that displacement has been driven by the complex interaction of conflict, persecution, and environment since the early 1990s, and at every phase multicausality has been present, albeit with significant geographical variation. By 2009, for example, UNHCR Somalia was recording monthly internally displaced persons (IDP) data through its Population Movement Tracking System, disaggregating the primary causes of displacement across different Somali territories.[4] Although the data it recorded on internal displacement did not provide a complete time series, a range of predominant factors could be differentiated: clan conflict, forced return, drought, livelihood insecurity, and IDP return. The data show tremendous variation even within the space of few days; factors such as fluctuation in rainfall and weather patterns, for instance, influenced the balance.

Throughout all three periods, what has driven displacement has not been any single cause but the way in which diverse causes have been mediated by the underlying weak governance in Somalia. I would therefore argue that since the early 1990s the movement of Somalis across borders cannot be reduced to flight from persecution or even from conflict. It amounts to a process of survival migration, a serious human rights–driven cross-border displacement that in many cases transcends the categories of the 1951 Refugee Convention (Tayler and Albin-Lackey 2009). In 2009, Peter Kusimba, director of Kenya's Department of Refugee Affairs, succinctly stated that most Somalis did not and had never fitted the 1951 Refugee Convention definition of a refugee based on individualized persecution: "Somalis are running into Kenya because of the generalized situation of insecurity—not individual but generalized."[5]

If there was any doubt, however, that these wider patterns of displacement have had complex causality even since 1991, then the famine of 2011 most starkly illustrates the limitations of the 1951 convention to address contemporary cross-border displacement and the relevance of survival migration as a concept. In April 2011, drought and famine struck Somalia as rains and crops failed for a second year in a row. Images appeared on television screens around the world of dead cattle, malnourished babies, and humanitarian aid agency vehicles.

Many of the scenes were reminiscent of the Ethiopian famine of 1984. The UN humanitarian coordinator for Somalia, Aeneas Chuma, claimed: "The humanitarian crisis we are facing is huge. It threatens lives, particularly those of the most vulnerable. It also threatens livelihoods and these must be protected as well" (IRIN 2011b). An MSF nurse, Alice Gude, claimed, "This is the worst drought that Somalia has seen for many years. People are dying in Somalia. Their crops have failed for many seasons and their livestock are all dying. . . . Twenty per cent would be in an intensive care unit if they were in Europe" (Gude 2011).

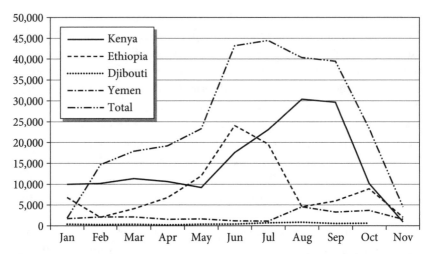

FIGURE 5. Survival migration per month across borders during the drought and famine in Somalia, January–November 2011. These statistics are based on UNHCR registrations, which came to an end on October 1, 2011, for the Dadaab refugee camps.

The events of 2011 starkly illustrate the role that factors beyond the scope of the existing refugee regime have played in contemporary Somali displacement. Anita Sacki, the MSF coordinator of nutritional assessment in the Dadaab camps, claimed: "The majority of new arrivals fled because they had nothing to eat, not just because their country has been at war for decades" (Médecins Sans Frontières 2011).

Although Somalis in Kenya have not generally been forcibly returned to their country of origin, their predicament—not only in 2011 but throughout the period since 1991—has placed them at the margins of the international refugee regime. The global regime's concept of a refugee—based on understanding refugees primarily as people fleeing individualized persecution—breaks down when confronted by the realities of Somali displacement.

Somali cross-border displacement has been driven by the complex interaction of conflict, persecution, and the environment. While the relative significance of these factors has varied temporally and spatially, the consistent feature—and the ultimate cause for cross-border displacement—has been weak governance. Conflict, persecution, or environmental change per se did not make displacement inevitable or necessary. Rather, these factors have been mediated through weak governance, which has meant that the state has been unwilling or unable to provide or ensure fundamental human rights, whether basic security, liberty, or subsistence.

Somali displacement has thus fallen beyond the boundaries of who is gener-ally recognized as a refugee by the international community. Throughout the pe-riod, it has defied the 1951 convention definition of a refugee, and has been based mainly on factors other than individualized persecution. While many of those fleeing generalized conflict and security have fit the regional OAU convention definition of a refugee, a significant proportion—particularly those primarily fleeing famine and drought—have fallen outside even this definition. Somali dis-placement is illustrative of forms of displacement that lie at the boundary of the refugee regime, and it draws attention to the arbitrariness of the 1951 convention in relation to contemporary patterns of displacement. The chapter now examines the response of the Kenyan government and the international community.

Kenya's Response

In many ways, Kenya's response to survival migration has been one of the most generous and open examined by this book. Rather than rounding up, detaining, and deporting those who have fallen outside the 1951 convention definition of a refugee, Kenya has generally recognized all Somalis as though they were refu-gees. On the other hand, the picture has been far from perfect. Although Somalis have been admitted to the territory, there has been a trade-off in terms of the limited sets of rights they have received in Kenya. In the language of this book, the Kenyan refugee regime has stretched to be inclusive—but at a cost, primarily in terms of restrictions placed on refugees' freedom of movement and access to livelihoods.

The Evolution of Asylum Policy

Before the Somali influx, Kenya conducted individual refugee status determi-nation interviews, applying the definition of the 1951 convention (Odhiamno-Abuya 2004), incorporated in its 1984 Immigration Act.[6] While imperfect and often influenced by an immigration control agenda (Verdirame and Harrell-Bond 2005), its policy had been government-led and had offered de facto in-tegration to all its refugees. However, up until 1991, the refugee population had not exceeded 10,000, and most had been skilled labor from Uganda and Rwanda (Milner 2009, 86).

With the fall of the Barre regime in 1989, there was a shift in Kenya's response to refugees. It initially engaged in forcible returns—or "push-backs"—at the bor-der. The Daniel Arap Moi regime began drafting national refugee legislation in 1990; however, because of the new circumstances on its border, this was put on hold until the middle of the first decade of the 2000s. By 1991, Kenya, which previously hosted a maximum of 14,500 refugees, was playing host to 130,000. Just over a year later, in 1992, this figure had skyrocketed to almost 400,000, including 285,000 Somalis and a significant number of Ethiopians fleeing the collapse of the Mengistu regime (Odhiamno-Abuya 2004, 188; Milner 2009, 86).

Arap Moi allowed large numbers of refugees from Somalia to cross the border in 1991 and 1992 and received great acclaim for it from the international community (Milner 2009, 84). He appealed to the international community for support, and seven new refugee camps were established in the extreme northeast of the country. A UNHCR emergency appeal brought in nearly $15 million, enabling the refugees to be consolidated within the camps, in which UNHCR provided assistance. Given the numbers involved and the inefficiency of providing individual refugee status determination, all Somalis except those suspected of being involved in the conflict were recognized on a prima facie basis (Albert 2010). By June 1993, the emergency was declared to be over.

However, the refugee camps were rife with insecurity, border incursions, and sexual and gender-based violence (Milner 2009, 87). In 1993, faced with concerns over security and dwindling international support after the initial emergency phase, the Kenyan government shifted its policy to one that James Milner (2009) has described as "abdication and containment," which has endured until the present day.

At the level of containment, Kenya adopted an encampment policy. Nearly all Somalis were relocated from the other camps in the country to the Dadaab camps (Ifo, Hagadera, Daghaley) in North Eastern Province (NEP). All refugees were henceforth obliged to reside in camps in order to qualify for assistance. Only those with travel documents, or "movement passes"—issued under very circumscribed conditions (e.g., urgent health problems or security problems that could not be dealt with in the camps)—would be permitted to leave the camps without risking arrest and deportation as illegal aliens (Lindley 2010, 96; Human Rights Watch 2010a, 48–49).

Kenya has taken the view that while it has been prepared to allow refugees on its territory, they should be the primary responsibility of the international community rather than the government of Kenya. In the words of the director of the Department of Refugee Affairs, Peter Kusimba, "the refugee business is not the business of the Kenyan government; it is the responsibility of the international community."[7] Verdirame (1999, 70) argues that this has effectively implied a delegation of sovereignty to the international community in the Dadaab camps, where UNHCR takes responsibility for providing basic services, overseeing a set of implementing partners with particular mandates.[8]

After the defeat of the Moi government in elections in late 2002, the incoming National Rainbow Coalition (NARC), led by Mwai Kibaki, made refugee legislation a priority. The Refugee Bill had been stalled since the 1990s by the Somali crisis. Stabilization in Somalia and the desire to reengage the donor community created an incentive to place it back on the agenda. Kenya's 2006 Refugee Act formalized many of the policies that had existed since the 1990s, institutionalizing much of the encampment policy. However, it was also the first and only refugee legislation in Africa to provide for prima facie recognition under the OAU Refugee Convention, creating an extremely inclusive basis on which to recognize all Somalis as though they were refugees (Albert 2010). The act also included provisions for the establishment of a Department of Refugee Affairs (DRA), which assumed administrative responsibilities for refugees in Kenya (Albert 2010, 12). The DRA has plans to eventually assume responsibility for aspects of refugee policy from UNHCR (Campbell and Oucho 2011).

Although the creation of the DRA has established a pro-refugee voice in the government, the DRA has been hampered as a result of being housed in the Ministry of State for Immigration and Registration of Persons, which is strongly influenced by concerns over internal security. Consequently, as the security situation within Somalia has deteriorated since 2006, Kenya's policy toward Somalis has become increasingly subject to a security and immigration-control agenda.

In January 2007, the Kenyan government officially closed the border with Somalia (Human Rights Watch 2009d). It also closed a UNHCR-run registration center at Liboi, near the border. This move—led by the Ministry of State for Provincial Administration and Internal Security and implemented by the police—highlights a split within the Kenyan government that has increasingly affected Kenyan asylum policy. On the one hand, the official legislation and the role of the DRA have been extremely inclusive compared with other cases outlined in this book, and once in the camps, the Somalis have been tolerated. In practice, though, other branches of government have made access to protection increasingly challenging for Somalis.

By the end of 2010, with 300,000 Somalis in the overcrowded Dadaab camps, an extension was agreed for 80,000 additional refugees at the Ifo camp, land was released by local authorities, and infrastructure work began. However, the government—notably the minister of state for provincial administration and internal security, George Saitoti—called a halt to the extension plan. Meanwhile, plans for a new, fourth Dadaab camp—Jarajilla—for 120,000 refugees were similarly scuttled by local and national political disagreement.

In October 2011, when there were more than 460,000 registered refugees, Kenya stopped registering refugees in the Dadaab, excluding new arrivals, from the services provided to registered refugees.[9] With the suspension of registration, it is difficult to know how the Kenyan military incursion into Somalia has affected the flows into the country. The presence of Kenyan troops may have hindered the ability of refugees to cross the border (Anderson 2012).

Although Kenya had tolerated the registration of Somalis fleeing famine and drought throughout much of 2011, the sheer numbers have led to a dramatic shift in policy: the government invaded Somalia in an attempt to restore stability along the border and create a safe haven within which to contain Somali IDPs. On October 16, 2011, Kenya sent two battalions into Somalia as part of Operation Linda Nhichi. The stated purpose of the military incursion was to eradicate al-Shabaab, which was blamed for a series of recent kidnappings and killings in Kenya, threatening its vital tourist industry.[10] Despite the official purpose, Kenyan deployment into Somalia is more a result of deep-seated security concerns associated with Somali refugees in Kenya and Kenyans of Somali ethnicity than an immediate need to address the threat posed by al-Shabaab to its tourism industry.[11]

The relationship between the military intervention and the large influx of 2011 was underscored in a speech by President Mwai Kibaki in February 2012 in which he described the presence of Somali refugees in Kenya as a "growing and serious security threat" to both Kenya and the region, and lamented their "adverse impact" on Kenya's socioeconomic life.[12] Although it was reported before his speech that there were no plans in place to close the camps,[13] Kibaki argued that the refugees should be sent to areas secured from the control of al-Shabaab. The president's proposal to close down the Dadaab camps, however serious, strongly resonates with Kenyans who are tired of "paying the Somali tax" for the past twenty years.[14]

Humanitarian Containment

The human consequences of the trade-off in Kenyan asylum policy are evident. Relative generosity in numbers is not matched by generosity in rights, and the result is a long-standing "humanitarian containment"—humanitarian in the sense of at least ensuring access to asylum for all Somalis, and containment in the sense of limiting rights and effectively imprisoning the majority in closed camps (and Verdirame and Harrell-Bond 2005). A senior UN aid worker at Dadaab described the camp as the "world's largest detention center" (Blatter 2011).

The dire conditions and insecurity in the Dadaab camps are well documented (Crisp 2000; Horst 2006; Verdirame and Harrell-Bond 2005; Helton 2002). Many Somalis have been in Dadaab since the early 1990s, without access to freedom of movement or the right to work. The camps are intentionally located in a remote and arid area just 80 kilometers from the Somali border. In the words of one senior NGO worker who has spent years working in the camps, "Dadaab is a dreadful place."[15]Cindy Horst (2006, 77) writes, "The refugees in Dadaab face insecurities of a physical, economic and existential nature that at times are similar to those they faced before and during the war in Somalia."

Somalis in the camps live with significant economic challenges, being dependent on humanitarian assistance. Such assistance often includes less than full food rations (Horst 2006, 82), which requires many to find informal sources of money either through low-paid work for the humanitarian agencies or, more commonly, through remittances sent from Nairobi or abroad.[16] While repeated efforts have been made to improve the security situation (Helton 2002, 156–57), levels of sexual and gender-based violence in the camps have remained high, and areas of the camps have been legal black holes typified by gun smuggling and banditry (Verdirame 1999; Crisp 2000). Security concerns in the camp leading up to the Kenyan military incursion into Somalia were highlighted by the abduction of two Spanish aid workers. Since October 2011, there have been several other incidents, including the discovery of improvised explosive devices (IEDs) and detonators, as well as the killing of two refugee leaders (Garvelink and Tahir 2012).[17]

Having been present for two decades, the Dadaab camps are more like a city than a series of camps (Agier 2010, 145; Helton 2002, 155). Yet they are not managed like cities, and instead the fiction of temporariness defines the boundaries of the possible in terms of improving conditions in Dadaab (Perouse de Montclos and Kagwanja 2000, 205). They are overcrowded and lack the necessary infrastructure for even the most basic health, water, sanitation, and education services that one would expect for a city of close to half a million people (Human Rights Watch 2010). Overcrowding resulting from the 2011 famine and drought has also contributed to outbreaks of diarrhea and cholera in the camps, and further exacerbated the insecurity (UN High Commissioner for Refugees 2011b).

In addition to the well-documented hardships in the camps, Somalis have faced increasing difficulties even accessing the camps. In 2010, Human Rights Watch published a report, "Welcome to Kenya," in which it highlighted the changing response of Kenyan police to Somalis after the border closure on January 3, 2007, and the Kenyan government's growing concern with border security. It notes that police have engaged in the "systematic interception, detention, abuse, deportation, and extortion of asylum seekers crossing the border from Somalia" (Human Rights Watch 2010, 10). It describes how police checkpoints have been set up at Liboi, near the HarHar border crossing, and around the Dadaab camps. Although the Refugee Act clearly states that asylum seekers have the right to enter freely and travel within thirty days to claim asylum at the nearest office of Kenya's refugee commissioner, "Kenya's notoriously corrupt and abusive police force" has used the Immigration Act's prohibition on illegal entry without a permit as a basis on which to make arrests, solicit bribes, and in some cases deport" (Human Rights Watch 2010, 23). As well as noting cases of *refoulement*, the report documents how Somalis have been openly accused of being "al-Qaeda," "al-Shabaab," and "terrorists," and how police have engaged in extortion, rape, sexual assault, unlawful arrest, and detention. It also documents abusive and inhumane conditions of detention, including of pregnant women. There have been reports of continued police abuse of Somali residents of the North Eastern Province since December 2011 (Human Rights Watch 2012).

Beyond the camps, the only other viable option for Somalis has been to live as urban refugees in Nairobi, which presents numerous challenges. Getting to Nairobi from Dadaab is difficult enough, given the limited conditions under which travel documents are available and the number of police checkpoints set up en route.[18] Furthermore, leaving informally usually means forfeiting assistance. In the words of the former head of the Refugee Consortium of Kenya, Judy Wakahiu, "The moment you leave the camp, you are effectively saying 'I can manage by myself.'"[19] Although in theory once refugees reach Nairobi they can register with UNHCR and be entitled to remain, in practice those who register do not get even the same minimal levels of assistance offered in the camps.

The main urban destination for Somalis is the Eastleigh district in Nairobi (Campbell 2005; Lindley 2010), which Anna Lindley (2010, 99) describes as a "place of both deprivation and entrepreneurial wealth." It is an overcrowded area with filthy muddy streets, thriving trade, and high levels of crime. It is "one of the most economically dynamic areas of Kenya,"[20] where many Somalis run small businesses and remit money to families in Dadaab or Somalia.[21]

There is also a challenging side to being in the city. According to a UNHCR consultant working in the community, "by being in the city, refugees are claiming to be self-sufficient."[22] In the overcrowded housing, six to seven people may share a room and sometimes are able to afford only one meal a day, and they often face economic exploitation by richer Kenyan Somalis.[23]

In the urban areas, there is very weak protection. According to the Danish Refugee Council, "The urban population is hardly supported or assisted. In some ways it is a very vulnerable population."[24] UNHCR works in Eastleigh through a range of implementing partners. Yet the health facilities provided by an MSF clinic and an IOM wellness center, the training offered by a UNHCR-funded Centre for Domestic Training and Development, the legal support provided by the NGO Kituo Cha Shariya, the educational role played by the GTZ, and the family tracing provided by the Kenyan Red Cross, for example, offer only very limited support to the most desperate.[25] In practice, while Kenya's urban Somalis at least have greater freedom of movement than those in the camp, they receive little assistance. Furthermore, after Kenya's military incursion into Somalia and security problems at Dadaab, Somalis in Nairobi have been the target of increasing xenophobia (Teff 2012).

The presence of such large numbers of refugees in Kenya over two decades has come at the cost of the depletion of the rights that refugees who are lawfully staying or resident are entitled to under the 1951 convention. James Hathaway (2005) argues that refugees physically present in the territory of the host state have a right to freedom from deprivation and to basic necessities. It is clear that Kenya has failed to grant many of the basic rights, such as the right to freedom of movement and residence and the right to self-employment and professional work. The longer refugees stay lawfully or are legally resident, the stronger the obligations of the state toward them (Hathaway 2005, 657). In Kenya, however, no such adjustment has occurred.

The International Community's Response

The role of the international community has been schizophrenic or—in the words of Verdirame and Harrell-Bond (2005)—"Janus-faced." On the one hand, UNHCR and its main donors have urged inclusivity, consistently trying to ensure that all Somalis are given access to territory and recognized as refugees. It has pushed the national refugee regime to stretch at the level of quantity of asylum. On the other hand, it has largely accepted containment as the price of asylum. Rather than openly criticize or actively seek to change the government's encampment policy, it has generally endorsed humanitarian containment. The outcome has been an implicit bargain in which quality of asylum has become the accepted price of regime stretching.

Since the onset of the initial influx, UNHCR has worked to ensure that Kenya has kept its borders open and provided access to territory. In 1991, this began with an early agreement to support the Moi government through offering international burden-sharing. Through its initial emergency appeal in 1992, UNHCR raised $14.7 million, enabling the Somalis to be housed initially in ten camps and later consolidated into Dadaab and Kakuma. Given Kenya's limited capacity to address the mass influx and the absence of national legislation or a national refugee bureaucracy, UNHCR agreed to take responsibility for refugee registration and assistance.

Taking on this role gave UNHCR the autonomy to determine the basis of refugee status determination. Though initially established partly to avoid the costly and unwieldy process of individualized refugee status determination, assuming control of refugee registration enabled UNHCR to maintain this form of status recognition, and hence to ensure inclusive recognition for all Somalis coming from south-central Somalia (Albert 2010).

Furthermore, UNHCR played an important role in pushing Kenya to institutionalize prima facie recognition under the more inclusive OAU convention in its 2006 Refugee Act. UNHCR's then representative to Kenya, George Okoth-Obbo, is widely credited with guiding the process and directly contributing to the drafting of the act. By engaging with the Kibaki government at a time of relative stability in Somalia, when repatriation was under way and when the Kenyan government was eager to re-engage the international community, UNHCR was able to help institutionalize a legal commitment to inclusivity at a particular moment.

It is worth underscoring that the Kenyan legislation was unprecedented in incorporating prima facie recognition under the OAU Refugee Convention. In other words, it committed the government to recognize—on the face of it—people fleeing situations involving, for example "events seriously disturbing public order." This meant that in terms of legislation, at least, the Kenyan government had perhaps the strongest legal commitment to inclusively protecting survival migrants of any state in the world.

Securing this legislative commitment subsequently enabled UNHCR to persuade Kenya to preserve access to asylum at crucial moments. For example, after the January 2007 border closure, Kenya tried to restrict access to its territory. As the Human Rights Watch report outlined above points out, the security focus of the government—together with the role of police corruption—has placed restrictions on access to asylum. Yet by highlighting Kenya's legislative commitments and the fact that the Immigration Act's prohibition on illegal aliens is overridden by the Refugee Act, allowing asylum seekers thirty days in which to register with DRA, UNHCR has been able to obtain concessions for Somali refugees. For example, at the height of the famine and drought in 2011, UNHCR was able to negotiate improved access and the reopening of a transit center at the border post of Liboi, which had previously been closed by the government.

However, securing a commitment to inclusivity has come at a price. UNHCR and the international community have accepted containment as the norm. There has been limited direct criticism of the Kenyan government's encampment policy. UNHCR and its core donors have broadly accepted and followed the government's policy, providing the financial and logistical support to maintain the Dadaab camps in ways that sustain the most minimum conditions of life—but little more.

The implicit Faustian bargain has been that Kenya has provided Somalis with access to territory but that protection and assistance have been enclosed in the Dadaab camps and made dependent on the voluntary support of donor states. With UNHCR placed between the rock of the Kenyan government and the hard place of limited international donor interest, protracted exile and confinement to Dadaab has become the "norm by default" (Helton 2002, 155). Horst (2006, 107) describes UNHCR as being in "a compromised position," playing the contradictory role of having to confront host states while being dependent on them.

UNHCR has also faced the challenge of having to consistently work with an underfunded budget for its Kenya operations. Food rations have been reduced in Dadaab simply due to resource constraints. Where there has been donor interest in the protection of Somali refugees, it has mainly been motivated by a desire to further entrench containment in the region in order to avert the onward movement of Somali refugees to Europe. In particular, Denmark, the Netherlands, and the United Kingdom—three of the biggest Northern state recipients of Somali asylum seekers—have funded a range of initiatives to support "protection in the region of origin," either bilaterally or through UNHCR. For example, between 2003 and 2005, UNHCR developed a so-called Comprehensive Plan of Action for Somali Refugees, which undertook a "protection gaps analysis" with funding from the Netherlands, Denmark, the United Kingdom, and the European Community. Although abandoned because of the deterioration of the security situation in Somalia, the plan was widely acknowledged as motivated by a desire to limit onward migration to Europe (Betts 2008).

Meanwhile, Kenya and Denmark have developed a multiyear capacity-building project, providing 2.7 million euros and seconding a migration expert to Nairobi as part of a "protection in the region of origin" project negotiated in 2004 and for which implementation was delayed until 2009 due to a disagreement over the substance of the agreement.[26] The project focuses on how livelihood opportunities might be strengthened to enable Somali refugees to be more self-sufficient. Yet even the Kenyan government has been cognizant of the underlying, unstated motivation: "This program of the naughty countries—Denmark, the Netherlands—they are all involved. They are saying 'keep refugees in the region.' They want refugees to be in the region so that when the situation improves, they can go back to their countries."[27]

In summary, then, the outcome has been an implicit bargain in which Kenya has admitted Somalis on an inclusive basis. However, the flip side of the deal has been a form of humanitarian containment in which only the most minimum conditions for life have been maintained. The insecure, overcrowded, and underfunded Dadaab camps have become a de facto prison in which Somalis have faced significant human rights deprivations. The chapter now turns to an explanation of why the humanitarian containment compromise has been adopted as the solution to survival migration in Kenya.

Explaining the Kenyan Government's Response

In his attempt to explain why the Kenyan government has imposed restrictions on asylum, Milner (2009) finds the explanation in the combination of concerns with security and the perceived limitations of international burden-sharing. However, the relevant question for the purposes of this book is not just to explain the restrictions but rather to ask why there has been relative openness in the quantity of asylum alongside restrictions in the quality of asylum. In other words, why has the national refugee regime stretched to include all Somalis, albeit with a trade-off in the depth of protection offered? The answer that this section provides is that there have been significant rewards for government elites from the international level for inclusivity but strong domestic incentives to ensure that Somalis are geographically confined.

At the international level, both Daniel Arap Moi and Mwai Kibaki—at the crucial stages of offering asylum to Somalis in the 1990s and passing refugee legislation in the early 2000s—recognized the political opportunities available from openness. During the Cold War, Moi had been predominantly an authoritarian leader, but his close relationship with the West averted international criticism. With the end of the Cold War, foreign aid was withheld and demands for political reform were made by the United States and other allies. The 1992 elections, in which Moi faced multiparty competition for the first time, were marred by interethnic violence, including government repression of the opposition in the regions of its main support base, the Western and Rift Valley provinces.

In this context, the Somali influx of the early 1990s offered Moi a way to relegitimate himself and the Kenya African National Union (KANU)-led regime in the eyes of the international community. Committing to refugee protection enabled the regime to demonstrate its human rights credentials. In turn, it created an opportunity not only to bring in humanitarian assistance but also to provide the legitimacy to attract development assistance and inward investment through improved relations with the West and the United Nations system.

After winning elections in 2002, Mwai Kibaki similarly recognized the international advantages of persevering with an open and inclusive policy and institutionalizing it with legislation. In order to defeat Uhuru Kenyatta and the KANU opposition, Kibaki had contested the election by working within the broad coalition of the National Rainbow Coalition (NARC). Part of Kibaki's ability to maintain this broad-based support relied on the external legitimacy conferred by the international community as well as the external resources to sustain the coalition, of which the refugee question was an important part

Pursuing these benefits alongside a policy of abdication and containment has meant that they could be achieved with relatively limited costs. Economically, the costs were borne primarily by the international community. Politically, the costs were limited because the Somali refugees were confined to the North Eastern Province, an area of the country peripheral to national politics; at the same time, developmental gains, primarily paid for by the international community, were showered on an otherwise impoverished region through the rehabilitation of roads and airstrips, the installation of water boreholes, the establishment of water and electricity, and the provision of medical care and environmental rehabilitation projects (Milner 2009, 95). Indeed, as Horst (2006, 78) observes, "the refugee camps have stimulated trade, created new jobs, and attracted humanitarian aid."

At the domestic level, however, there have been strong incentives to ensure that the way in which protection is carried out has been geographically confined and based on a policy of containment and abdication. There has been a long-standing politicization of Somalis in Kenya. During the colonial era, there was significant free movement by Somali pastoralists across what is today the border of Somalia and Kenya. The NEP—formerly known as the Northern Frontier District of Kenya (Castagno 1964) and where the Dadaab camps are located—has historically been populated by a majority of ethnic Somali pastoralists. As part of British East Africa, it was largely a buffer zone with Italian Somalia. With the unification and independence of Somalia in 1960, there was a campaign for the incorporation of the NEP within Somalia; however, the British instead made it part of Kenya. In opposition, a low-level secession war took place known as the Shifta (bandit) War between 1963 and 1967 with the aim of incorporating the Northern Frontier District into a greater Somalia.

Consequently, there has been a consistent narrative of anti-Somali xenophobia in national Kenyan politics. In contrast to the NEP, where Somali refugees have generally been tolerated by Somali Kenyans, at the level of national politics the fear of ongoing *shifta* activity in pursuit of a "pan Somali dream" has exacerbated intolerance (Horst 2006, 117). This has made it politically costly for the government to go beyond confining Somalis to the few areas of the country where they are tolerated. Since the 1990s, this anti-Somali strand of national Kenyan politics has been exacerbated by the putative link between Somalis and terrorism (Juma and Kagwanja 2008).

On August 7, 1998, the bombings of U.S. embassy in Nairobi (and Dar es Salaam) by al-Qaeda operatives was linked to Somalia (Haynes 2005). Fear of Somali-connected terrorist possibilities led the Kenyan government to attempt to pass counterterrorist legislation in 2003 and 2006, but both drafts failed to receive support because of their wide interpretation of terrorism and the extensive powers given to the police. Nevertheless, some of these powers have been used by the Anti-Terrorist Police Unit, leading to "increasingly tense relations between the central government and the Muslim community" (Bachmann and Hönke

2009, 108). By 2009, the Kenyan government was in partnership with the TFG to engage in counterterrorist activities against al-Shabaab.[28] In 2009, there were media reports that Somalis in refugee camps were being recruited by the Kenyan government to fight Islamists in Somalia (Tayler and Albin-Lackey 2009). On July 11, 2010, two bombings in Kampala were carried out by al-Shabaab, killing 74. The bombings constituted the first strike by al-Shabaab outside Somalia, raising fears of attack within Kenya.[29]

Fears of terrorism and the spillover of conflict have influenced the Kenyan government's response to Somali refugees. Refugees have increasingly been accused of being terrorists by police (Human Rights Watch 2010b). Kenya's joint military-police disarmament operation among Somali communities in NEP, launched in late 2008, has even been accused of torture (Human Rights Watch 2010b, 16). The shift has coincided with a rise in the forcible deportation of Somalis back to their homeland by Kenyan authorities, in violation of international law (Human Rights Watch 2010b). By the end of 2011, Kenya had closed the border with Somalia and even stationed soldiers on the Somali side of the border in order to reduce armed incursions. Police and military presence has since increased in and around the Dadaab camps (Anderson 2012).

A key to understanding how the concern with national security has affected asylum policy is the division of responsibility in government. On the one hand, UNHCR has been able to operate with a supportive Department of Refugee Affairs, which has worked to preserve asylum space for Somalis. On the other hand, this support has been counterbalanced by the branches of government dealing with immigration and internal security, which have had different priorities.

As we have seen, George Saitoti has been central to this split. As minister of state for provincial administration and internal security since 2008, he has pushed for significant restrictions on the movement of Somalis and has frequently overridden the DRA. Saitoti is a populist and a career politician who has consistently played on citizens' concerns about security in order to advance his popularity. The split between Refugee Affairs and Internal Security has been widely noted. Judy Wakahiu, head of the Refugee Consortium of Kenya, noted, "The Refugee Secretariat and the Immigration Ministry do not have any clout within the government. The Minister of State for Internal Security is the obstacle."[30]

Even Peter Kusimba, head of the DRA, acknowledged: "The problem is that a number of government agencies look at you differently. . . . We want to treat refugees as they are supposed to be treated. . . . The Ministry of Internal Security views them as security risks."[31] It is Saitoti who has upheld the border closure, closed the Liboi transit center, and supported the provincial commissioners' clamp-down on Somalis outside the Dadaab camps. He has also been accused of obstructing full implementation of the 2006 Refugee Act.[32] In the words of

Peter Klansoe of the Danish Refugee Council: "Peter Kusimba is effective, but his task is not high on the agenda. . . . It is the minister of the interior who closed the border. He is also the one who restricts decisions on expanding Dadaab. It is not the prime minister; it is not the president. It is this guy. I can remember the first time I came to Kenya, which was twenty-three years ago; he was the vice president. So he is the most powerful minister, and he is taking the decisions. He is very difficult to come in contact with. The concern is whether he has the real information and what his interest is in."[33] It is this division in government that partly explains a stark disjuncture between an inclusive policy—mandated by the Refugee Act and supported by the DRA—and an increasingly restrictive and repressive implementation. On the one hand, UNHCR has been able to use the Refugee Act as an important advocacy tool, and to work through the DRA in order to preserve a legally recognized right for all Somalis to be recognized as refugees. On the other hand, it has been forced to operate within the constraints of an increasingly security-focused government policy that has made clear that the Dadaab camps are the only area in which Somali refugees will be tolerated.

The Kenyan invasion of Somalia in October 2011 was the latest illustration of the growing dominance of certain branches of the government over the DRA. The minister of state for defense, Yusuf Haji, had strongly promoted the intervention as a means of testing the Kenyan army's military capability. Business interests have also promoted the invasion, with a return to stability in the NEP being seen as a means to facilitate the construction of oil pipelines from Uganda and South Sudan in the region (Throup 2012). President Mwai Kibaki has seen the invasion primarily as a way to restore stability to the border region and to enable some of the refugees to be protected within the territory of Somalia (Anderson 2012). The intervention has become the latest means of promoting humanitarian containment—but this time through creating an extra-territorial protection space.

Explaining the International Community's Response

On many levels, humanitarian containment has also suited the international community. A genuine protection motive has been coupled with the desire to ensure that a perceived migration and terrorism threat from the region does not spill over from South to North. The legacy of international failure in Somalia in the early 1990s and the limitations of protection space in south-central Somalia (Abild 2009) have continued to impel international donors to push for inclusive recognition of Somalis in Kenya. However, concern over onward movement of a globally stigmatized refugee population has predisposed the international community to try to ensure that displaced Somalis remain protected within the region of origin.

Since the early 1990s, there has been a need to ensure a humanitarian space in which Somalis can receive access to international protection. This has been assumed to be a basic obligation of the international community because the United States and the UN system were implicated in the failures of humanitarian intervention in the early 1990s. The 1992–93 UNOSOM missions and the withdrawal of U.S. soldiers following Black Hawk Down made humanitarianism the international community's fig leaf for engaging with the problems of Somalia. After withdrawal, the United States, not surprisingly, contributed more than 50 percent of emergency appeal contributions to UNHCR in Kenya during the initial mass influx. While levels of humanitarian assistance channeled through UNHCR fell in the early 2000s, UNHCR's main donors have continued to prioritize earmarking contributions to UNHCR's Dadaab operations. Meanwhile, the humanitarian industry of NGOs working in the camps has continued to provide a strong lobby to maintain these operations.

On the other hand, there has been countervailing pressure to engage in containment not only from the host government but also from UNHCR's core donor states. Since the 1990s, Somali mixed migration to Europe has increased, and Somalis have become the subject of xenophobia in some northern European states. Most notably, Denmark, the Netherlands, the United Kingdom, and the European Commission have pushed UNHCR to explore ways of developing the concept of protection in the region of origin (Betts 2009; Lindley 2010, 109–113). The basis of this concept has been to seek ways in which development assistance might be used to enhance the quality of protection available to Somalis in Kenya as a means of reducing the need for them to move onward in search of asylum in Europe.

One of the leading states in this endeavor has been Denmark, which exemplifies UNHCR's European donor states' concerns with Somali mixed migration. Bettina Gollander-Jensen, the Danish government's minister counselor in Nairobi, explained: "In 2003, Denmark started a Regions of Origin program, and the objective of that program was to really control migration."[34] It focused on Kenya and Somaliland. Klansoe, of the Danish Refugee Council, concurred: "The minister of course has an interest. It is 'support refugees in their region of origin' . . . but clearly with the political aim of 'keep people in there.' . . . If you want to deal with displacement and refugee issues, Kenya is the place to be."[35] Meanwhile, the Netherlands has been conferring with the Danes about building on this work. The United Kingdom has also actively sought to establish a bilateral partnership on mixed migration from the region. Its embassies and high commissions have attached new migration officers, and the U.K. Home Office has supported the new EAC Centre of Excellence for Training Migration Officials.

The U.S. government has also funded International Organization for Migration (IOM) research on Somali smuggling routes to South Africa.[36] At the multilateral level, the concern with the mixed migration of Somalis has led to the creation of a Mixed Migration Task Force (MMTF), in which UNHCR, IOM, and the Danish Refugee Council, in particular, are collaborating with donors to understand and limit the onward movement of Somalis, whether across the Gulf of Aden or toward South Africa.[37]

This trend in donor support for the containment of Somali refugees has in turn been exacerbated by a global concern with the link between Somalia and terrorism, mirroring that in Kenya (Juma and Kagwanja 2008). The August 1998 bombings of U.S. embassies in Nairobi and Dar es Salaam, the announcement by then president George W. Bush of an East African counterterrorism initiative in June 2003, the January 2007 Battle of Ras Kamboni in which the United States attacked al-Qaeda suspects in southern Somalia all illustrated key turning points at which Kenya—and its Somali refugees—became increasingly central to the West's counterterrorism strategy. Kenya has become an important ally in the "war on terror," receiving external support for its counterterrorism efforts mainly from the U.S., U.K., and Danish governments (Juma and Kagwanja 2008, 101). As Bachmann and Hönke (2009, 101) explain, after the September 11 terrorist attacks: "Development and security policies merged into an agenda of conflict prevention and peacekeeping in which stable states such as Kenya received new strategic importance as regional anchor states. . . . A problematic blurring of the lines between developmental and classical security instruments in the practice of reactive conflict management interventions soon became evident. The process intensified with regard to the functionality of development projects in the fight against terrorism." UNHCR has been placed in a position in which it is caught between donor and host states with a coincidence of interests: to provide an inclusive humanitarian space for Somalis—yes—but also to contain them in a way that aligns with perceptions of national and international security. This concession to security is implicit in the comment of UNHCR's Kenya Representative Elike Segbor during the 2011 survival migration influx: "With a refugee population of over 400,000, compared to the host community's 100,000, only 80 km from a border of a country at war, you can imagine there are security concerns" (IRIN 2011b).

Conclusion

From a certain perspective, the refugee regime in Kenya has stretched to an exceptional degree. Relative to other cases explored in this book, Kenya has assumed a broad and inclusive definition of a refugee. Since the early 1990s, it has recognized all people fleeing south-central Somalia as refugees, irrespective of the proximate cause. What began as a pragmatic policy for addressing a large-scale mass influx was enshrined in legislation in 2006. By becoming the only state in Africa to incorporate prima facie recognition under the OAU refugee definition, Kenya formally adopted perhaps the most inclusive refugee definition of any government in Africa. Even during the 2011 famine and drought, when many people were fleeing causes that arguably fell outside even the OAU definition, the Kenyan refugee regime remained inclusive.

The reasons why regime stretching has taken place can be attributed to a set of incentives of key elites within the government at critical historical junctures. The initial influx came at a point when the Moi regime needed international legitimacy and development assistance because it could no longer count on the same unconditional support it had received in the context of the Cold War. The revival of debates on inclusive refugee legislation came at a time when Kibaki was similarly seeking greater international recognition and support. Ensuring that refugees received protection offered a means to demonstrate the human rights credentials of both leaders and to bring in international assistance.

Furthermore, the option to effectively contain and outsource the cost of protection to the international community massively reduced the domestic political costs of hosting. NEP already had a population dominated by ethnic Somalis. Provided that the international community not only paid the refugee protection bill but also extended benefits to the host community, it could be conceived as beneficial. There has been a coincidence of interests between the government's concerns and those of the international donor community. Inclusive recognition has suited UNHCR. During the initial mass influx, prima facie recognition was more pragmatic and cost-effective given the large numbers of Somalis, while at later stages introducing individualized screening would have risked *refoulement*.

Regime stretching, however, has come at a cost. There has been a trade-off between the quantity and quality of asylum. The combination of anti-Somali xenophobia and rising concerns with terrorism has reinforced government restrictions on freedom of movement and livelihood opportunities. The overwhelming majority of Somalis have been forced to remain indefinitely in the overcrowded Dadaab camps, where conditions have deteriorated over time. Government elites like George Saitoti have exploited the "Somali question" for electoral gain, pushing for greater security restrictions on Somalis since 2007. However, the 2006 Refugee Act and the Department of Refugee Affairs have at least created an institutional safeguard that has prevented any systematic attempt to engage in deportation. The government's ongoing concern with international legitimacy has led it to broadly continue to respect the 2006 act and to retain inclusivity toward all displaced Somalis even during the 2011 crisis.

By the end of 2011, however, this commitment had begun to erode. The increasingly large numbers of Somali refugees in Kenya, coupled with already existing tensions with Kenya's resident Somali community, played a significant role in contributing to Kenya's invasion of Somalia in late 2011. Although the military deployment was framed as a response to the immediate threat of al-Shabaab to Kenya, and despite the commercial and political gains Kenya stands to make as a consequence of its military involvement in Somalia, the invasion is clearly also a way to begin to close the Dadaab camps. This is most clearly illustrated in President Kibaki's speech in London in February 2012, in which he suggested that the territories freed from al-Shabaab should be used for the return of Somali refugees.

In summary, international support and the incentives of elites at key moments have enabled the refugee regime to stretch to protect all Somali survival migrants, regardless of the proximate cause of their flight. However, this inclusivity has come at a price: a trade-off between numbers and rights. In admitting large numbers, Kenya has simultaneously sought to contain the population movement in ways that have compromised the human rights of those in exile. While Somalis may not yet have been deported in large numbers, they certainly have not received all the rights to which they would be entitled as refugees, or even under international human rights law (Human Rights Watch 2010b). Furthermore, the invasion of Somalia—and the search for an internal flight alternative—indicates that the government's generosity may have been pushed to its limits.

YEMEN

Contrasting Responses to Somalis and Ethiopians

Somalis have dispersed throughout their own region and beyond because of the failure of their state. Just across the Gulf of Aden, Yemen has been the most immediate destination outside East Africa. It hosts an estimated 220,000 Somalis,[1] and it represents a transit country on the way to the Middle East, the Gulf states, and Europe. The opportunity for transit coupled with a sizable and well-integrated Somali diaspora makes it an attractive destination. Somalis fleeing to Yemen face a treacherous route, however, as they travel northward across Somalia to coastal ports such as Bosaso or even Djibouti. Using smuggling networks, they cross at the narrowest points of the choppy and shark-infested Gulf of Aden, often on insecure and rickety boats. They face significant risks, and there are hundreds of drownings per year.

In Yemen, the government's response toward the Somalis has traditionally been tolerant. Like Kenya, it has recognized all Somalis as refugees on a prima facie basis. Unlike Kenya, it has not even insisted on the encampment of Somali refugees, and most are de facto locally integrated in urban areas, albeit with limited assistance. Of the 130,000 Somalis assisted by UNHCR in the country,[2] only around 14,000 live in the country's main al-Kharaz camp; the majority live in urban areas in Sana'a and around the al-Basateen district in Aden, where they have freedom of movement and a degree of self-sufficiency.[3] In that sense, the response of the national and international refugee regime has been to stretch to protect all Somalis.

Yemen's traditional openness can be explained by a combination of domestic and international incentives on the country's elites. Domestically, the long-standing presence of the well-integrated Somali diaspora within Yemen, and its positive economic impact and close social ties with nationals, has contributed to a willingness of the government to retain openness. In contrast to democracies like Kenya, authoritarianism in Yemen has insulated Somali immigration, preventing it from becoming contested in national political debates. Meanwhile, at the international level, UNHCR has provided the financial support to maintain prima facie recognition, with the international community underwriting most of the limited humanitarian assistance available to Somali refugees. Historically, the Somalis have been easy guests.

However, in recent years, the traditional generosity of the government toward Somalis has gradually come under threat. While Somalis are still given immediate refugee status in Yemen, there are increasingly restrictive policies as well as persistent rumors that the government will soon introduce refugee status determination for Somalis in order to separate "refugees" from "migrants," a process that already exists in Yemen for all other nationalities.[4] There has been a perceptible shift in domestic attitudes toward foreigners, tracking a perceived increase in terrorist operations in both Yemen and Somalia as well as growing competition for resources and jobs. Furthermore, the international community has focused increasingly on the management of Somali "mixed migrants." Concerned to triage between refugees and "other migrants," the European Union in particular has been engaging more with Somali mixed migration on both sides of the Gulf of Aden.

Yet even with these shifts, protection for Somali survival migrants has continued to be far stronger than it has for another numerically significant population seeking sanctuary in the country: Ethiopians. While Somalis fleeing a variety of proximate causes beyond individualized persecution have received sanctuary in Yemen, Oromo and Ogaden Ethiopians, often fearing persecution and insecurity within Ethiopia, have been given short shrift and have generally faced roundup, detention, and deportation by the Yemeni authorities. Somalis and Ethiopians have been routinely separated at arrival points along the Red Sea and have been subject to different procedures and levels of assistance. The reason underlying the contrast: a very different domestic perception of Somalis and Ethiopians, coupled with a strong bilateral relationship between Yemen and Ethiopia, which has created international political incentives to limit sanctuary for the Oromo.

This chapter explores these contrasting and changing approaches to implementing the refugee regime in Yemen. It demonstrates that they have been driven by national politics, which shapes what international law means at the national level, rather than by international law per se.

The Journey to Yemen

The journey across the Gulf of Aden has historically been a significant migration route for Somalis. In the 1970s, for example, Somali laborers migrated to Yemen and other Gulf countries to seek employment after the oil boom there (Gundel 2002). During the same decade, after General Mohamed Siad Barre overthrew the Somali government in a military coup in 1969, many of his opponents fled into political exile in Yemen and other neighboring countries (Kleist 2004). These and earlier historical movements created the basis of an ethnic Somali population in Yemen. Yet emigration to Yemen on a mass scale began only after the start of civil war and the collapse of Siad Barre's regime in 1991. Since the 1990s, state failure has exacerbated successive waves of conflict, persecution, famine, and drought across south-central Somalia.

Significantly, while most have fled desperate conditions and state failure, a recent survey of Somalis arriving in Yemen revealed that a majority identified themselves as leaving for reasons outside the refugee definition. According to the Mixed Migration Task Force (MMTF), in December 2011 the primary motivation that Somalis reported as their reason for flight continued to be lack of economic opportunities (50 percent) followed by insecurity (39 percent) (Regional Mixed Migration Secretariat 2012).

Somalis leaving for Yemen have faced the same broad structural conditions as those leaving for Kenya and other neighboring states such as Ethiopian and Djibouti. Yet their journey and reception have been different (Jureidini 2010, 3).[5] Many of the Somalis who have chosen to move to Yemen, as opposed to other neighboring states, appear to be members of families of refugees, who rely on remittances from abroad as the primary source of funding for the journey, allowing them to pay the fees of human smugglers (Jureidini 2010, 5). The vast majority of Somali migrants to Yemen begin their journey from the south-central region of Somalia, especially around Mogadishu.

Most migrants traveling from Somalia to Yemen are alone (Jureidini 2010, 8). They travel first to Mogadishu from elsewhere in Banadir and the neighboring regions of the south-central zone, where they get access to the main overland routes to the coast, from Mogadishu to Jowhar and onward to Garoowe. From Garoowe, the route branches off to the east to the Puntland coast and Bosaso, or to the west to the Somaliland coast toward Hargeysa and up the coast to Djibouti (Jureidini 2010, 5). Along the main roads northward, more than three hundred checkpoints across south-central Somalia offer smugglers and criminals ample opportunity to harass migrants and to extort payments for safe passage (Mixed Migration Task Force 2008, 5).

Migrants traveling in Somalia toward the Red Sea ports of Bosaso and Djibouti face multiple dangers, including harassment, extortion, and robbery, as well as difficulties finding accommodation and food. Militias and armed groups often threaten travelers at road checkpoints and along the coast. Ray Jureidini reported incidents of physical assault and rape at all the major stops and checkpoints from Mogadishu en route to the Red Sea (Jureidini 2010, 7).

Migrants are typically driven to departure points by smugglers, separated by nationality, and guarded by gunmen until loading (Mixed Migration Task Force 2008, 8). Passengers are lined up on the shore and then, under the supervision of guards, walk through shallow water to the waiting boats. Smuggling agents frequently mislead boat passengers regarding the risks involved in the journey, as well as the opportunities for onward travel from Yemen (Mixed Migration Task Force 2008). In 2011, some 131 individuals died crossing the Gulf of Aden; in 2010, the total was 14; and in 2009, the total was 289. This trend appears to track the sharp reduction and later increase in migration flows from Somalia to Yemen between 2009 and 2011 (Regional Mixed Migration Secretariat 2012).

UNHCR and the interagency MMTF provide estimates on the number of migrants who leave Somalia and arrive in Yemen along the coast. The coastal monitoring network involves coordination by UNHCR, the International Organization for Migration (IOM), and local NGOs, and it extends across most of the southern Red Sea coast.[6] During 2011, Yemen received the highest number of migrants recorded since 2006 (Regional Mixed Migration Secretariat 2012), 103,154 Somalis and non-Somalis, a figure attributable partly to the drought and famine in Somalia. This is almost double the number of migrants arriving in 2010 (53,000); in 2009, the figure was 78,000.[7]

New arrivals disembark at a variety of entry points along the coasts of the Red Sea and the Gulf of Aden (Mixed Migration Task Force 2008, 8–9). If they land near Bel Har or Bir Ali, they tend to be taken to a temporary transit center before being transported to the UNHCR reception center at Mayfa'ah. If they arrive on the coast of the Abyan Governorate, they are taken to the UNHCR reception center in Ahwar. The al-Kharaz refugee camp receives migrants arriving in Dudab and Al Mohka along the Red Sea coast. In each reception center, new arrivals are offered food, water, medical treatment, and a few days' rest.

On arrival at transit centers, Somalis have been recognized on a prima facie basis and registered by UNHCR in collaboration with the National Committee for Refugee Affairs (ONARS). Only a minority—generally the most vulnerable—go to the camp. The majority instead travel to urban areas, where they are locally integrated and, with limited assistance, generally reliant on their own networks and access to the informal economy.

The Government's Response

Yemen has traditionally had a comparatively generous policy toward Somalis, at least in terms of allowing them access to territory. It is the only country on the Arabian Peninsula that has signed the 1951 Refugee Convention and its 1967 protocol. It does not have a domestic asylum or refugee law,[8] and its consultative National Committee for Refugee Affairs, established in 2000, has no formal power and can act only as a consultant on refugee policy (US Committee for Refugees and Immigrants 2009; Moret, Baglioni, and Efionayi-Mäder 2006). Nevertheless, Yemen's refugee policy is broadly supportive of Somali refugees (Mixed Migration Task Force 2008, 8–9).

There have been some moves toward creating more refugee policy instruments and institutions, but so far work has not substantially extended beyond stated commitments. In particular, since 1988, Somalis have been accepted as prima facie refugees. The fact that people come from Somalia is taken as enough evidence that they are in need of international protection and should be treated as though they are refugees.

This is not to say that there are perfect standards of protection and assistance for Somalis. There are not. Although Somalis are generally not deported, they face a range of obstacles and challenges in practice. Most Somalis have been outside the al-Kharaz refugee camp, living in urban areas in Sana'a and Aden. The al-Basateen district of Aden in some ways parallels the Eastleigh district of Nairobi. It represents a major hub for Somali activity and enterprise, but there are significant levels of poverty among Somali families. In urban areas, protection and assistance are weak, and in reality most Somalis rely on their own networks and entrepreneurialism to survive.

Yemeni police officers often do not receive adequate training in asylum protection, and consequently Somalis living outside refugee camps risk violence and extortion (US Committee for Refugees and Immigrants 2009). Meanwhile, although refugee identification cards, which offer access to health services, education, travel, and limited forms of informal employment, are far more readily available to Somalis than to other groups, they remain extremely limited in number (Jureidini 2010, 5). Somalis thus face significant challenges getting access to basic services.

Nevertheless, compared with other survival migrant populations fleeing fragile and failed states for reasons not directly connected to persecution and violence, Somalis in Yemen have received an open and welcoming response. This relative generosity is in stark contrast with the Yemeni response to another population, the Ethiopians, who since 2009 have constituted the largest proportion of new arrivals in the country (Regional Mixed Migration Secretariat 2012). In the words of Human Rights Watch (2009b, 1): "The government of Yemen has displayed an extraordinary generosity towards Somalis, granting all of them prima facie refugee status because of the conflict raging in their country. But for Ethiopians the opposite is true. Whether they are economic migrants or asylum seekers in need of protection, the policy of the central government is to track them down, arrest them, and deport them." Unlike Somalia, Ethiopia has a stable and recognized government. However, there are parallels between the human rights violations faced by Somalis and Ethiopians. The majority of Ethiopians coming to Yemen have been from the contested and secessionist Oromo and Ogaden regions, where they have suffered a combination of persecution, low-level conflict, and drought. Indeed, an MMTF survey in December 2011, immediately after the declared end to the 2011 Horn of Africa famine and drought, showed that Somalis and Ethiopians arriving in Yemen described their primary motivation for coming to Yemen very similarly. Somalis continued to report a lack of economic opportunities (50 percent), followed by insecurity (39 percent) (Regional Mixed Migration Secretariat 2012). Correspondingly, 48 percent of Ethiopian migrants cited lack of economic opportunities, and 37 percent listed insecurity.

Yet while Somalis have been accepted as prima facie refugees, Ethiopians are required to undergo individual refugee status determination procedures, handled by UNHCR on the government's behalf. The Yemeni government has refused to issue identification documents to a majority of Ethiopian and other non-Somali asylum seekers (Human Rights Watch 2009b, 3). Even for the minority of Ethiopians who do receive mandate refugee status from UNHCR, the level of services is not equal to that of Somalis. For example, the UNHCR refugee identity card provided to Ethiopians states that the holder is not eligible for financial assistance or resettlement (Jureidini 2010, 4). In particular, Ethiopian refugees perceived to be involved in political community organizing activities have been threatened with violence. Non-Somalis experience periodic harassment and extortion by security forces. Little provision is made for basic needs; food, accommodation, education, and health-care services remain inadequate. As a result, some Ethiopians claim to be Somali in an attempt to gain access to protections associated with refugee status (Jureidini 2010).

While their motivations are broadly similar, the level of assistance received by Ethiopians differs widely from that received by Somalis. Almost all Somalis who register with UNHCR (and it is estimated that over 95 percent do) receive some assistance from UNHCR and its implementing partners.[9] In contrast, the majority of Ethiopians surveyed by RMMS report receiving little to no assistance in Yemen. In interviews, many Ethiopians complained of the unequal treatment they were receiving from UNHCR compared with that of the Somalis. NGO assistance was also more available for Somalis: 68 percent of Somalis reported receiving NGO assistance, but almost none of the Ethiopians reported NGO assistance in Yemen (Regional Mixed Migration Secretariat 2012). Overall, the government, religious organizations, and refugee communities provided very little assistance to Ethiopians (Jureidini 2010, 9).

The government of Yemen has been extremely resistant to allowing Ethiopians to register for asylum.[10] The vast majority of Ethiopian migrants originate from Oromia (Regional Mixed Migration Secretariat 2012), the largest and most populous region in Ethiopia. Oromia is also the site of contestation between the ruling Ethiopian People's Revolutionary Democratic Front (EPRDF) and nationalist groups, the most extreme of which is the Oromo Liberation Front (OLF), which pursues secession by military means. The Oromo majority played a dominant role in the centralist, federalist, and nationalist movements in Ethiopia during the nineteenth and twentieth centuries. A number of Oromo groups now seek to create an independent Oromo nation and demand respect for their languages.[11] In 2008, an opposition party to the government, the Oromo Federalist Democratic Movement (OFDM), condemned the government's indirect role in the deaths of hundreds of Oromos in western Ethiopia.[12]

Compared with the situation for many Somalis, there are substantially more deportations of Ethiopians.[13] Many Ethiopians seek to enter Saudi Arabia to pursue domestic work. Because of robust monitoring by Saudi border guards, Ethiopian migrants remain stranded in North Yemen around the city of Harad. The IOM provides a "voluntary assisted return" program to Ethiopians stranded in Yemen. In 2010–2011, IOM returned 6,169 Ethiopians to their country of origin (Regional Mixed Migration Secretariat 2012). Throughout the region, there are also reports from Ethiopians of kidnappings and even assassinations by Ethiopian security services working in collaboration with neighboring states.[14] When I put the allegation to the Ethiopian attorney-general, I was told simply, "We reserve the right to pursue people we deem to be criminals, both within and beyond the boundaries of the state."[15]

The contrast with the response to Ethiopians serves to highlight the relative tolerance of Yemen toward Somalis as a group. However, the special status enjoyed by Somalis may be coming under threat. There are persistent rumors that the government is considering introducing refugee status determination for Somalis to separate "refugees" from "other migrants,"[16] and while there has been no confirmation of these rumors, the government periodically sponsors policies designed to more effectively monitor Somali migration. For example, in 2009, Yemen began creating a database of all Somali refugees, offering a two-month registration deadline for those not yet registered with the state.[17] By virtue of presidential decree in 2010, the Bureau of Refugees was established to support the documentation of refugees and asylum seekers.[18] On January 18, 2010,

Yemen issued a two-month deadline for all unregistered Somalis to register with UNHCR or risk deportation.[19]

This shift toward increased documentation and monitoring, and the emergence of a debate on whether to introduce refugee status determination to triage Somali refugees from other migrants, has paralleled and been shaped by increasing concern with terrorism and the international community's growing focus on mixed migration (US Committee for Refugees and Immigrants 2009). Yet this apparent evolution toward a possible triage of refugees and migrants has stalled in the context of the Arab Spring. Early in 2012, President Saleh ceded power, and elections installed a new government on February 21. Although the country saw a doubling in mixed migrants and asylum seekers in 2011, the focus of the government on transition has meant that—for now at least—policies toward the Somalis have remained broadly constant.[20]

The International Response

UNHCR began operations in Yemen in 1992 in response to the large-scale influx of Somali refugees fleeing civil war in their country.[21] Since that time, UNHCR has applauded the Yemeni government for recognizing Somali refugees on a prima facie basis.[22] Its role with the Somalis has been relatively straightforward; it works with other UN and NGO partners to provide assistance in the main refugee camp and in urban areas. Alongside this assistance role, UNHCR has supported the development of the basic refugee bureaucracy established by Yemen.

The al-Kharaz refugee camp is run by UNHCR in coordination with other UN agencies and various local and international partners. UNHCR provides education until the eighth grade in two schools, one using the Yemeni curriculum and the other a Somali-Yemeni curriculum. The dropout rate is reportedly high, however, especially for girls (US Committee for Refugees and Immigrants 2009). The camp has limited shelters, in part because land disputes with host communities have led to a shortage in the supply of shelters for refugees.[23] Finally, the camp is located in a remote area of the Lahaj region and offers few opportunities for employment.[24] In urban areas, UNHCR has provided some support through its community services teams and a range of NGO implementing partners, particularly in Sana'a and Aden. However, it has faced challenges in reaching and assisting urban Somalis.

To some extent, UNHCR has also urged greater access for Ethiopians and other non-Somalis to refugee channels. However, responding to Ethiopian survival migrants who have been viewed as primarily leaving for economic reasons has been problematic. For example, as one member of the RMMS team asked,

"When you have large groups of Ethiopians not registering, is it UNHCR's responsibility to go to them if they're economic migrants?"[25] Another obstacle to engaging in the protection of the Ethiopians has been the resource and political constraints created by UNHCR's work with Yemeni internally displaced persons (IDPs). There are ten IDP camps (six in Saada, three in Hajjah, and one in Amran Governorate), and UNHCR has needed to retain good relations with the Yemeni government in order to preserve access to the IDP populations.[26] If UNHCR were under fewer material and political constraints, it might have urged the Yemeni government more strongly to treat Somali and non-Somali asylum applicants equally.[27] Human Rights Watch (2009b, 4) in particular has criticized UNHCR's failure to press Yemen's government to permit asylum seekers to apply for refugee status regardless of their nationality and for not demanding access to detained Ethiopian asylum seekers.

Over time, UNHCR has come under more pressure from donors to separate refugees from other migrants arriving in Yemen from the Horn of Africa. The emergence of the Mixed Migration Task Force (MMTF) in Somalia and Yemen offers the best example of a renewed attempt by the international community to engage with the challenge of mixed migration by seeking ways to distinguish between types of migrants. The MMTF, and its successor, the Regional Mixed Migration Secretariat (RMMS), includes UNHCR, the International Organization for Migration (IOM), the UN Organization for Coordinating Humanitarian Affairs (OCHA), the Danish Refugee Council (DRC), and the Norwegian Refugee Council (NRC), and was established to work in Somalia in early 2007 after Yemen received a spike in migrants in 2006. Its purpose was "to develop a rights-based strategy to respond to protection and humanitarian needs of migrants and asylum seekers transiting through Somalia" (Mixed Migration Task Force 2008, 2). A similar MMTF task force was created in Yemen in 2008.

MMTF and its successor offer coastal monitoring, advise government officials, and provide protection to mixed migrants.[28] The task force offers a way in which responsibility for different categories of migrants—notably "refugees" and "other migrants"—can be divided up across agencies with different mandates. Gradually, rather than see all Somalis as refugees, UNHCR is beginning to examine ways to deter the movement of Somalis from relatively more secure areas such as Somaliland and Puntland.

Explaining the Responses

Why is it that the national response to Somalis has been so relatively generous while the one toward Ethiopians has been almost the opposite? And why has the openness toward Somalis begun to come under threat? The answer to these questions can once again be found in the diverging—and gradually changing—incentives on elites in government. Strong domestic and international incentives in favor of the protection of Somalis have contrasted with those relating to the Ethiopians. Yet as the set of positive incentives on the elites for the protection of Somalis has begun to wane, there has been a gradual shift in the terms of the debate.

At the domestic level, Somalis have generally been welcomed by the public. Somali communities have lived in Yemen for a long time, and there has always been movement across the Gulf of Aden. This sizable diaspora is recognized by the Yemeni government as socially well integrated and as making an important economic contribution. Yemen is ethnically diverse, tribal, and Muslim, which enables Somalis to integrate comparatively easily, even if those not speaking Arabic initially face language barriers. In addition to the Somali refugees, there is a large mixed Somali-Yemeni population. The al-Basateen area of Aden, which hosts a significant proportion of the Somalis, is squalid and poor,[29] but Somalis are well integrated and often perceived to be one of the most entrepreneurial groups.

The public response to Somalis has contrasted markedly with the response to Ethiopians, who have traditionally been discriminated against. In Yemen, the most stigmatized Yemeni nationals are the tribesmen known as al-Akhdam (in Arabic, literally "servant"). In popular discourse, they are claimed to have originally had Ethiopian heritage. Much of this discrimination carries across to the xenophobic response to Ethiopians. In a Muslim society, there is additional xenophobia directed toward Ethiopians as Coptic Christians. They are seen as labor migrants who compete for jobs, and they face abuse at every level of society. There are sporadic attacks on the Ethiopian community. In one case, on December 20, 2008, the head of an Oromo Ethiopian refugee community organization was murdered in Yemen (Human Rights Watch 2009b, 45).

The international incentives on the government are also different in the Somali and Ethiopian cases. The Yemeni government has effectively been able to outsource to the international community the costs of protecting and assisting the Somalis. UNHCR and its implementing partners have assumed responsibility for registering the Somalis and offer assistance in the camp and in urban areas. At almost no cost, the government has thereby received significant international recognition and legitimacy on the basis of its openness toward to Somalis.

In contrast, the government has faced strong incentives not to recognize Ethiopians. The Saleh regime in Yemen worked hard to improve its relations with Ethiopia, especially in the areas of trade and regional security. Given this political agenda, then, it may be unsurprising that Yemeni national elites appear indifferent, if not hostile, to Ethiopians fleeing the government of Ethiopia. As mentioned previously, the vast majority of Ethiopians arriving in Yemen travel from Oromia, where secessionist groups such as the Oromo Liberation Front are based (Jureidini 2010, 4). Oromo migrants continue to report that their reason for fleeing is the threat of arbitrary arrest and other harassment by Ethiopian authorities, who perceive them as OLF members (Regional Mixed Migration Secretariat 2012). Interviews with Ethiopian refugees across the region highlight a pervasive fear that a strong alliance between the Ethiopian, Yemeni, and Djiboutian governments will take steps to combat OLF secessionism.[30]

Although the Yemeni response to Somalis has been notably tolerant, not least in comparison to the Ethiopians, the gradual shift in the terms of the debate can be attributed to changes in domestic and international incentives that have underpinned openness. In particular, there has been a gradual rise in xenophobic attitudes toward the Somalis and an increasing concern with potential terrorist links between Somalia and Yemen.

As the political and economic climate has worsened with civil war and the fall of Saleh, there has been a general increase in antagonistic feeling toward non-nationals.[31] Host communities close to refugee reception centers—such as the Harad district in northern Yemen or Dudab and al-Mohka, close to al-Kharaz refugee camp—have become increasingly sensitive to perceived threats by asylum seekers and refugees (Regional Mixed Migration Secretariat 2012). Moreover, with unemployment rates in Yemen as high as 50 percent, many Yemeni citizens see the Somalis as potential threats in the labor market.[32]

The Yemeni government is also very concerned about extremism among incoming migrants. The country continues to experience insecurity, and Islamic extremists such as Ansar al-Sharia and other groups have gained control over parts of Yemen, particularly in the north. In early 2012, al-Shabaab formally affiliated itself with al-Qaeda.[33] There have been media reports in Yemen that al-Shabaab terrorists come into the country through asylum channels. Although those reports remain unsubstantiated, they illustrate a pervasive concern with the potential terrorist link between the two states.[34] It remains uncertain to what extent rising xenophobia and concerns with terrorism will influence responses to the Somalis over time.

The response of the international community has relatively clearly mapped onto that of the national government, and UNHCR in particular has been accused of being overly compliant with the Yemeni government. Human Rights Watch (2009b, 8), for example, has complained:

> UNHCR has an excellent relationship with the government of Yemen on the issue of Somali refugees and preserving that good relationship

is important. But favorable treatment of one refugee group should not come at the expense of another, especially when this involves systematic refoulement and other abuses directed against the disfavored group. UNHCR faces a government disinclined to change its policies regarding Ethiopians and other non-Somalis, but too often the refugee agency has acted as though the plight of these refugees and asylum seekers in Yemen is a secondary issue.

Indeed, UNHCR's relationship with Yemen has been strained. For many years, UNHCR has struggled to achieve open dialogue with the government, and the absence of a national refugee law or relevant national institutions beyond ONARS has complicated UNHCR's work.[35] On the one hand, UNHCR has sought to influence the government. On the other hand, it has been extremely dependent on the government in order to preserve protection space for the Somalis, which has made it reluctant to be overly critical of the response to the Ethiopians. This dependence on the government has been further complicated in the context of the civil war and UNHCR's growing role in protecting the estimated 144,000 IDPs resulting from internal conflict (Regional Mixed Migration Secretariat 2012).

Conclusion

Yemen's national refugee regime has stretched to offer protection to all Somalis arriving in Yemen since 1988, recognizing them on a prima facie basis. It has offered protection to Somalis just by virtue of their having left a failed state, regardless of whether the proximate cause of flight is more closely related to persecution, conflict, or livelihoods. Even though conditions of assistance in the Al-Kharaz refugee camp and urban areas such as Al-Basateen have been imperfect, Yemen has allowed Somalis access to territory and a significant degree of freedom of movement. Although that generosity has come under threat—with an emerging debate about the reintroduction of refugee status determination amid growing concern about terrorism and mixed migration—inclusive recognition of all Somalis as though they are refugees has been maintained.

However, the contrasting response to Ethiopians illuminates the role of politics—rather than human rights—in shaping who gets access to asylum and protection and who does not. In recent surveys the two groups reveal similar sets of reasons for coming to Yemen. Furthermore, many of the Ethiopians fleeing the Oromia region have arguably fled conditions of persecution that more clearly fit the 1951 convention, while others have fled low-level conflict or the consequences of famine and drought in ways that are analogous to the experiences of the Somali survival migrants. Yet despite the overlapping reasons for flight and the commonalities in the underlying human rights violations faced by many Ethiopians and Somalis, Ethiopians have routinely been rounded up, detained, and deported, sometimes without even being given access to asylum procedures.

What has explained the different responses is not international law or human rights but politics. Elites in the government of Yemen have faced contrasting incentives in their respective treatment of Somalis and Ethiopians. At the domestic level, Somalis have been well integrated and positively received by Yemeni communities while Ethiopians have encountered discrimination at all levels of society. At the international level, Yemen has received significant praise and financial assistance for its hospitality toward the Somalis but diplomatic inducements from the government of Ethiopia not to accommodate its citizens in exile.

The international community in general and UNHCR in particular have uncritically accepted—and reinforced—many of the distinctions created by domestic politics. Overall, the case of Yemen shows that even where one group of survival migrants fleeing state failure gets access to protection—in this case, Somalis—contradictions may remain. While these contradictions appear arbitrary from a human rights perspective, they are anything but arbitrary from a political perspective. In the absence of legal precision, political interests shape what the national refugee regime does in practice.

IMPROVING THE REFUGEE PROTECTION REGIME

The six previous chapters highlight an immense regional and global challenge. People who flee state persecution across international borders are relatively consistently recognized as refugees, but those who flee serious rights deprivations face a much more inconsistent response. While those who flee targeted violations by the government generally obtain access to asylum, those who flee the state's inability or unwillingness to ensure people's rights face a far more mixed and uncertain response.

This matters because although the number of repressive states in the world may be in decline, the number of weak states—so-called fragile and failed states—represents a growing international challenge. Beyond the African context, people are fleeing crisis and insecurity in fragile states such as Haiti, Libya, and Afghanistan. The threats that people face due to environmental change, food insecurity, or generalized violence, which might be more easily addressed domestically by a stronger state, can compel people to seek their basic rights by crossing international borders.

The cases in the previous chapters starkly illustrate the desperate situation faced by hundreds of thousands of people who have fled Zimbabwe, the Democratic Republic of Congo, and Somalia. Despite fleeing different situations, they have in common that they have been fleeing serious existential threats that, for the majority, have not been due to persecution per se. Although some have nevertheless received protection as refugees, others have instead faced detention and deportation by the neighboring host states.

What explains this inconsistent response is not principle but politics. Elite interests—rather than law—are determining whether people fleeing deprivation rather than persecution receive access to international protection. Even though regional instruments and international human rights law standards fill some of these gaps in some regions and countries, there are no universally accepted standards on how such people should be protected. Consequently, where there is ambiguity in law, discretion enables politics to define what happens in practice.

This gap is something that the international community should be concerned about. It is based on an arbitrary—and historically anachronistic—distinction between people fleeing persecution and people fleeing a state's unwillingness or inability to ensure basic rights. Both entail a severance of the assumed state-citizen relationship and require a surrogate provider of basic rights until such time as the country of origin is able to ensure such rights. Moreover, in addition to the human rights consequences, the inconsistent and incoherent responses may have implications for a state's own interests. Without coherent responses, people fleeing may be forced to resort to informal transnational networks in ways that may have national and international security implications.

Recognizing these gaps and inconsistencies, and their consequences for human rights and security, raises the question of how global governance can and should adapt to the changing nature of cross-border displacement. How can and should international institutions such as UNHCR ensure more consistent and principled protection in relation to people fleeing serious basic rights deprivations in fragile and failed states?

The challenge is how to make the refugee protection regime, created in the aftermath of the Second World War, meet the needs of a very different world from the one into which it was born. The regime's underlying purpose was never to protect people fleeing particular causes of movement. It was rather to ensure that, in an international society of states, all individuals would have a state willing and able to provide their most fundamental human rights. The refugee regime was created in order to serve as a check and balance against the inevitable failure of some states to protect their own citizens. Protection against persecution served this function in post–Second World War Europe; it no longer does in the contemporary world.

However, making the global refugee regime better able to fulfill its underlying purpose is not simply about creating new treaties or abstract instruments in Geneva or New York. What matters is also what happens at the levels of institutionalization and implementation of existing norms and international organizations. International institutions adapt—and hence can also be reformed—at each of these different levels. This recognition is important because it highlights that, by themselves, interstate agreements at the global level may do very little in practice, but also because it suggests that, even if there is not the political will for wholesale reform, there is still a range of ways in which institutions can adapt and be made more effective.

The theoretical framework set out in this book offers a template for thinking about how to reform the refugee protection regime in response to the changing nature of cross-border displacement. According to the principle of subsidiarity, it makes sense to consider what can be improved at lower levels of governance before working up to higher levels. If protection can be improved by focusing on implementation, it makes sense to begin at that level. Then, if that does not work, we should consider the role of institutionalization before considering the need for reform at the global level. As this chapter argues, making the refugee regime applicable to the modern world requires consideration of practical measures at all three levels: implementation, institutionalization, and international agreements.

Implementation

The case studies highlight that even where states have signed and ratified international agreements, and even where these are theoretically incorporated into law or policy, this may not be sufficient to determine what actually happens in practice. Even states that have similar levels of institutionalization of international agreements may have radically different practices of refugee protection. What lies between adopting agreements and practice is a process of implementation mediated by politics and bureaucracy. Understanding implementation as a discrete phase during which international norms and international organization mandates are contested and recontested is crucial for effective international public policy.

Where international norms have a degree of ambiguity or imprecision, politics will shape how they are implemented in practice. As we see in the cases in this book, there is a national politics of international institutions, especially in contexts in which the law leaves states with a degree of discretion. A range of factors will inevitably matter for implementation, including state capacity (VanDeveer and Dabelko 2001), the national legal system (Simmons 2009), bureaucratic identity (Checkel 2005), and cultural context (Acharya 2004). However, what stands out most clearly from the case chapters is the importance of interests in shaping implementation. Incentives on elites with the power to influence implementation will significantly determine what happens in practice. As Steve Krasner (1999) has argued at the global level, where norms are ambiguous or contested, interests will determine how these clashes and ambiguities are reconciled.

Explaining what these incentives are and how they matter is important for international public policy. If the processes that shape implementation can be understood, then they can be influenced. The kinds of incentives that have mattered at the domestic level include public opinion, electoral politics, the role of civil society, and business interests. At the international level, incentives have come from international financial assistance and the importance of international legitimacy. In many cases, these incentives have changed over time even within a particular country context, and often in ways that have been or could have been influenced by public policymakers.

The reason why national refugee regimes have sometimes been broad and sometimes narrow in their interpretation of who is a refugee is the incentive structure created by domestic politics and international politics. At the domestic level, there may be a limit to what international actors can do, but supporting civil society groups or transnational advocacy groups may be one way to redefine the contours of domestic debate and how refugee and migrant rights issues enter electoral politics in democracies or patrimonial politics in authoritarian states.

At the international level, there is more that can be done. Where national refugee regimes have stretched to protect survival migrants, it has often been because of positive incentives such as international assistance, either from humanitarianism or from linked areas such as development assistance. Dependency on external sources of financial assistance in states like Kenya and Tanzania has given UNHCR more leverage than in middle-income states like Botswana and Angola, which are less beholden to the international community. Even in these cases, though, international interactions have shaped incentives. Investment strategies by multinational corporations in Angola have had adverse effects on migrant rights in the diamond mining provinces. South Africa's bilateral relationship with Zimbabwe and its role as a key Southern African Development Community (SADC) mediator over Zimbabwe have compromised its willingness to protect Zimbabweans. Yemen's bilateral relationship with Ethiopia has similarly undermined its willingness to protect Ethiopians.

The cases reveal in a whole variety of ways that the actions and inactions of the international community can shape the incentives of elites in government. Some of these incentives—such as international burden sharing to support the cost of hosting refugees—lie within the scope of the refugee regime (Milner 2009). Other incentives lie outside the scope of an organization like UNHCR to control or directly influence. Nevertheless, being aware of and understanding the incentives and interests that shape how national politics interacts with norms and international law is an important part of effective implementation of the refugee regime.

Engaging with domestic politics is, of course, a central part of the work of UNHCR representatives in every refugee-hosting country in the world. Trying to effectively influence and persuade states to create protection space is what UNHCR does on a daily basis. However, the cases analyzed in this book suggest that UNHCR's impact on host state policies relating to survival migration has been limited. In every single case, rather than lead or fundamentally shape states' responses, UNHCR's own response to survival migration has been shaped by and followed the host states' own policies.

Although UNHCR undoubtedly has influence on states' behavior in many contexts, at the level of implementation in the six case study chapters it has been what social scientists call "epiphenomenal." Its role has had limited independent causal effect on whether or not the national regime has stretched to be inclusive of survival migrants fleeing for reasons other than persecution. In all the cases, UNHCR's work at the national level has been fundamentally constrained by a combination of factors. First, it has been reliant on the invitation of the government to operate in the country. When the UNHCR representative in Botswana was seen as outspoken or critical, for instance, he was expelled. Second, it has faced a set of conflicts of interest across different populations of concern. For example, in Yemen, its concern to safeguard protection space for internally displaced persons (IDPs) and the Somalis has compromised its ability to criticize the government's response to Ethiopians. In South Africa, its concern to maintain its refugee and IDP protection activities in Zimbabwe has limited its willingness to be seen to directly or indirectly criticize the government. Third, its degree of influence has varied between less-developed countries and middle-income countries, in which international legitimacy has been less important to government elites.

There are a range of things that UNHCR can do to better engage with the national politics of implementation. The most obvious is to improve the quality of its political analysis. Understanding the sets of interests that shape what national refugee regimes do in practice offers a means to identify levers through which to influence and change those interests. To explain a causal relationship is to offer a potential policy lever. Of course, protection officers within UNHCR are already actively engaged in interpreting and responding to domestic politics. However, the organization lacks a coherent infrastructure to engage in the kind of political analysis that is integral to understanding how international law actually relates to practice.

There are practical ways in which UNHCR could better influence the politics of implementation. As well as relying on its national representatives, it might appoint special envoys of the High Commissioner, for instance, to work on particular refugee situations or displacement crises, and to engage directly with the national politics of government responses. Even when there are areas of national politics and government policy that lie outside the influence or mandate of UNHCR, it could more systematically build informal or formal partnerships with other actors to facilitate implementation. At the global level, this might involve partnering with other actors within and beyond the UN system capable of realigning the incentives on government elites, such as development and security actors in the UN system. At the local level, it might simply involve closer relationships with civil society or the "hidden protection actors," such as faith-based humanitarian actors who currently fill some of the protection gaps described in this book.

Institutionalization

Beyond engaging with the politics and practice of implementation, more can be done to institutionalize existing international instruments. Across the cases, if host states had fully incorporated within their policies the international refugee law and human rights law standards to which they are signatories, then a much higher proportion of survival migrants would have received access to protection.

The OAU Convention

The 1969 OAU Convention Governing the Specific Aspects of Refugee Problems has been much underused in the African context to address the challenges of survival migration. While all the African states included in the book have signed the OAU convention, and all except Botswana have ratified the convention, only Kenya has fully applied it to protect survival migrants fleeing fragile and failed states. Indeed, Kenya is the only state in Africa to explicitly incorporate prima facie recognition under the OAU convention in national legislation (Albert 2010).

Significantly, the OAU convention expands the definition of a refugee found in the 1951 convention. Article I(2) of the OAU convention states:

> The term refugee shall also apply to every person who, owing to external aggression, occupation, foreign domination or events seriously disturbing public order in either part or the whole of his country of origin or nationality, is compelled to leave his place of habitual residence in order to seek refuge in another place outside his country of origin or nationality.

The two key phrases in this are "events seriously disturbing public order" and "in either part or the whole of his country of origin." These phrases could be interpreted as offering refugee status to all the survival migrants described as fleeing Zimbabwe, the DRC, and Somalia in this book. The first phrase opens up an array of causes of movement far beyond persecution, which may include a whole range of serious threats to human security. The second phrase shows that these threats need not necessarily exist throughout the country and that if the existence of "events seriously disturbing public order" in one part of the country were to have secondary effects—for example, on socioeconomic conditions—in another part of the country which "compelled" movement, then this would be sufficient to justify refugee status.

In other words, the OAU convention offers a basis on which to protect many survival migrants in Africa. Yet surprisingly, UNHCR has offered very little guidance to states on how to apply it, nor has it systematically advocated for its application in relation to mass influx situations caused by survival migrations. For example, UNHCR did not push the government of South Africa to implement the OAU convention to protect Zimbabwean survival migrants (Crisp and Kiragu 2010; Schreier 2008).

Promoting the use of the OAU convention could therefore address some of the challenges of survival migration in Africa. By itself, however, the OAU convention is not a panacea for the challenges of survival migration. While the cases in this book focus on the African context, the challenges they highlight extend beyond Africa to states in which there is no equivalent regional convention to supplement the international 1951 convention (Wood 2012).

The 1951 Convention

The 1951 Convention on the Status of Refugees was conceived as a living document. Even though it was created in a particular historical and geographical context, the drafters envisaged that it would adapt over time and be interpreted in its historical context (Goodwin-Gill and McAdam 2007). This organic quality means that the line between refugees and other survival migrants can never be understood as fixed because the refugee in international law is subject to interpretation.[1] In theory, all survival migrants could be interpreted as refugees under the 1951 convention—although it currently seems unlikely.

Indeed, the idea of persecution in Article 1A(2) of the convention is complex and has been interpreted in different ways over time. National courts and UNHCR Executive Committee (Excom) conclusions have offered insights into the meaning and scope of "persecution," as has some domestic legislation.[2] For example, in some jurisdictions it has been argued to encompass acts of persecution by nonstate actors or to include the omissions of states, especially where these may be understood to be discriminatory.

Michelle Foster (2007)'s pioneering work has examined "refuge from depriva-tion" in international law, arguing that even the 1951 convention has the scope to be applied to protect people fleeing economic and social rights deprivations. She suggests that the assumption that the 1951 convention can protect only people fleeing civil and political rights violations is mistaken. Following Foster's argu-ments, there is far more that UNHCR might do to offer guidance on the appli-cation of the 1951 convention to people seeking asylum based on deprivation rather than persecution.

Human Rights Law

Perhaps most important, international human rights law could be used to pro-vide sources of complementary protection to people who fall outside the refugee definition. A range of regional and international jurisprudence in the European Court of Human Rights (ECtHR), the UN Committee against Torture, and the UN Human Rights Committee has indicated that many people who are not rec-ognized as refugees under international refugee law may nevertheless be enti-tled not to be forcibly returned to their country of origin for reasons relating to human rights (McAdam 2007).

The European Convention on Human Rights (ECHR) offers the most de-veloped jurisprudence on the application of human rights law to the principle of *non-refoulement*. Article 3 states: "No one shall be subjected to torture or to inhuman or degrading treatment or punishment." A significant and growing proportion of this jurisprudence on the ECHR has broadened the interpretation of "inhuman, cruel and degrading treatment" to include some people fleeing so-cioeconomic deprivations. The case of *D. v. United Kingdom* (1997)[3] ruled that a failed asylum seeker with HIV/AIDS could not be returned to Saint Kitts–Nevis: "in view of these exceptional circumstances and bearing in mind the critical stage now reached in the applicant's fatal illness, the implementation of the decision to remove him to St Kitts would amount to inhuman treatment by the respondent State in violation of Article 3."

The case of *Sufi and Elmi v. United Kingdom* (2011)[4] illustrates the applica-tion of ECHR Article 3 to protect people fleeing failed and fragile states in Africa who are judged to fall outside the scope of the 1951 convention. In this case, two Somali asylum seekers were declined refugee status on the broad grounds of not facing persecution as a result of being part of a minority clan and having scope for an internal flight alternative. The U.K. government had therefore proposed returning them to Mogadishu. However, the ECtHR ruled that returning them to Somalia would leave them to face dire humanitarian conditions reaching the threshold of "inhuman, cruel and degrading treatment."

The idea that people facing "dire humanitarian conditions" reach the threshold of "inhuman, cruel and degrading treatment" has been developed in jurisprudence across a number of ECtHR cases, including *N. v. United Kingdom* (2008)[5], *M.S.S. v. Belgium and Greece* (2011)[6], and *Hirsi Jamaa and Others v. Italy* (2012).[7] It thereby begins to flesh out the basis of a human rights–based standard for *non-refoulement* founded on a threshold—albeit a very high one—of rights violations that may entitle individuals, even those who fall outside the framework of international law, to asylum.

However, complementary protection based on human rights law remains extremely limited. The ECtHR's jurisprudence is developing rapidly, and yet the threshold for providing asylum remains prohibitively high. Furthermore, its decisions are applicable only in the European context, applying only to members of the Council of Europe. In other parts of the world, many national and regional courts have not even begun to consider the application of international human rights law in relation to *non-refoulement*.

While other regional human rights courts, such as the African Court of Human and People's Rights, might conceivably consider cases relating to asylum, no such jurisprudence currently exists. The slow pace and regional variation in the development of jurisprudence concerning complementary protection therefore pose major challenges for how to better mobilize human rights law to protect the rights of survival migrants in regions beyond Europe, including in Africa.

International Agreements

Nevertheless, important gaps remain at the global level. There is no clear and authoritative set of guidelines on the implications of international human rights law for the rights of vulnerable irregular migrants. Nor is there a clear division of responsibility among international organizations for the protection of vulnerable migrants at the margins of the refugee regime.[8] Addressing these gaps requires (1) an authoritative clarification of the relevant normative frameworks governing protection in the context of cross-border movements and (2) a clear division of interagency responsibility for migrant protection.

In terms of the normative framework, new treaties are not necessarily required. One of the emerging trends in policy debates has been to consider the need for a new intergovernmental treaty on environmental displacement in the context of climate change. Such a response is problematic. It is debatable whether a new treaty is actually necessary. In theory, existing standards in refugee law, humanitarian law, and human rights law have the potential to highlight the conditions under which people have an entitlement to protection or to *non-refoulement*. More important, though, it would be a mistake to supplement the existing refugee regime by looking at particular causes of cross-border displacement—whether the environment or anything else—in isolation. From a protection perspective, what should matter in determining the right to asylum or temporary protection is not the particular cause of movement. What should matter is the underlying threshold of human rights, which when unavailable in a country of origin necessitates flight as a last resort, irrespective of the cause.

The cases analyzed in this book show the existing ambiguity and inconsistencies in the interpretation of law relating to survival migrants who cross international borders for reasons other than persecution. Although international refugee law and international human rights law have a contribution to make, there is an absence of clear and universal acceptance of what these standards mean for people crossing borders for reasons other than persecution. Who—beyond those covered by the 1951 convention—should be entitled to *non-refoulement*? Of those who can be returned, what forms of treatment can they and should they expect from the receiving state? One response to these questions is to wait for national and regional courts to gradually build jurisprudence on these issues. The problem, however, is that this process is slow and patchy, and reinforces inconsistencies. What is needed is greater clarity and guidance at the international level. As this book has shown, where there is no clarity at the global level, then national politics will fill the gap and define outcomes.

Soft Law and Guiding Principles

One way of clarifying both the entitlement to *non-refoulement* and the rights of vulnerable migrants who may be returnable would be to develop a set of guiding principles at the international level in the form of what is often referred to as "soft law." Soft law represents a form of nonbinding normative framework in which existing norms from other sources are consolidated within a single document. Soft law guidelines may, for example, be compiled through drawing on experts or facilitating an interstate agreement on the interpretation of how existing legal norms apply to a particular area. The value of soft law is that it can provide clear and authoritative guidelines in given areas without the need to negotiate new binding norms.

The development of a soft law framework has been applied to address gaps in international protection in the past. In particular, there was a long-standing recognition that there were gaps in IDP protection, which ultimately led to the development and negotiation of a set of Guiding Principles on Internally Displaced Persons between 1992 and 1998. During that period, the representative of the UN Secretary-General for IDPs, Francis Deng, worked with the legal support

of Walter Kaelin and the backing of a small number of states to identify existing normative gaps in IDP protection. Having identified the gaps, they drew on
existing international human rights and international humanitarian law norms
to draft a set of guiding principles that were subsequently adopted by states as
a nonbinding framework for interpreting their obligations toward IDPs. These
principles have been relatively effective in filling protection gaps and meeting the
demand of states for clear guidelines and a clear institutional division of responsibility for IDP protection.

In many ways, the situation of survival migrants is analogous. The international community has reached the point at which there is consensus that the
international protection of vulnerable migrants is no longer simply about people
fleeing persecution. There is a growing recognition that there is a significant
gap—at both the normative and especially the operational level—with respect
to a range of vulnerable irregular migrants, many of whom might have a right to
non-refoulement. However, as with the IDP case, the relevant human rights norms
already exist; they simply require consolidation and application, and a clear division of operational responsibility between international organizations. As with
the development of the guidelines on IDP protection, a soft law framework for
the protection of vulnerable migrants would have two main features: it would be
nonbinding, and it would clarify the application of the existing legal and normative obligations to people crossing borders for reasons other than persecution.

The current historical juncture does not represent an auspicious political climate in which to develop new norms. Few powerful states are predisposed to
the negotiation of binding, multilateral norms through a UN framework, and in
the context of state concern with migration and security, this reluctance is even
greater with respect to negotiating binding agreements in relation to the rights of
noncitizens. In the area of migration, states' reticence to engage in the development of binding norms is evident in several areas. The limited number of ratifying states for the United Nations International Convention on the Protection of
the Rights of All Migrant Workers and Members of Their Families, the voting
patterns at the UN General Assembly in relation to the outcome of the first Global
Forum on Migration and Development (GFMD), and the growing use of informal regional consultative processes (RCPs) that bypass multilateral forums all
exemplify the resistance of states to agree to new norms in relation to migration.

In the case of the protection of vulnerable migrants, however, there is no need
to develop new norms through multilateral agreement. The norms within international human rights law already exist. As was the case with IDPs, nonbinding
guidelines are required on the application of those norms to the context of cross-
border movements. The guidelines would help states by offering an authoritative
and agreed-on interpretation of the existing standards and by identifying any

normative or operational gaps. Over time, these guidelines may become hard law as states adopt them in domestic legislation, as has occurred with IDPs. While there is no guarantee that international standards would translate into institutionalization and implementation at the regional and national levels, authoritative guidance has an important contribution to make.

Interagency Collaboration

In addition to developing a clear and authoritative interpretation of the application of existing human rights norms to people who cross international borders for reasons other than persecution, there is a need to establish who is responsible for "doing" protection. At the level of international organizations, there remains an operational gap with respect to the protection of vulnerable migrants. Which organizations should (a) have responsibility for interpreting the application of rights and obligations in particular situations, and (b) have responsibility for being present in the field to ensure access to rights? As it stands, no organization has a clear mandate for the identification, referral, and protection of vulnerable irregular migrants who are adjudged not to be refugees.

Here again, the IDP precedent is instructive. Alongside the guiding principles, the process of IDP norm development during the 1990s led to the creation of an interorganizational division of labor for implementing the rights of IDPs. Initially, a collaborative approach was created in which a range of UN and non-UN agencies shared responsibility for IDP protection. The approach was based on the recognition that IDP protection needed a coordinated response across different international agencies. It lasted until 2005, when in the context of humanitarian reform across the UN system, a new approach to interagency coordination was created known as the cluster approach.

The cluster approach divides up interagency responsibility for different areas of humanitarian response—for all populations—across various sectors. Based on an agreement in the Inter-Agency Standing Committee (IASC), the approach created nine thematic clusters—at both the global and the national level—in which particular agencies take on a lead coordination role. These areas are protection; camp coordination and camp management; health; shelter; nutrition; water, sanitation, and hygiene; early recovery; logistics; and emergency telecommunications. In each area there is an agency or agencies assigned responsibility for being the global cluster lead. For example, UNHCR coordinates the global protection cluster and co-chairs the camp coordination and camp management cluster with the International Organization for Migration (IOM).

One of the great ambiguities of the cluster approach, however, is the allocation of responsibility for humanitarian response in the context of cross-border migration and displacement. "Refugees" is the one area of humanitarian response that is not yet "clusterized" and remains the exclusive competence of a single organization, UNHCR. Although the cluster approach addresses displacement across its nine sectors, and no longer explicitly mentions IDPs, the reality is that its displacement focus is predominantly internal. This means that there continues to be the risk of a gap in the humanitarian system for cross-border displacement. It remains unclear whether migration related to humanitarian crises should fall within UNHCR's refugee mandate or be part of the wider cluster approach. At the moment, it appears to be neither fully within UNHCR's mandate nor within the cluster approach.

Regardless of whether the humanitarian response to cross-border displacement is understood as inside or outside the scope of the cluster approach, improving protection for survival migrants fleeing reasons other than persecution will require interagency coordination and a much clearer allocation of responsibility than currently exists at the global or the field level. In particular, such improvement relies on four organizations to determine the scope of their role in this area and to coordinate appropriately: UNHCR, IOM, the International Federation of the Red Cross and Red Crescent Societies (IFRC), and the Office of the High Commissioner for Human Rights (OHCHR), all of which work on the protection of vulnerable migrant populations but none of which currently offers fully predictable or consistent responses in relation to migrant protection.

Next Steps

The underlying purpose of the global refugee regime is not to protect people fleeing particular causes of movement across international borders, whether persecution or climate change. Rather, it is premised on a simple understanding: in a civilized international system, all people have an entitlement to a state that can ensure their most basic rights. States have primary responsibility for ensuring these rights for their own citizens. Sometimes, though, the relationship between citizen and state breaks down. The refugee regime was created to ensure that when the state is unable or unwilling to provide protection, and there is no other means to access those rights within the state, people can seek surrogate protection in another country. At the moment, the refugee regime fails to adequately fulfill this function because it arbitrarily excludes many people who are in need of surrogate protection due to the omissions rather than the targeted acts of their own state.

The policy challenge is to identify ways to make the refugee regime better meet its underlying purpose. States recognize in their wider practices that flight from serious basic rights deprivations should be grounds for international protection. This idea is present in much of international human rights law. The distinction between persecution and deprivation does not exist in the way in which states respond to internal refugees—internally displaced persons—who are recognized as such whether they are fleeing the acts or omissions of the state. Furthermore, in many regions, jurisprudence is emerging to protect people outside their country of origin because of existential threats other than persecution, and the scope of who is a refugee is expanding. However, the definition of a refugee is growing slowly, unevenly, and in ways that leave significant gaps.

In a world in which states' commitment to offer asylum—even to those fleeing persecution—is under threat, there is little appetite for new international treaties or for fundamental reform of the global refugee regime. But addressing the gaps identified in this book need not necessarily require wholesale institutional reform. It is a matter of making existing institutions work better—across implementation, institutionalization, and international agreements—rather than fundamentally transforming those that already exist.

Law can do some of this work. In theory, a range of international instruments exist that can and should be strengthened at every level. Had regional instruments like the OAU convention been more clearly understood, institutionalized, and implemented, the African responses in this book could have been improved, although this would still leave significant gaps outside that context. Similarly, if international human rights law had been more strongly institutionalized and implemented in the African region, it might have been used to protect survival migrants. However, making international human rights law work in the context of asylum is a major challenge in regions other than Europe, where jurisprudence on human rights–based complementary protection remains limited but is still far ahead of many other areas of the world.

An important starting point would be to clearly define the normative standards and institutional arrangements that should guide responses to survival migration. On a normative level, one way of doing this would be to draw on the precedent of the Guiding Principles on Internal Displacement in order to develop a consolidated and authoritative set of guidelines relating to survival migration or, more broadly, the protection of vulnerable irregular migrants. On an institutional level, a much clearer division of institutional responsibility is required in relation to the protection of migrant rights around the margins of the refugee regime. UNHCR, IOM, and OHCHR, in particular, should work to ensure that gaps are addressed.

In areas in which normative standards do not exist or remain contested, politics will also have an important role to play. Although UNHCR consistently emphasizes its nonpolitical character, there are few things that are more political than protecting the rights of noncitizens. The six cases in this book show how an understanding of the national politics of the refugee regime is crucial for influencing outcomes. Better political analysis and mobilization of the entire United Nations system to realign the incentives faced by government elites has the potential to open up additional protection space, even in areas in which international law is inadequate or contested.

IMPLEMENTATION MATTERS

This book began with a simple observation. Many people are fleeing fragile and failed states across international borders because they cannot access their most fundamental human rights at home. And yet because the modern refugee regime was created at a particular historical juncture and for a particular period, its definition of a refugee excludes large numbers of these people. While one would imagine that people facing a serious threshold of human rights deprivations for which they have no access to a domestic remedy would be refugees, in practice many are not. The refugee regime was created to protect people fleeing individualized persecution by their own governments. The protection afforded to people deprived of equally fundamental human rights due to deprivations rather than violations, omissions rather than acts of states, and socioeconomic rather than simply civil and political reasons is patchy and inconsistent at best.

The concept of survival migration highlights the situation of people who are running for their lives across international borders and yet are at the margins of the refugee regime, falling outside the dominant interpretation of a refugee under the international framework created after the Second World War. This book has defined survival migrants as persons who are outside their country of origin because of an existential threat to which they have no access to a domestic remedy or resolution. It suggests that the concept might be grounded in the ethical notion of basic rights or in international human rights law as a way of defining those in need of asylum and international protection on the basis of a threshold of rights rather than on the arbitrary basis of particular causes of displacement.

From Refugees to Survival Migration

The exact line between refugees and other survival migrants is blurred by the fact that the refugee in international law is an evolving concept that is subject to jurisprudence and the interpretation of law. Nevertheless, a clear area of analytical separation lies in the distinction between people whose reason for flight is based on persecution and those for whom it is based on deprivation. For Matthew Price (2009), a refugee is and should be someone fleeing persecution. He argues this on the basis that persecution indicates a severance of the assumed link between state and citizen, and so requires a form of surrogate protection in another state— albeit one that might be temporary. For Price, there is a difference between people fleeing violations and those fleeing deprivations, those fleeing the targeted acts of states and those fleeing the omissions of states, and those fleeing a lack of civil and political rights and those fleeing a lack of socioeconomic rights. This distinction highlights the analytical line between refugees and survival migrants.

This book has argued, contra Price, that to privilege protection of those fleeing targeted acts of the state over and above those fleeing omissions of the state is normatively arbitrary. Whether a certain set of basic rights is unavailable to an individual because of the targeted acts of the state or because of the unwillingness or inability of the state to ensure a certain minimum threshold of rights does not make a difference to the affected individual. If a state is unable or unwilling to provide that basic threshold of rights, then the same severance in the assumed state-citizen relationship takes place, the state fails to protect basic rights, and there is an equal need for substitute protection.

International law has partly adapted to protect survival migrants who are fleeing rights deprivations rather than persecution. Complementary protection standards, derived from both regional instruments and international human rights law, recognize that some rights deprivations resulting from a state's unwillingness and inability to ensure fundamental rights may sometimes justify asylum (McAdam 2007). However, unlike for refugees fleeing persecution, there is far more legal ambiguity and state variation in responses to survival migrants fleeing basic rights deprivations resulting from states' unwillingness and inability to protect.

Flight from fragile and failed states most starkly illustrates the differences in response. Across the world, states with weak governance from Haiti to Libya to Afghanistan are unable to ensure the basic rights of their citizens. In Africa, the states of Zimbabwe, the Democratic Republic of Congo, and Somalia represent three of the most fragile in the world. The majority of people fleeing these states are not fleeing persecution and so do not easily fit the dominant definition of who is a refugee under the 1951 Refugee Convention. Most have instead been fleeing extreme socioeconomic deprivations. These deprivations have been the result of the breakdown of the state and its unwillingness or inability to mitigate a range of threats to human security.

Reflecting ambiguity in international law, there has been significant variation in national and international responses to survival migrants fleeing basic rights deprivations in fragile and failed states. The responses in the six case studies explored in this book have varied along a spectrum. Although none of the responses has been ideal, and every case illustrates significant weaknesses in the protection of survival migrants, they nevertheless show considerable variation. At one end of the spectrum, the national regimes in Kenya and Tanzania have stretched to provide protection to survival migrants. At the opposite end of the spectrum, Botswana and Angola have rounded up, detained, and deported survival migrants. In between, Yemen and South Africa have, to different degrees, partly stretched their national refugee regimes to offer some protection to survival migrants but on an inadequate and inconsistent basis. In each case, the international response has largely followed that of the national government, and UNHCR has become involved in protection only to the extent that the government's position has placed people within the orbit of the organization's refugee protection mandate.

Explaining Variation in National Responses

In addition to illustrating the range of institutional responses and their human consequences, the book has attempted to explain the politics underlying this variation. Its central argument is that when international law has been imprecise or ambiguous, national politics has determined what international law actually means in practice. Insofar as international law enables discretion, politics defines what happens in the translation from global to national to local levels. In the refugee context, while states' obligations to refugees fleeing persecution have been relatively clear, their obligations toward other survival migrants has been far more ambiguous, and so politics has shaped variation in whether and to what extent national refugee regimes have stretched (or not) beyond their primary purpose of protecting those fleeing persecution.

The concept of regime stretching sheds light on this process. It illustrates how an international regime, comprising both norms and international organizations, created at a particular juncture of history and for a particular purpose, may sometimes adapt to new circumstances at the national level. In the refugee context, the regime, created primarily to protect people fleeing persecution, has stretched to protect survival migrants when it has been in the interests of elites in the national government. Where domestic or international incentives have made stretching the national regime in the interests of elites, the regime has stretched. Where domestic or international incentives have been against a more expansive interpretation of refugee protection, survival migrants have lacked protection and sometimes been subject to deportation.

In other words, there has been a separate national politics of international institutions, defining what international norms and international organizations actually do in practice. In the six cases examined in the book, government elites have responded to domestic and international incentives. Where elites have had positive incentives, regime stretching has taken place; where there have been negative incentives, the national regime has taken a more restrictive interpretation of international law. The kinds of incentives that have mattered at the domestic level have included public opinion, electoral politics, the role of civil society, and business interests. At the international level, incentives have come from international financial assistance and the importance of international legitimacy.

In addition to explaining variation across the cases, changes in domestic and international incentives account for temporal shifts in the cases such as Somalia's increasingly exclusionary policies in 2011, South Africa's temporary introduction of a moratorium for Zimbabweans in 2009, Yemen's gradual move toward more exclusionary policies, and Angola's fluctuations in methods of deportation between 2003 and 2009.

Revisiting Alternative Explanations

In order to substantiate this interest-driven account of institutional variation and adaptation, the book set up three alternative explanations for variation in regime stretching. Each of these has mattered, but not to the same extent as the role of elite interests within government.

The first alternative explanation was that variation in regime stretching is caused by variation in institutionalization. However, all six of the case countries have had similar levels of institutionalization of the core refugee instruments, with only some degree of variation. All six are signatories of the 1951 convention and its 1967 protocol, and all allow UNHCR to operate on their territory. All the African states except Botswana have signed and ratified the OAU convention. The only outliers in terms of institutionalization are Kenya, as the only one of the states that uniformly and consistently applies the OAU convention in its response to Somalis, and Yemen and Botswana, as the only states that are not signatories to the OAU convention. Yet the fact that Kenya and Yemen have both offered prima facie recognition to Somali survival migrants suggests that this outlying variation in institutionalization is insufficient for explaining variation in responses. Rather, even given constant institutionalization, there is variation in how international institutions play out in practice. This can be understood only by recognizing implementation as an additional phase at which norms and international organizations are contested at the national level.

The second alternative explanation was that the role of international organizations accounts for the variation in regime stretching. Yet in each of the cases UNHCR's role in influencing variation in response appears to have been negligible. Rather than influence states' response, UNHCR has mainly followed or mirrored state choices. Where states have sought an expanded role for UNHCR, it has obliged. But where states have sought to exclude survival migrants from refugee protection, UNHCR has generally followed. In some states, UNHCR has been more influential than in others: in less-developed states in which authority has been centralized, such as Kenya, UNHCR appears to have had some influence on the government's willingness to refrain from deporting Somalis during the famine and drought of 2011. Yet even in Kenya, where elite preferences have been sufficiently strong, they have gradually outweighed UNHCR's influence. For example, the government's decisions to keep the border closed and to seek ways to develop an internal flight alternative for Somalis in south-central Somalia have been in defiance of UNHCR recommendations.

In the middle-income countries of Botswana, South Africa, Angola, and Yemen, UNHCR's leverage over governments has been extremely limited. Its ability to influence host states' policies toward particular populations of survival migrants has been constrained by its need to maintain good relations with the government in order to preserve protection for other populations, such as refugees fleeing persecution or internally displaced persons. These trade-offs have been especially evident in South Africa, Yemen, and Botswana, where UNHCR has been compromised by its desire to preserve protection space for other groups and so has been largely silent on, for example, Yemen's treatment of Ethiopians, Botswana's treatment of Zimbabweans, and South Africa's response to Zimbabweans. Where UNHCR has spoken out against a state, it has risked being sanctioned, as Botswana's expulsion of the UNHCR representative in 2009 illustrates. In that sense, it appears that the role of the international organization has been epiphenomenal in explaining variation in how the refugee regime has been implemented at the national level. National politics rather than international organizations defines what regimes do at the level of implementation.

The third alternative explanation for variation in regime stretching has been the importance of national context and political and legal culture. Variation in legal culture does not seem to have mattered, however, because across all six cases there have been similar levels of institutionalization of international norms. Instead, it has been politics and bureaucratic decision making and not the courts that have influenced access to asylum. Unlike, for example, Europe, none of the countries in these cases has been significantly influenced by domestic or regional jurisprudence. However, there is some evidence that regime type is important. The cases exhibit some variation in being authoritarian or democratic and in being less-developed or middle-income countries. As an authoritarian state, Yemen would have been more insulated from electoral politics than the other, procedurally democratic states, in which the immigration issue was key in elections. Yet even so, diverging public opinions about Somalis and Ethiopians have shaped responses. The less-developed countries of Kenya and Tanzania have been more receptive to certain international incentives relating to legitimacy and development assistance, whereas the middle-income countries have been more insulated from international carrots and sticks. However, this variation in national context seems to matter only insofar as it changes the incentives to which elites in government are responsive, rather than as an explanation that challenges the centrality of elite interests for explaining variation in national response.

Implications for Theories of Global Governance

Beyond the context of survival migration, the analysis has implications for how we understand global governance more broadly. In contrast to a significant proportion of the literature in international relations, the book shows that international institutions do not exist just as abstract entities based in Geneva or New York. Instead, they need to be understood as having national and local manifestations that potentially diverge and deviate from the global context. While the insight that international institutions have different national and local manifestations is not new (see Acharya 2004; Autesserre 2006; Busby 2007; Cortell and Davis 2000; Schmidt 2006; Stone Sweet, Sandholtz, and Fligstein 2001; Wiener 2009, 2010), this is one of the first books to systematically examine the processes of how international institutions adapt at the national level within a comparative, multicountry framework.

International institutions—norms and international organizations—can adapt (and vary) at three different levels: international bargaining, institutionalization, and implementation. The book has empirically shown how, even with constant international bargaining and constant institutionalization, both norms and international organizations can and do adapt and vary at the level of implementation. In other words, there is a distinct national politics of international institutions at which both norms and international organizations may be recontested.

This insight may help researchers in international relations to better understand processes of adaptation in international institutions. Temporally, it shows how institutions may adapt over time at any one of these levels—international bargaining, institutionalization, and implementation—independently of the other. Spatially, it highlights how there may be variation in adaptation across states. Even given constant international institutions and states with the same institutionalization of international norms, there may nevertheless be significant variation in what actually happens in practice. We can understand these temporal and spatial variations only by looking at the level of implementation.

This matters for theory because it fundamentally challenges the view of global governance implicit to a great deal of international relations literature as something "global" and "static." Instead, global governance is inherently based on different levels of governance that adapt dynamically and interact with one another over time. While this book has looked mainly at the linear way in which implementation follows from international bargaining and institutionalization, it hints at the importance of understanding two-directional feedbacks from implementation back up to institutionalization and international bargaining (Legro 2005). Indeed, some of the national debates relating to the challenges of survival migration at the national level appear to have fed back up to policy debates at the global level. One analytical question that follows from this observation is, at what point do recurring, unforeseen challenges to a regime at the national level lead to fundamental reassessment at the global level?

These insights speak back to the constructivist international relations literature on international norms. The analysis highlights the need to consider implementation as an additional fourth stage in Finnemore and Sikkink (1998)'s highly influential norm life cycle model. Their ground-breaking model captures the way in which norms emerge, cascade, and are internalized by states. It shows the process of institutionalization. However, it implicitly assumes that the story ends at that stage. Yet as this book has shown, states with the same levels of institutionalization of international norms can exhibit significant variation in practice, which we can explain only by turning to the level of implementation. The findings do not in any way discredit Finnemore and Sikkink's model, but they imply the need for an additional stage if we are to trace how norms actually influence practice.[1]

The analysis also offers insights into how we understand international organizations (IOs). Until now, most international relations scholarship on IOs has looked at them as predominantly global actors. In contrast, the national politics of IOs and relations between headquarters and the field have rarely been integrated into theoretical analysis. This book highlights why this distinction matters. While international relations literature has consistently shown that international organizations—including UNHCR—can exert autonomous influence on world politics, these studies have rarely drawn a distinction between the degrees and types of influence that IOs have on politics at different levels (Barnett and Finnemore 2004). UNHCR has been shown to have autonomous influence on states at the levels of institutional bargaining or institutionalization (Betts 2009; Loescher 2001), but it appears to have been largely epiphenomenal at the level of implementation across the six country cases. Although this insight cannot be generalized for UNHCR, let alone for all IOs, it nevertheless points to the need to consider the influence of IOs on states differently across international bargaining, institutionalization, and implementation.

Implications for the Practice of Global Governance

In addition to theory, the insights of the book have implications for the global refugee regime, global migration governance, and international public policy-makers more generally.

First, the analysis poses fundamental questions about who in the contemporary world should be permitted to cross an international border on human rights grounds. On the one hand, who should be granted asylum or temporary protection? On the other hand, who is it legitimate for states to detain and deport? At the moment, there is international consensus around the imperative to protect refugees fleeing persecution by states. However, there is far less consensus on whether and how to protect people fleeing fundamental human rights deprivations resulting from the inability or unwillingness of states to ensure those rights.

In a world in which new threats to human security are emerging from environmental change, food insecurity, and generalized violence, it is imperative to have a clear and principled basis on which to determine who should have the right to flee across a border. At the moment, politics rather than principle determines the conditions under which millions of people leaving desperate situations in failed and fragile states get access to international protection. As the cases in this book show, that patchy and inconsistent response has major implications for both human rights and international security.

Some degree of adaptation can take place at the level of implementation. Occasionally, faced with the right sets of national and international incentives, governments will be prepared to expand protection to people who fall outside the core 1951 convention definition of a refugee. Similarly, there is scope for adaptation at the level of institutionalization. In the African context, if existing refugee protection instruments such as the OAU convention had been more systematically institutionalized within domestic legal and policy frameworks, some of the protection gaps might have been filled. However, even though much can be done on these levels, providing universal protection coverage for people running for their lives will inevitably require major rethinking at the global level.

If and when states and international public policymakers consider reforming the global refugee regime, reformers should not make the mistake of focusing on particular causes of displacement such as climate change or environmental migration. In discussions about institutional responses to cross-border displacement, to focus on particular causes of movement in isolation from one another would risk replicating the arbitrariness and exclusions of the status quo. Instead, the only nonarbitrary basis on which to allocate asylum or temporary protection is to consider not causes but the underlying threshold of human rights which when unavailable in a country of origin necessitates asylum or temporary protection.

Second, the challenge of how to allocate asylum in a changing world represents just one part of the broader question of global migration governance. Even beyond the global refugee regime and UNHCR, the international community faces the challenge of how to develop international institutional mechanisms to better ensure the protection of vulnerable migrants. The mechanisms for ensuring the protection of international migrants who fall outside the refugee framework represent one of the weakest parts of the international human rights system. While in theory all migrants have human rights as human beings, in practice those who fall outside the asylum system often face rights violations at the hands of host states.

Part of the problem is that irregular migrants are often the least able to access human rights mechanisms at the domestic or the international level. They are in an inherently vulnerable position. Yet, at the international level, they fall between the mandates of different organizations. Too often, as this book has shown, they fall outside the refugee protection mandate of UNHCR. OHCHR, as the organization responsible for human rights, has limited operational capacity or expertise on migration. IOM, which frequently works on the protection of migrant rights, lacks a clear and consistent migrant protection mandate. At the moment, the lack of coherence across international organizations means that in practice many vulnerable irregular migrants are reliant on hidden protection actors such as faith-based humanitarian organizations or the networks of such organizations as Médecins Sans Frontières and the national Red Cross societies to fill gaps.

Survival migration draws attention not only to the question of who should be entitled to asylum but also to the broader issue of how to ensure the human rights of even those who are—and in some cases should be—outside the asylum system. It is important to build better mechanisms not just to ensure that the right to *non-refoulement* is upheld but also to ensure that migrants who are not in need of its protection have their other human rights respected. In other words, even if the line of who gets access to asylum or temporary protection is redrawn, it does not and should not justify human rights violations against those who are judged to be on the wrong side of that line.

Third, the analysis arguably also has broader insights for the general practice of global governance. It highlights the need for international public policymakers in general to think differently about processes of institutional reform. The conceptual framework developed and applied in this book shows how when new challenges arise, old institutions may adapt. Understanding that institutional adaptation and change can take place across at least three different levels—international bargaining, institutionalization, and implementation—potentially allows international public policymakers to make existing institutions work better, even when wholesale reform at the global level may not be immediately possible. In a world that is changing more rapidly than its international institutions, understanding these causal mechanisms may allow global governance to adapt better to emerging challenges.

Notes

INTRODUCTION

1. The international refugee regime has a history that precedes the United Nations system, most notably with the development of the League of Nations High Commissioner for Refugees (LNHCR) during the interwar years (Haddad 2008; Loescher 2001; Skran 1995).

2. It should be noted that states' practices on asylum, even toward those fleeing persecution, also vary enormously, although not to the same extent as for those fleeing serious human rights deprivations. Ramji-Nogales, Schoenholtz, and Schrag (2009) have developed the term "refugee roulette" to describe this inconsistency even in asylum decisions relating to persecution.

3. Michelle Foster (2009, 236–90) has also highlighted that, under certain conditions, some forms of deprivation might also be interpreted as persecution and hence be grounds for protection under the 1951 convention.

CHAPTER 1

1. This definition is the Inter-Agency Standing Committee (IASC)'s working definition of "protection." See, for example, IASC, "IASC Operational Guidelines on the Protection of Persons in Situations of Natural Disaster" (Geneva: IASC), 5.

2. The logic is exemplified by the international community's development of the Responsibility-to-Protect (R2P). For an elaboration of R2P and its relevance to refugee protection, see Martin 2010.

3. This definition is found in Article 1(A) of the 1951 Convention Relating to the Status of Refugees (Goodwin-Gill and McAdam 2007, 573).

4. See Article 1(2) of the 1969 OAU Convention Governing the Specific Aspects of Refugee Problems in Africa.

5. See Conclusion 3 of the 1984 Cartagena Declaration on Refugees.

6. See Article 15 of the *Council Directive 2004/83/EC of 29 April 2004 on Minimum Standards for the Qualification and Status of Third Country Nationals or Stateless Persons as Refugees or as Persons Who Otherwise Need International Protection and the Content of the Protection Granted*, 19 May 2004, 2004/83/EC.

7. For an overview of complementary protection standards, see McAdam 2007, 2011.

8. The decision in *R. (Adam, Limbuela and Tesema) v. Home Secretary* [2005] UKHL 66 provides a good example of the application of ECHR to cover economic and social rights. In that matter, the House of Lords held that an asylum applicant was subject to inhuman or degrading treatment when he was left without any support from the state because he failed to apply for asylum in the prescribed time period. Lord Bingham (paras. 7–8) held: "A general public duty to house the homeless or to provide for the destitute cannot be spelled out of article 3. But I have no doubt that the threshold may be crossed if a late applicant with no means and no alternative sources of support, unable to support himself, is, by the deliberate action of the state, denied shelter, food or the most basic necessities of life. . . . When does the Secretary of State's duty . . . arise? The answer must in my opinion be: when it appears on a fair and objective assessment of all the relevant facts and circumstances that an individual applicant faces an imminent prospect of

serious suffering caused or materially aggravated by denial of shelter, food or the most basic necessities of life."

9. In 2010, for example, UNHCR (2010) claimed that "displacement scenarios continue to evolve.... The drivers appearing today include population growth, urbanization, governance failures, food and energy insecurity, water scarcity, natural disasters, climate change and the impact of the international economic crisis and recession."

10. Numerous intergovernmental initiatives have begun to look at environmental migration and displacement. Paragraph 14(f) of the Cancun Adaptation Framework adopted in 2010 in the context of the UN Framework Convention on Climate Change identifies migration as a climate change adaptation strategy. In February 2011, UNHCR convened the Bellagio Expert Meeting on Climate Change and Displacement, recognizing that "displacement is likely to be a significant consequence of global climate change." In June 2011 the Nansen Conference on Climate Change and Displacement adopted ten principles to guide future responses. Since the end of 2012, the Nansen Initiative represents an intergovernmental process that is examining cross-border displacement in the context of natural disasters.

11. Even the U.K. government's (2011) Foresight report on environmental migration recognizes within its conceptual framework that governance is one of the most important intervening variables determining how environmental change affects migration.

12. This term was used, for example, by UNHCR in the context of the International Conference on Refugees in Central America (CIREFCA) in the 1980s and 1990s.

13. The idea of survival migration is not entirely new, and has been used in different contexts such as Oded Stark and Edward Taylor's (e.g., 1989) work on the "new economics of migration," in which they see migration as part of a household "survival strategy." However, this book's application of the concept to institutional questions of response to externally displaced people is new.

14. It is worth noting that this definition is not necessarily hugely expansive and need not necessarily imply permanent protection. Rather, it is intended to highlight the situations in which a fundamental set of rights is simply unavailable within the country of origin and can be sought only in another country—but in a way that does not arbitrarily exclude certain types of rights violations.

15. Adapted from Trygve G. Nordby, IFRC Special Envoy on Migration, Keynote Speech, High Commissioner's Dialogue on Protection Challenges, Geneva, December 11–12, 2007.

2. NATIONAL POLITICS OF INTERNATIONAL INSTITUTIONS

1. The concept of implementation has been explored—implicitly or explicitly—in international relations in the work of Sandholtz and Stiles 2008; Deere-Birkbeck 2008; Wiener 2009; Victor, Raustiala, and Skolnikoff 2008; and Schmidt 2006. However, this work still requires conceptual development.

2. The decision to frame the independent variable as the interests of national elites rather than the state is based on the recognition that in many states—including those examined in this chapter—the interests of the actors within government may not be in any way representative of a wider national interest. See, for example, the work of Ayoob 1995; Clapham 1996; Jackson 1990; Lemke 2002; and Olson 2000 for a discussion of the distinction between the interests of the state as an actor and the national elites in government.

3. Stephen Krasner—author of the original regime definition—acknowledges in conversation (2010) that seeing regimes as having norms and international organizations makes more sense, especially in empirical application. Other authors, such as Gary Goertz, have also argued for a more minimalist concept of a regime. Goertz (2003, 19) states that "for my purposes, norms, principles, decision-making procedures, and rules can be seen

as synonymous," arguing that the logical form of these norms is broadly reducible to the idea of a norm (as a single standard of behavior)—although it may be useful to distinguish between those norms that define action and those that define organizational procedures.

4. These categories broadly follow Ostrom (1990), who has three levels of analysis—constitutional, directive, and operational—in looking at collective action.

5. Finnemore and Sikkink (1998, 893) accord a role to the domestic level, noting that "international norms must always work their influence through the filter of domestic structures and domestic norms, which can produce important variations in compliance and interpretation of these norms." However, they argue that domestic influences "are strongest at the early stages" and that these "lessen significantly once a norm has become institutionalized in the international system."

6. All the states are subject to the same broad global refugee regime.

7. All the states have signed and ratified the 1951 Convention on the Status of Refugees and its 1967 protocol, and have incorporated them within their legislative and/or administrative frameworks on refugees. In addition, all the states except Botswana and Yemen have signed and ratified the 1969 OAU Refugee Convention.

8. Interview with Alex Tyler, Protection Officer, UNHCR Somalia, Nairobi, May 15, 2009.

9. Interview with Peter Klansoe, Regional Director, Danish Refugee Council, Nairobi, May 14, 2009.

10. Interviews with UNHCR Community Service partners in Eastleigh Estate, Nairobi, May 18, 2009.

11. Interview with Geoffrey Carliez, UNHCR Assistant External Relations Officer, Kigoma, Tanzania, September 16, 2009.

12. Interview with Hans Hartmark, Protection Officer, UNHCR, Kigoma, September 15, 2009; interview with Mr. Chuleha, Assistant Zonal Coordinator, Department of Refugee Affairs, Kigoma, September 15, 2009.

13. Interview with Chuleha.

14. Interview with Hartmark.

15. Interview with Kazuhiro Kaneko, Head of Field Office, UNHCR Kasulu, September 16, 2009.

16. Interview with Jerome Seregni, Mass Information Officer, UNHCR Field Office Kasulu, September 16, 2009.

17. Interview with Kaneko.

18. Interview with Florencia Belvedere, Department of Home Affairs, Johannesburg, April 1, 2009.

19. Interview with Kajaal Ramjathan-Keogh, Head of Refugee and Migrant Rights Programme, Lawyers for Human Rights (LHR), Johannesburg, March 18, 2009.

20. For a history of Zimbabwe, see Meredith 2002; interview with Ambassador Simon K. Moyo, Zimbabwe House, Pretoria, March 30, 2009.

21. Interview with Gelafele Beleme, UNHCR Botswana, Gaborone, March 28, 2009.

22. Interview with Alice Mogwe, Director of Ditshwanelo, Gaborone, March 25, 2009.

23. Interview with Beleme.

24. Ibid.

25. Interview with Marcus Betts, Deputy Representative to Botswana, UNICEF, Gaborone, March 25, 2009.

26. Interview with Fabienne de Laval, Deputy Director, MSF-B, October 1, 2009; interview with Helene Lorinquer, Coordinator of the Analysis and Advocacy Unit, MSF-B, in 2007, October 1, 2009.

27. Interview with Emanuel Lampeart, Medical Focal Point, Pool d'Urgence Congo (PUC), MSF-B, Kinshasa, November 3, 2009.

28. Again, this is drawing on the definition of institutionalization set out above, which is implicit to Finnemore and Sikkink (1998).

29. Interview with Betina Gollander-Jensen, Counselor, Danish Embassy to Kenya, Nairobi, May 19, 2009.

30. Interview with Carliez.

31. Ibid.

32. Interview with Hartmark.

33. Interview with Lily Sanya, International Organization for Migration Technical Advisor to Intergovernmental Authority on Development (IGAD), Djibouti City, May 26, 2009.

34. See Mixed Migration Task Force website for details: http://www.mmyemen.org/.

35. Interview with Moyo.

36. Interview with Advocate D. Mashabane and Andries Ousthuizen, Humanitarian Affairs, Department of Foreign Affairs, Pretoria, March 18, 2009.

37. Interview with G. Burton Joseph, Director of Immigration Policy, Department of Home Affairs, Pretoria, March 19, 2009.

38. Interview with Sanda Kimbimbi, Regional Representative, UNHCR, Pretoria, March 17, 2009.

39. Correspondence with Roy Hermann, former UNHCR Representative to Botswana; interview with Khin-Sandi Lwin, Representative (and UN Resident Coordinator), United Nations Development Programme (UNDP), March 24, 2009.

40. Interview with Mogwe.

41. Ibid.

42. Interview with Mohamed Toure, Assistant Regional Representative, UNHCR, Kinshasa, November 11, 2009.

43. Furthermore, there are sound reasons to suggest that the African cases are more likely to be representative than Barnett and Finnemore's (2004) own case. Barnett and Finnemore look at Burmese Rohingas in the Asian context, an exceptional case because it relates to a situation in which the host state is not a signatory of the 1951 convention and hence refugee status determination is fully devolved to UNHCR.

44. In April and May 2009, in response to increasing international pressure, the government of South Africa announced a series of policy measures to increase protection to the Zimbabweans, most notably suspending deportations.

45. In February 2007, following the release of an MSF document published at simultaneous press conferences in Brussels, Johannesburg, and Kinshasa, the government of Angola reduced the levels of brutality in its subsequent deportations.

46. In Yemen, in response to growing domestic xenophobia and international pressure to address onward migration to Europe, there has been an increasingly restrictive policy response since 2009.

3. SOUTH AFRICA

1. Interview with Kajaal Ramjathan-Keogh, Head of Refugee and Migrant Rights Programme, Lawyers for Human Rights (LHR), Johannesburg, March 18, 2009.

2. For a history of Zimbabwe, see Meredith 2002.

3. Interview with Ambassador Simon K. Moyo, Zimbabwe House, Pretoria, March 30, 2009.

4. *The Times*, "From Africa's bread basket to economic basket case, life in Mugabe's Zimbabwe," May 15, 2007, http://business.timesonline.co.uk/tol/business/markets/africa/article1790223.ece.

5. *The Economist*, "Zimbabwe: Please Do Something—But What?" December 11, 2008, http://www.economist.com/node/12773105.

6. Interview with Moyo.

7. Interview with Florencia Belvedere, Department of Home Affairs, Johannesburg, April 1, 2009.

8. Ibid.

9. Ibid.

10. Interview with Florencia Belvedere, Department of Home Affairs, Johannesburg, March 30, 2009.

11. Interview with Sabelo Sibanda, Lawyers for Human Rights, Musina, April 3, 2009; interviews with Zimbabwean migrants, Musina, April 3, 2009.

12. Interview with Sibanda.

13. Interviews with Zimbabwean migrants in Musina.

14. Based on a visit to the Central Methodist Church, Johannesburg, April 1, 2009.

15. Interviews with Zimbabwean migrants, Central Methodist Church, Johannesburg, April 1, 2009.

16. Interview with Belvedere.

17. Interview with Sanda Kimbimbi, Regional Representative, UNHCR, Pretoria, March 17, 2009.

18. Interview with Mohammed Hasan, International Organization for Migration, Musina, April 3, 2009.

19. Interview with Mandisa Kalako-Williams, President, South African Red Cross (SARC), Pretoria, March 31, 2009; interview with Kyetsta Nara and John Shiburi, SARC, Polokwane, April 3, 2009.

20. Interview with G. Burton Joseph, Director of Immigration Policy, Department of Home Affairs, Pretoria, March 19, 2009.

21. Interview with Mahlomola Skhosana, Executive Manager, International Relations, Africa Desk, Department of Labour, Pretoria, March 19, 2009.

22. Interview with Advocate Doctor Mashabane, Director of Humanitarian Affairs, Department of Foreign Affairs, Pretoria, March 18, 2009.

23. Interview with Ramjathan-Keogh.

24. Interview with Peter, twenty-three-year-old white restaurant manager, Johannesburg.

25. Interview with Kimbimbi.

26. Interview with NGO staff member working on the protection of Zimbabweans in South Africa.

4. BOTSWANA

1. Interview with Alice Mogwe, Director of Ditshwanelo, Gaborone, March 25, 2009.

2. Interview with Mary Ratau, Ditshwanelo, Gaborone, March 25, 2009.

3. Ibid.

4. Ibid.

5. Interview with Gelafele Beleme, UNHCR Botswana, Gaborone, March 28, 2009; interview with Khin-Sandi Lwin, Representative (and UN Resident Coordinator), United Nations Development Programme (UNDP), Gaborone, March 24, 2009; interview with Marcus Betts, Deputy Representative to Botswana, UNICEF, Gaborone, March 25, 2009.

6. Barnaby Phillips, "Zimbabwe Crisis Spills over Border," BBC News, March 30, 2004, http://news.bbc.co.uk/1/hi/world/africa/3582459.stm.

7. Interview with Beleme.

8. Interview with Ratau.

9. Interview with Monica Kiwanuka, University of the Witwatersrand, Johannesburg, March 17, 2009.

10. In 2009, there was an effort by some non-UN groups to institute the private treatment of HIV-positive migrants, though it was expected that they would have difficulty getting government approval. They wanted to provide Prevention of Mother to Child Transmission (PMTCT) to all pregnant HIV-positive mothers, legal or illegal. Personal correspondence with Roy Hermann, UNHCR Representative to Botswana, May 25, 2009.

11. Interview with Mogwe.

12. Interview with Betts.

13. This is based on UNHCR statistics of the number of refugees and the proportion that are children. However, extrapolation from the refugee population to the undocumented migrant population is problematic because the proportion of children may be higher in the refugee population, whereas undocumented migrants may be more likely to be individuals seeking employment than families.

14. "World's Barriers: Botswana-Zimbabwe," BBC News, November 5, 2009, http://news.bbc.co.uk/1/hi/world/africa/8343505.stm.

15. Interview with Beleme.

16. Ibid.

17. Quote from the vice president of Botswana in May 2009. Information provided by Roy Hermann, UNHCR Representative, Gaborone, personal correspondence, May 25, 2009.

18. Interview with Samuel Chakwera, Senior Desk Officer, Southern Africa Operations, UNHCR, Geneva, January 19, 2012.

19. The total number of forcibly returned people assisted by IOM at the Plumtree Reception and Support Centre between 2008 and April 2012 is 150,151. Between January and April 2012, the number was 5,448. E-mail correspondence with Natalia Perez y Andersen, Acting Chief of Mission, IOM Harare, Zimbabwe.

20. Interview with Mogwe.

21. Interview with Beleme.

22. Ibid.

23. Information provided by Hermann, May 25, 2009.

24. Interview with Betts.

25. Interview with Ratau.

26. Interview with Chakwera.

27. Ibid.

28. Interview with Mogwe.

29. Interview with UNHCR staff member.

30. Conversation with national staff member of a UN organization.

31. Interview with Lwin.

32. Ibid.

33. Interview with Beleme.

34. Interview with Chakwera.

35. Interview with Beleme.

36. Interview with Chakwera.

37. Interview with Lwin.

5. ANGOLA

1. UN, "Rapport de la mission inter-agences d'évaluation des besoins humanitaires des populations des 2ZS du territoire de Kahemba," September 2007.

2. Interview with doctor, MSF, Kinshasa, November 9, 2009.

3. Médecins Sans Frontières, PUC Internal Document, November 2007.

4. Concession holders, in turn, have delegated these powers to private security firms. The three principal firms all have strong connections to the Angolan security establish-

ment. (1) K&P, founded in 2002, boasts among its six owners four senior officers of the Angolan National Police, including the general commander, Commissar José Alfredo. (2) Among its eight owners, Teleservice counts six FAA generals, two of them former chiefs of staff. (3) Alfa-5 is 30 percent owned by Endiama and also counts active generals and close relatives of the general staff among its owners. See Partnership Africa-Canada 2007.

5. Médecins Sans Frontières–Belgium, PUC Internal Document, November 2007."

6. Médecins Sans Frontières–Belgium, "Refoules d'Angola: Résumé des datas a ce jour," April 27, 2004, internal document.

7. "Congo miners 'tortured' in Angola," BBC News, April 22, 2004, http://news.bbc.co.uk/1/hi/3650655.stm; "Angolan Troops Reportedly Kill Congolese Miners," Reuters, April 22, 2004, www.queensu.ca/samp/migrationnews/2004/apr.htm#Angola.

8. Response by MSF to editorial April 30 comment, May 12, 2004.

9. Luis Raya, OCHA Mexico, to Paola Carosi, OCHA Angola, "Missao de accompanhemento de 'Operacao Brilhante,' nas provincias de Lunda Sul e Lunda Norte," May 18, 2004.

10. Médecins Sans Frontières–Belgium, "Refoules d'Angola."

11. Document on file with the author.

12. Interview with Brice de la Vigne, head of PUC in 2007, Médecins Sans Frontières–Belgium, Brussels, October 1, 2009.

13. See also Médecins Sans Frontières–Belgium, "PUC Memo."

14. Interview with Fabienne de Laval, Deputy Director, Médecins Sans Frontières–Belgium, Brussels, October 10, 2010. She was the head of mission in the DRC at the time and gave the press conference in Kinshasa on December 5.

15. Ibid.

16. Office of the High Commissioner for Human Rights, Speech delivered to mark the 59th anniversary of the UDHR, OHCHR Angola Office, Luanda, December 10, 2007.

17. Interview with Helene Lorinquer, Coordinator of the Analysis and Advocacy Unit, Médecins Sans Frontières–Belgium, October 1, 2009.

18. Médecins Sans Frontières–Belgium, Pool d'Urgence Congo (PUC), May 30, 2008.

19. Ibid.

20. See also Médecins Sans Frontières–Belgium, "PUC: Draft Mission Explo Refoules d'Angola a Kahungula," June 5, 2008.

21. Ibid.

22. UN, "Draft rapport de mission inter-agences d'évaluation de la situation des congolais expuses d'Angola dans le territoire de Luiza, province du Kasai Occidental, 5–10 Juillet 2008."

23. Interview with Mohamed Toure, Assistant Regional Representative, UNHCR, Kinshasa, November 11, 2009.

24. Interview with Ebba Kalondo, Deputy Head, F24/RFI Africa Service, Kinshasa, November 9, 2009.

25. On file with the author.

26. Interview with Toure.

27. Interview with Aurelie Ponthieu, Humanitarian Adviser on Displacement, Médecins Sans Frontières–Belgium, Brussels, July 12, 2012.

28. The GoA introduced administrative and legislative reforms in 2011 to strengthen its control over immigration: Presidential Decree No. 108/11 of 25 May on the Legal Framework Relating to Foreigners, and Law No. 2/07 of 31 August on the Legal Framework Relating to Foreigners on the Territory of Angola.

29. The majority of the victims of violence have been returned to Western Kasai; twothirds of the victims are in the Kamako zone of Tshikapa, most arriving at Kandjaji and Kamako. Interview with Ponthieu.

30. CISP database, as of May 8, 2012, on file with the author.

31. Interviewed by MSF in May 2012. Médecins Sans Frontières–Belgium, "Rapport de visite—Support AAU a la Mission Exploratoire Frontière RDC/Angola" (internal document), 2012.

32. Interview with Ponthieu.

33. Anonymous statement, Office for the Coordination of Humanitarian Affairs, Kinshasa, November 2009.

34. Interview with Felly Ntumba, Office for the Coordination of Humanitarian Affairs, Kinshasa, November 14, 2009.

35. Interview with Kalondo.

36. Interviews with three members of OCHA staff in Kinshasa, November 2009.

37. UN News Centre, "DR Congo Mass Rape Verdicts Send Strong Signal to Perpetrators—UN Envoy," February 21, 2011, http://www.un.org/apps/news/story. asp?NewsID=37580&Cr=sexual#.UHiX7a4U6uI.

38. Interview with Ponthieu.

39. Ibid.

40. Médecins Sans Frontières–Belgium, "Rapport de Visite."

41. Ibid.

6. TANZANIA

1. Tanzania is composed of twenty-six administrative units called *mikoa*, meaning regions or provinces. Each of these units is further divided into various districts. This chapter uses the word "region" to refer to the administrative province of Kigoma.

2. Although the peace process was undertaken in several steps, the inauguration of the transitional government on June 30, 2006, is widely agreed to mark the end of the war and the beginning of the postconflict phase (see Reyntjens 2007, 310).

3. "The Silent Cost of Child Malnutrition in the Democratic Republic of the Congo," *Guardian*, http://www.guardian.co.uk/global-development/poverty-matters/2012/feb/15/silent-cost-child-malnutrition-congo.

4. Interview with Fatima Sherif-Nor, Head of Sub-Office, Kigoma, September 25, 2009.

5. Interviews with Congolese refugees in Nyargusu refugee camp, Kigoma, Tanzania, September 16, 2009.

6. A more alarmist estimate of forty-eight rapes per day is cited by the *Guardian*: Joe Adentunji, "Forty-Eight Women Raped Every Hour in Congo, Study Finds," *Guardian*, May 12, 2011, http://www.guardian.co.uk/world/2011/may/12/48-women-raped-hour-congo.

7. IRIN, "DRC: Treating the Sexually Abused in South Kivu," March 5, 2009, http://www.irinnews.org/Report/83321/DRC-Treating-the-sexually-abused-in-South-Kivu.

8. Interview with Chris Tomlinson, journalist, University of Texas at Austin, November 26, 2010.

9. Interview with Professor Bonaventure Rutinwa, University of Dar es Salaam, Dar es Salaam, September 11, 2009.

10. Interview with Hans Hartmark, Protection Officer, UNHCR, Kigoma, September 15, 2009.

11. Interview with Dr. Yacoub el Hillo, Country Representative, UNHCR Tanzania, Dar Es Salaam, September 11, 2009.

12. Interview with el Hillo.

13. Interview with Hartmark.

14. Interview with Sherif-Nor.

15. Interview with Kazuhiro Kaneko, Head of Field Office, UNHCR, Kasulu, September 16, 2009.

16. Interviews with refugees, Nyarugusu refugee camp, Kigoma, Tanzania, September 16, 2009.

17. Interview with Mr. Chuleha, Assistant Zonal Coordinator, Department of Refugee Affairs, Government of Tanzania, Kigoma, September 15, 2009.

18. Interview with Hartmark.

19. The administrative entity of the region of Kigoma consists of four districts: Kigoma Urban, Kigoma Rural, Kasulu, and Kibondo.

20. Interview with Hamdani Hamisi, Deputy Immigration Officer, Kigoma, September 15, 2009.

21. Interview with Hamisi; visit to Kigoma Immigration Office.

22. Interview with Kaneko.

23. Interview with Geoffrey Carliez, Assistant External Relations Officer, UNHCR, Kigoma, Tanzania, September 16, 2009; interview with Rutinwa.

24. Interview with Hartmark.

25. On June 30, 2012, a group of 71 Congolese fleeing violence in Rutshuru traveled in the direction of Goma-Bukavu-Uvira and crossed Lake Tanganyika on a boat. Claiming asylum on their arrival, they were denied access to asylum procedures and immediately put on the private boat *MV Alphonsine* and returned to Baraka on July 12. E-mail correspondence, Evariste Mfaume, Executive Director, Syndicaat van Vlaamse Huisartsen vzw (SVH), Baraka-Fizi, Democratic Republic of Congo, July 13, 2012.

26. Interview with Sherif-Nor.

27. Interview with Jerome Seregni, Mass Information Officer, UNHCR Field Office Kasulu, September 16, 2009.

28. Ralf Gruenert, Deputy UNHCR Representative for Protection, DRC, cited in UNHCR, "South Kivu Returns to Start October 15," 2005, http://www.unhcr.org/cgi-bin/texis/vtx/news/opendoc.htm?id=43258dee4&tbl=NEWS.

29. Interview with Seregni.

30. Interview with Hartmark.

31. Interview with Rutinwa; interview with el Hillo.

32. Interview with Kaneko.

33. Interview with Rutinwa.

34. Interview with Kaneko.

35. Ibid.

36. Interview with Hartmark.

37. Interview with Kaneko.

38. Interview with Paul Jansen, Belgian Ambassador to Tanzania, Dar es Salaam, September 18, 2009.

39. Interview with Hartmark; interview with Carliez.

40. Interview with Rutinwa.

41. Interview with el Hillo; interview with Indrika Ratwatte. Deputy Representative, UNHCR, Dar es Salaam, September 11, 2009.

42. Interview with Sherif-Nor.

7. KENYA

1. See UNHCR (2011, 81) for the variation among European states of the treatment of Somalis seeking protection from indiscriminate violence under Article 15(c) of the European Council Directive 2004/83/EC of April 29, 2004, on minimum standards for the qualification and status of third-country nationals or stateless persons as refugees or

as persons who otherwise need international protection and the content of the protection granted. Countries such as Belgium and Sweden, for example, maintain that indiscriminate violence in south and central Somalia is at too high a level for a person to be returned there, but the United Kingdom and Netherlands do not.

2. In *Sufi and Elmi v. United Kingdom* (Applications nos. 8319/07 and 11449/07, Council of Europe: European Court of Human Rights, June 28, 2011), for instance, the court ruled that the "general violence in Mogadishu is sufficiently intense" that it constitutes a risk that any person returning to Mogadishu faces a real risk of inhuman or degrading ill-treatment such that it would breach Article 3 of the European Convention of Human Rights (para. 249). Furthermore, the court ruled that Article 3 would be similarly breached were a person to return to an internally displaced persons (IDP) camp such as Afgooye Corridor or a refugee camp such as the Dadaab (para. 295).

3. UNHCR country operations profile, Somalia 2011. http://www.unhcr.org/pages/49e483ad7.html.

4. Interview with Alexander Tyler, Protection Officer, UNHCR for Somalia, Nairobi, May 18, 2009.

5. Interview with Peter Kusimba, Director, Department of Refugee Affairs, Nairobi, May 15, 2009.

6. A refugee is listed in entry permit Class M. http://www.kenyalaw.org/Downloads/Acts/Immigration%20Act%20%28Cap.%20172%29.pdf.

7. Interview with Kusimba.

8. The Canadian section of CARE for food distribution; the World Food Programme (WFP) for food provision; Médecins Sans Frontières–Belgium for medical aid; and Gemeinschaft für Technologische Zusammenarbeit (GTZ) for improvement of environmental degradation.

9. "Kenya Must Resume Registration of Somali Refugees," Refugees International Press Release, February 15, 2012, http://refugeesinternational.org/press-room/press-release/kenya-must-resume-registration-somali-refugees.

10. On September 11, a British tourist was kidnapped and her husband shot dead at an exclusive resort. A French resident of Manda was kidnapped on October 1 and later died in captivity. On October 13, 2011, an aid worker was kidnapped and killed in the Dadaab.

11. See blog entry by Abi Guled on the release of the Judith Tebutt: http://www.huffingtonpost.com/2012/03/21/judith-tebbutt-freed-somali-pirates_n_1369342.html.

12. Mwai Kibaki, "A Defining Moment in the History of Somalia," speech at the London Conference on Somalia, February 23, 2012, http://www.fco.gov.uk/en/news/latest-news/?view=Speech&id=733696082.

13. Clar ni Chongile, "Kenya Denies Planning to Close World's Largest Refugee Camp," *Guardian,* February 22, 2012.

14. Randall Smith, "Kenya: Time to Shut Down Dadaab Refugee Camp," *Daily Nation,* February 24, 2012, http://allafrica.com/stories/201202241668.html.

15. Interview with Peter Klansoe, Regional Director, Danish Refugee Council, Nairobi, May 14, 2009.

16. Interview with Ibrahim, Somali refugee, Eastleigh, Nairobi, May 20, 2009.

17. See also "Kenya-Somalia: Paying High Price for Military Incursion," IRIN, January 13, 2012, http://www.irinnews.org/Report/94641/KENYA-SOMALIA-Paying-high-price-for-military-incursion.

18. Interview with Judy Wakahiu, Executive Director, Refugee Consortium of Kenya, May 13, 2009.

19. Ibid.

20. Interview with Klansoe.

21. Interview with Ibrahim.

22. Interview with Anita Anwuar, UNHCR, Nairobi, May 20, 2009.

23. Interview with Aaminaa, Somali refugee, Eastleigh, Nairobi, May 20, 2009.

24. Interview with Catherine-Lune Grayson, Regional Advisor on Migration and Protection, Danish Refugee Council, Nairobi, May 14, 2009.

25. Interview with Louise Aubin, Deputy Representative, UNHCR, Nairobi; interview with Moses Chege Kabatti, Kituo Cha Shariya, Nairobi, May 20, 2009.

26. Interview with Bettina Gollander-Jensen, Counselor, Regions of Origin Initiative, Danish Embassy, Nairobi, May 19, 2009.

27. Interview with Kusimba.

28. "Kenya to Help Fight Somali Rebels," *Daily Nation,* May 28, 2009, http://www.nation.co.ke/News/-/1056/604268/-/ujptmp/-/index.html.

29. "'Somali Link' as 74 World Cup Fans Die in Uganda Blasts," BBC News, July 12, 2010, http://www.bbc.co.uk/news/10593771.

30. Interview with Wakahiu.

31. Interview with Kusimba.

32. Interview with Wakahiu.

33. Interview with Klansoe.

34. Interview with Gollander-Jensen.

35. Interview with Klansoe.

36. Interview with Tal Raviv, Regional Programme Development Officer for East and Central Africa, IOM, Nairobi, May 19, 2009.

37. Telephone interview with Christopher Horwood, Regional Mixed Migration Task Force, February 15, 2012.

8. YEMEN

1. UNHCR, "2012 UNHCR Country Operations Profile: Yemen," http://www.unhcr.org/pages/49e486ba6.html.

2. Ibid.

3. "UNHCR Yemen Factsheet, October 2010," http://www.mmyemen.org/resources.

4. See, for example, IRIN, "Yemen-Somalia: Somalis Set to Lose Automatic Refugee Status," August 9, 2010, http://www.irinnews.org/Report/90103/YEMEN-SOMALIA-Somalis-set-to-lose-automatic-refugee-status.

5. Ray Jureidini's 2010 study, commissioned by the Mixed Migration Task Force (MMTF), collected data by means of a structured questionnaire given to 955 Somalis and Ethiopians (479 males and 476 females) aged 15–66 years living in Yemen and Turkey. Respondents included new arrivals, migrants who had resided in Yemen and Turkey for more than one month and less than one year, and a smaller group of migrants who had stayed for longer than a year.

6. Interview with Christopher Horwood, Director, Regional Mixed Migration Task Force, February 15, 2012.

7. "Record Number of Refugees, Migrants Risked Lives to Reach Yemen in 2011—UN," UN News Centre, January 20, 2012, http://www.un.org/apps/news/story.asp?NewsID=40987&Cr=refugees&Cr1.

8. Yemen's 1991 Law on the Entry and Residence of Aliens governs all foreigners, and while it exempts refugees from residence requirements, it is generally applied to refugees as well. Law on the Entry and Residence of Aliens [Yemen] (April 15, 1991), http://www.unhcr.org/refworld/docid/3ae6b4d110.html.

9. Interview with Horwood.

10. Ibid.

11. "Ethiopia's Largest Ethnicity Group Deprived of Linguistic and Cultural Sensitive Media Outlets," African Press Network for the 21st Century (RAP21), January 10, 2008, http://www.rap21.org/article19870.html?var_recherche=Ethiopia%27s+Largest+Ethnicity+Group+Deprived+of+Linguistic+and+Cultural+Sensitive+Media+Outlets.

12. "OFDM Press Release: The Massacre of May, 2008," *Yeroo-Jimma Times*, June 21, 2008, http://www.jimmatimes.com/article.cfm?articleID=31292. The *Yeroo-Jimma Times* is a noted ethnic Oromo newspaper.

13. Telephone interview with Ann Maymann, Assistant Representative/Protection, UNHCR Sana'a, February 24, 2012.

14. Interviews with Ethiopian refugees at the Ali-Addeh Refugee Camp, Djibouti, May 25, 2009.

15. Interview with Minelik Alemu, Attorney-General for International Law and Consular Affairs, Ministry of Foreign Affairs, Addis-Ababa, May 29, 2009.

16. See, for example, IRIN, "Yemen-Somalia: Somalis Set to Lose Automatic Refugee Status."

17. IRIN, "Somalia-Yemen: Registration Programme 'to Weed Out Illegal Migrants,'" IRIN, July 22, 2009, http://www.irinnews.org/Report/85383/SOMALIA-YEMEN-Registration-programme-to-weed-out-illegal-migrants.

18. "UNHCR Yemen Factsheet, July 2011,"http://www.mmyemen.org/c/document_library/get_file?p_l_id=10800&folderId=13856&name=DLFE-1602.pdf.

19. IRIN, "Yemen: Ministry Announces Refugee Registration Deadline," January 20, 2010, http://www.irinnews.org/Report/87805/YEMEN-Ministry-announces-refugee-registration-deadline.

20. Interview with Horwood.

21. "UNHCR Yemen Factsheet, July 2011."

22. Interview with Maymann.

23. IRIN, "Yemen: IDP/Refugee Camps—Facts and Figures," September 21, 2010, http://www.irinnews.org/Report/90531/YEMEN-IDP-refugee-camps-facts-and-figures.

24. Ibid.

25. Interview with Horwood.

26. IRIN, "Yemen: IDP/Refugee Camps."

27. E-mail correspondence with Allen Jelich, Country Director, Danish Refugee Council, Sana'a, March 2, 2012.

28. Ibid.

29. IRIN, "Somalia-Yemen: Over 3,000 Somalis Living in Harsh Conditions, Community Leader Says," October 21, 2007, http://www.irinnews.org/Report/74891/SOMALIA-YEMEN-Over-3000-Somalis-living-in-harsh-conditions-community-leader-says.

30. Interviews with Ethiopian refugees.

31. E-mail correspondence with Jelich.

32. Interview with Horwood.

33. CNN, "Al-Shabaab Joining al Qaeda, Monitor Group Says," February 9, 2012, http://articles.cnn.com/2012-02-09/africa/world_africa_somalia-shabaab-qaeda_1_al-zawahiri-qaeda-somali-americans?_s=PM:AFRICA.

34. E-mail correspondence with Jelich.

35. Participant observation, based on working with UNHCR, August–December 2005.

9. IMPROVING THE REFUGEE PROTECTION REGIME

1. The definition of a refugee is subject to interpretation within the scope of the definition in article 1A(2), which must be interpreted in light of the scope and purpose of the treaty (Goodwin-Gill 2010).

2. For example, Australia's Migration Act defines "persecution."

3. *D. v. United Kingdom*, 146/1996/767/964, Council of Europe: European Court of Human Rights, May 2, 1997.

4. *Sufi and Elmi v. United Kingdom*, Applications nos. 8319/07 and 11449/07, Council of Europe: European Court of Human Rights, June 28, 2011.

5. *N. v. United Kingdom*, Appl. No. 26565/05, Council of Europe: European Court of Human Rights, May 27, 2008.

6. *M.S.S. v. Belgium and Greece*, Application no. 30696/09, Council of Europe: European Court of Human Rights, January 21, 2011.

7. *Hirsi Jamaa and Others v. Italy*, Application no. 27765/09, Council of Europe: European Court of Human Rights, February 23, 2012.

8. The United Nations International Convention on the Protection of the Rights of All Migrant Workers and Members of Their Families, while relevant, is ratified by extremely few predominantly migrant-receiving states, and so does little to fill this gap.

CONCLUSION

1. While authors such as Amitav Acharya and Séverine Autesserre offer important conceptual and empirical insights into the transformation of norms at the domestic level, Acharya (2004)'s work on norm localization does so at a very high level of abstraction, looking at how international norms are changed in the ways they "fit" or "graft onto" pre-existing national and local norms. Autesserre's (2010) analysis of peacekeeping norms in the Congo offers a fascinating but largely descriptive account of how norms change at the national and local levels based on very in-depth ethnographic work. I have tried to take the middle ground between these methodological and conceptual approaches by adopting a positivist, comparative framework but one that nevertheless draws on the insights of systematic fieldwork.

References

Abild, Erik. 2009. *Creating Humanitarian Space in Somalia*. New Issues in Refugee Research, no. 184. December. Geneva: UNHCR.

Acharya, Amitav. 2004. "How Ideas Spread: Whose Norms Matter? Norm Localization and Institutional Change in Asian Regionalism." *International Organization* 58 (2): 239–275.

ADEPAE (Action pour le Développement et la Paix Endogènes) and SVH (Solidarité des Volontaires pour l'Humanité). 2011. *Congolese Refugees from South Kivu: Challenges of Return in the Territories of Fizi and Uvira*. June.

Africa Inland Mission Canada and Butoke. 2008. "Narrative Project Report: Food Security and Nutrition Project in Western Kasai, March 2007–February 2008." http://www.butoke.org/AIM_Final_Report.pdf.

Aggarwal, Vinod K. 1998. *Institutional Designs for a Complex World: Bargaining, Linkages, and Nesting*. Ithaca: Cornell University Press.

Agier, Michel. 2010. *Managing the Undesirables: Refugee Camps and Humanitarian Government*. Cambridge: Polity.

Akokpari, John K. 1998. "The State, Refugees and Migration in Sub-Saharan Africa." *International Migration* 36 (2): 211–234.

Albert, Matthew. 2010. *Prima Facie Determination of Refugee Legal Status: An Overview of Its Legal Foundation*. RSC Working Paper Series, no. 55. Oxford: Refugee Studies Centre, University of Oxford.

Alter, Karen J., and Sophie Meunier. 2009. "The Politics of International Regime Complexity." *Perspectives on Politics* 7 (1): 13–24.

Amit, Roni. 2010. *Protection and Pragmatism: Addressing Administrative Failures in South Africa's Refugee Status Determination Decision*. FMSP Report. April. Johannesburg: Forced Migration Studies Programme, University of the Witwatersrand.

Amnesty International. 2011. "South Africa: Call for South Africa to Fulfil Its International and Domestic Obligations in the Protection of the Rights of Refugees and Asylum Seekers." Public statement. December 20. www.amnesty.org/fr/library/asset/AFR53/007/2011/fr/555b8c2b-ae0c-4ac9-9078-0c4073d40aa8/afr530072011en.pdf.

Anderson, David. 2012. "Kenya's Somali Invasion." Public lecture. African Studies Seminar Series, University of Oxford. February 23.

Araia, Tesfalem. 2009. *Report on Human Smuggling across the South Africa/Zimbabwe Border*. Migrant Rights Monitoring Project Occasional Report. Johannesburg: Forced Migration Studies Programme.

Association des Congolais de Lunda. 2004. *Rapport adresse aux Médecins Sans Frontières a Kahungula/RDC pour dénoncer les traitements inhumains et dégradant subis par les Congolais durant leur séjour en Angola et pendant leur refoulement*. April 19.

Autesserre, Séverine. 2006. "Local Violence, National Peace? Postwar 'Settlement' in the Eastern D.R. Congo (2003–2006)." *African Studies Review* 49 (3): 1–29.

———. 2009. "Hobbes and the Congo: Frames, Local Violence, and International Intervention." *International Organization* 63 (2): 249–280.

———. 2010. *The Trouble with the Congo: Local Violence and the Failure of International Peacebuilding.* Cambridge Studies in International Relations. Cambridge: Cambridge University Press.

Ayiera, Eva. 2007. "Bold Advocacy Finally Strengthens Refugee Protection in Kenya." *Forced Migration Review* 28: 26–28.

Ayoob, Mohammed. 1995. *The Third World Security Predicament: State Making, Regional Conflict, and the International System.* Boulder, Colo.: Lynne Rienner.

Bachmann, Jan, and Janna Hönke. 2009. "'Peace and Security' as Counterterrorism? The Political Effects of Liberal Interventions in Kenya." *African Affairs* 109 (434): 97–114.

Baptiste, Raymond. 2010. "Land, IDPs, and Mediation." *Forced Migration Review* 36: 20–21.

Barnett, Michael N., and Martha Finnemore. 2004. *Rules for the World: International Organizations in Global Politics.* Ithaca: Cornell University Press.

Berle, Adolf Augustus, and Gardiner Coit Means. 1932. *The Modern Corporation of Private Property.* New York: Macmillan.

Betts, Alexander. 2008. "Historical Lessons for Overcoming Protracted Refugee Situations." In *Protracted Refugee Situations: Political, Human Rights, and Security Implications,* ed. Gil Loeschner, James Milner, Edward Newman, and Gary G. Troeller. Tokyo: United Nations University.

———. 2009. "Institutional Proliferation in the Refugee Regime." *Perspectives on Politics* 7 (1): 53–58.

———. 2010a. "Survival Migration: A New Protection Framework." *Global Governance* 16 (3): 361–382.

———. 2010b. "Towards a Soft Law Framework for Protection of Vulnerable Irregular Migrants." *International Journal of Refugee Law* 22 (2): 209–236.

Betts, Alexander, and Esra Kaytaz. 2009. *National and International Responses to the Zimbabwean Exodus: Implications for the Refugee Protection Regime.* New Issues in Refugee Research, no. 175. July. Geneva: UNHCR.

Betts, Alexander, and James Milner. 2006. *The Externalization of EU Asylum Policy: The Position of African States.* COMPAS Working Paper Series. Oxford: Centre on Migration, Policy and Society.

Betts, Alexander, and Phil Orchard. 2013. "The Normative Institutionalization-Implementation Gap." In *Implementation and World Politics: How International Norms Change Practice,* edited by Alexander Betts and Phil Orchard. Under review.

Black, Richard. 2001. *Environmental Refugees: Myth or Reality.* New Issues in Refugee Research no. 43. March. Geneva: UNHCR.

Blatter, Ariele. 2011. "The World's Largest Detention Center." *Refugees International Blog,* October 12. http://www.refugeesinternational.org/blog/world%E2%80%99s-largest-detention-center.

Blyth, Mark. 2002. *Great Transformations: Economic Ideas and Institutional Change in the Twentieth Century.* Cambridge: Cambridge University Press.

Boano, Camillo, Roger Zetter, and Tim Morris. 2008. *Environmentally Displaced People: Understanding the Linkages between Environmental Change, Livelihoods and Forced Migration.* RSC Forced Migration Policy Briefing, no. 1. Oxford: Refugee Studies Centre, University of Oxford.

Brown, Oli. 2008. *Migration and Climate Change.* IOM Migration Research Series, no. 31. Geneva: International Organization for Migration.

Brown, Vanessa N. 2010. "Foundations for Repatriation and Peace in DRC." *Forced Migration Review* 36: 54–55.

Busby, Joshua William. 2007. "Bono Made Jesse Helms Cry: Jubilee 2000, Debt Relief, and Modern International Politics." *International Studies Quarterly* 51 (2): 247–275.

Butoke. 2008. "Butoke Update: September 21, 2008." http://www.butoke.org/Update_Sept.%2021_2008.htm.

———. 2009. "Butoke Update: April 30, 2009." http://www.butoke.org/Update_2009-04-30.htm.

Campbell, Elizabeth H. 2005. *Urban Refugees in Nairobi: Protection, Survival and Integration.* Migration Studies Working Paper Series, no. 23. Johannesburg: University of the Witwatersrand.

Campbell, Elizabeth H., Jeff Crisp, and Esther Kiragu. 2011. *Navigating Nairobi: A Review of the Implementation of UNHCR's Urban Refugee Policy in Kenya's Capital City.* Geneva: UNHCR Policy Development and Evaluation Service.

Campbell, Eugene K., and John O. Oucho. 2003. *Changing Attitudes to Immigration and Refugee Policy in Botswana.* Migration Policy Series 28. Cape Town and Toronto: Southern African Migration Project.

———. 2011. *Navigating Nairobi: A Review of the Implementation of UNHCR's Urban Refugee Policy in Kenya's Capital City.* UNHCR Policy Development and Evaluation Service, Geneva, UNHCR. http://www.unhcr.org/4d5511209.pdf.

Castagno, Alphonse A. 1964. "The Somali-Kenyan Controversy: Implications for the Future." *Journal of Modern African Studies* 2 (2): 165–188.

Castles, Stephen. 2002. *Environmental Change and Forced Migration: Making Sense of the Debate.* New Issues in Refugee Research, no. 70. October. Geneva: UNHCR.

Chaulia, Sreeram Sundar. 2003. "The Politics of Refugee Hosting in Tanzania: From Open Door to Unsustainability, Insecurity and Receding Receptivity." *Journal of Refugee Studies* 16 (2): 147–166.

Checkel, Jeffrey T. 1997. "International Norms and Domestic Politics: Bridging the Rationalist—Constructivist Divide." *European Journal of International Relations* 3 (4): 473–495.

———. 1999. "Norms, Institutions and National Identity in Contemporary Europe." *International Studies Quarterly* 43 (1): 84–114.

———. 2005. "International Institutions and Socialization in Europe: Introduction and Framework." *International Organization* 59 (4): 801–826.

Clapham, Christopher S. 1996. *Africa and the International System: The Politics of State Survival.* Cambridge: Cambridge University Press.

Collinson, Sarah. 1999. *Globalization and the Dynamics of International Migration: Implications for the Refugee Regime.* New Issues in Refugee Research, no. 1. May. Geneva: UNHCR.

Consortium of Refugees and Migrants in South Africa (CoRMSA). 2008. *Protecting Refugees, Asylum Seekers and Migrants in South Africa.* June 18. Johannesburg: CoRMSA.

———. 2011. *Protecting Refugees, Asylum Seekers and Migrants in South Africa.* April. Johannesburg: CoRMSA.

Cortell, Andrew P., and James W. Davis. 2000. "Understanding the Domestic Impact of International Norms: A Research Agenda." *International Studies Review* 2 (1): 65–87.

Crisp, Jeff. 2000. "A State of Insecurity: The Political Economy of Violence in Kenya's Refugee Camps." *African Affairs* 99 (397): 601–632.

————. 2008. *Beyond the Nexus: UNHCR's Evolving Perspective on Refugee Protection and International Migration.* New Issues in Refugee Research, no. 155. April. Geneva: UNHCR.

Crisp, Jeff, and Esther Kiragu. 2010. *Refugee Protection and International Migration: A Review of UNHCR's Role in Malawi, Mozambique and South Africa.* Geneva: UNHCR Policy Development and Evaluation Service.

Crush, Jonathan, and Daniel S. Tevera. 2010. *Zimbabwe's Exodus: Crisis, Migration, Survival.* Cape Town: Southern African Migration Project; Ottawa: International Development Research Centre.

de Boeck, Filip. 2001. "Garimpeiro Worlds: Digging, Dying and 'Hunting' for Diamonds in Angola." *Review of African Political Economy* 28 (90): 548–562.

Deere-Birkbeck, Carolyn. 2008. *The Implementation Game: The Trips Agreement and the Global Politics of Intellectual Property Reform in Developing Countries.* Oxford: Oxford University Press.

de Oliveira, Ricardo Soares. 2011. "Illiberal Peacebuilding in Angola." *Journal of Modern African Studies* 49 (2): 287–314.

Diehl, Paul F., Charlotte Ku, and Daniel Zamora. 2003. "The Dynamics of International Law: The Interaction of Normative and Operating Systems." *International Organization* 57 (1): 43–75.

Drezner, Daniel W. 2007. *All Politics Is Global: Explaining International Regulatory Regimes.* Princeton, N.J.: Princeton University Press.

Emizet, Kisangani N. F. 2000. "The Massacre of Refugees in Congo: A Case of UN Peacekeeping Failure and International Law." *Journal of Modern African Studies* 38 (2): 163–202.

Fanning, Emma. 2010. "Challenges of Protection." *Forced Migration Review* 36: 37–38.

Finnemore, Martha, and Kathryn Sikkink. 1998. "International Norm Dynamics and Political Change." *International Organization* 52 (4): 887–917.

Flockhart, Trine. 2005. *Socializing Democratic Norms: The Role of International Organizations for the Construction of Europe.* Basingstoke, U.K.: Palgrave Macmillan.

Foster, Michelle. 2007. *International Refugee Law and Socio-Economic Rights: Refuge from Deprivation.* Cambridge Studies in International and Comparative Law. Cambridge: Cambridge University Press.

————. 2009. "Non-Refoulement on the Basis of Socio-Economic Deprivation: The Scope of Complementary Protection in International Human Rights Law." *New Zealand Law Review* [2009] Part II: 257–310.

Franck, Thomas M. 2006. "The Power of Legitimacy and the Legitimacy of Power: International Law in an Age of Power Disequilibrium." *American Journal of International Law* 100 (1): 88–106.

Garvelink, William J., and Farha Tahir. 2012. "The Dadaab Refugee Complex: A Power Keg and It's Giving Off Sparks." Centre for Strategic and International Studies. http://csis.org/publication/dadaab-refugee-complex-powder-keg-and-its-giving-sparks.

Gasarasi, Charles. 1990. "The Mass Naturalization and Further Integration of Rwandese Refugees in Tanzania: Process, Problems and Prospects." *Journal of Refugee Studies* 3 (3): 88–109.

Gemenne, François. 2009. "L'environnement: Nouveau facteur de migrations?" In *L'enjeu mondial: Les migrations,* edited by Christophe Jaffrelot and Christian Lequesne, 137–145. Paris: Presses de Sciences Po.

Gibney, Matthew. 2004. *The Ethics and Politics of Asylum: Liberal Democracy and the Response to Refugees.* Cambridge: Cambridge University Press.

Goertz, Gary. 2003. *International Norms and Decision Making: A Punctuated Equilibrium Model.* Lanham, Md.: Rowman & Littlefield.

Goodwin-Gill, Guy. 1986. "Non-Refoulement and the New Asylum Seekers." *Virginia Journal of International Law* 26 (4): 897–918.

———. 2010. "The Search for the One, True Meaning . . ." In *The Limits of Transnational Law: Refugee Law, Policy Harmonization and Judicial Dialogue in the European Union*, edited by Guy Goodwin-Gill and Helene Lambert, 204–241. Cambridge: Cambridge University Press.

Goodwin-Gill, Guy, and Jane McAdam. 2007. *The Refugee in International Law.* Oxford: Oxford University Press.

Government, U.K. 2011. *Foresight: Migration and Global Environmental Change.* London: Government Office for Science.

Greenhill, Kelly. 2010. *Weapons of Mass Migration: Forced Displacement, Coercion, and Foreign Policy.* Ithaca: Cornell University Press.

Gude, Alice. 2011. "Horn of Africa: A Situation Which Is Tragic Beyond Words." *Letters from the Field* (blog). http://www.msf.org.uk/Alice_Gude.letter?lId=a2f362ec-bc3b-4e55-89b5-7db03e1a1e42.

Gundel, Joakim. 2002. "The Migration-Development Nexus: Somalia Case Study." *International Migration* 40 (special issue 2): 255–281.

Hacker, Jacob. 2004. "Privatizing Risk without Privatizing the Welfare State: The Hidden Politics of Social Policy Retrenchment in the United States." *American Political Science Review* 98 (2): 243–260.

Haddad, Emma. 2008. *The Refugee in International Society: Between Sovereigns.* Cambridge: Cambridge University Press.

Hall, Peter A., and Kathleen Ann Thelen. 2009. "Institutional Change in Varieties of Capitalism." *Changing Institutions in Developed Democracies: Economics, Politics and Welfare.* Special issue, *Socio-Economic Review* 7 (1): 7–34.

Hammar, Amanda, JoAnn McGregor, and Loren B. Landau. 2010. "Introduction: Displacing Zimbabwe; Crisis and Construction in Southern Africa." *Journal of Southern African Studies* 36 (2): 263–283.

Harvard Humanitarian Initiative (HHI). 2010. "Now, the World Is without Me—An Investigation of Sexual Violence in Eastern DRC." Harvard Humanitarian Initiative, OXFAM US. http://www.oxfam.org/en/policy/now-world-without-me.

Hathaway, James C. 1997. "Is Refugee Status Really Elitist? An Answer to the Ethical Challenge." In *Europe and Refugees: A Challenge*, edited by Jean-Yves Carlier and Dirk Vanheule. The Hague: Kluwer Law International.

———. 2005. *Rights of Refugees under International Law.* Cambridge: Cambridge University Press.

———. 2007. "Forced Migration Studies: Could We Agree Just to 'Date'?" *Journal of Refugee Studies* 20 (3): 349–369.

Hawkins, Darren G., David A. Lake, Daniel L. Nielson, and Michael J. Tierney. 2006. *Delegation and Agency in International Organizations.* Cambridge: Cambridge University Press.

Haynes, Jeffrey. 2005. "Islamic Militancy in East Africa." *Third World Quarterly* 26 (8): 1321–1339.

Hege, Steve. 2010. "Of Tripartites, Peace and Return." *Forced Migration Review* 36: 51–53.

Helton, Arthur C. 2002. *The Price of Indifference: Refugees and Humanitarian Action in the New Century.* Oxford: Oxford University Press.

Holmes, John. 2010. "A Scandal That Needs to End." *Forced Migration Review* 36: 4–5. http://www.fmreview.org/DRCongo/holmes.htm.

Hopgood, Stephen. 2006. *Keepers of the Flame: Understanding Amnesty International.* Ithaca: Cornell University Press.

Horst, Cindy. 2006. *Transnational Nomads: How Somalis Cope with Refugee Life in the Dadaab Camps of Kenya.* New York: Berghahn.

Human Rights Watch (HRW). 2004. "Angola: Congolese Migrants Face Brutal Body Searches." April 23. www.hrw.org/news/2004/04/22/angola-congolese-migrants-face-brutal-body-searches.

———. 2008. "They Beat Me Like a Dog: Political Persecution of Opposition Activists and Supporters in Zimbabwe." August 12.

———. 2009a. "Crisis without Limits: Human Rights and Humanitarian Consequences of Political Repression in Zimbabwe." January 22.

———. 2009b. "Hostile Shores—Abuse and Refoulement of Asylum Seekers and Refugees in Yemen." December 20.

———. 2009c. "Kenya: End Abuse and Neglect of Somali Refugees." March 30.

———. 2009d. "From Horror to Hopelessness: Kenya's Forgotten Somali Refugee Crisis." March 30.

———. 2010a. "'Welcome to Kenya': Police Abuse of Somali Refugees." June 17. http://www.hrw.org/reports/2010/06/17/welcome-kenya-0.

———. 2010b. "Kenya: Stop Deportations to War-Torn Somalia." December 7.

———. 2012. "Kenya: Security Forces Abusing Civilians near Somalia Border." January 12.

Hurd, Ian. 2005. "Strategic Use of Liberal Internationalism: Libya and the UN Sanctions." *International Organization* 59 (3): 495–526.

———. 2007. *After Anarchy: Legitimacy and Power in the UN Security Council.* Princeton, N.J.: Princeton University Press.

International Crisis Group (ICG). 2012. *The Kenyan Military Intervention in Somalia.* ICG Africa Report, no. 184. February 15. Nairobi: ICG.

International Federation for the Red Cross and Red Crescent Societies (IFRC). 2009. "Angola: Population Movement." October 29. International Federation of the Red Cross, Disaster Relief Emergency Fund (DREF). http://www.ifrc.org/docs/Appeals/09/MDRAO004.pdf.

International Organization for Migration (IOM). 2010. *Wolves in Sheep's Skin: A Rapid Assessment of Human Trafficking in Musina, Limpopo Province of South Africa.* Geneva: IOM.

IRIN. 2011a. "South Africa: Deportations of Zimbabweans Set to Resume." www.irinnews.org/Report/93912/SOUTH-AFRICA-Deportations-of-Zimbabwean-migrants-set-to-resume.

———. 2011b. "Fourth Dadaab Camp Yet to Open Despite Government Pledge." www.irinnews.org/Report/93347/KENYA-SOMALIA-Fourth-Dadaab-camp-yet-to-open-despite-government-pledge.

Jackson, Robert H. 1990. *Quasi-States: Sovereignty, International Relations and the Third World.* Cambridge: Cambridge University Press.

Jacquemot, Pierre. 2010. "The Dynamics of Instability in Eastern RC." *Forced Migration Review* 36: 6–7.

Jansen, Bram J. 2008. "Between Vulnerability and Assertiveness: Negotiating Resettlement in Kakuma Refugee Camp, Kenya." *African Affairs* 107 (429): 569–587.

Jepperson, Ronald, Alexander Wendt, and Peter J. Katzenstein. 1996. "Norms, Identity, and Culture in National Security." In *The Culture of National Security: Norms and Identity in World Politics,* edited by Peter J. Katzenstein and Social Science Research Council (U.S.) Committee on International Peace and Security, 33–75. New York: Columbia University Press.

Jones, Jeremy L. 2010. "'Nothing Is Straight in Zimbabwe': The Rise of the Kukiya-Kiya Economy, 2000–2008." *Journal of Southern African Studies* 36 (2): 285–299.

Juma, Monica, and Peter Kagwanja. 2008. "Somali Refugees: Protracted Exile and Shifting Security Frontiers." In *Protracted Refugee Situations: Political, Human Rights, and Security Implications*, edited by Gil Loescher et al. Tokyo: United Nations University Press.

Jureidini, Ray. 2010. *Mixed Migration Flows: Somali and Ethiopian Migration to Yemen and Turkey*. Final Report to the Mixed Migration Task Force. Cairo: Center for Migration and Refugee Studies, American University in Cairo.

Kamanga, Khoti. 2005. "The (Tanzania) Refugees Act of 1998: Some Legal and Policy Implications." *Journal of Refugee Studies* 18 (1): 100–116.

Keck, Margaret, and Kathryn Sikkink. 1998. *Activists beyond Borders: Advocacy Networks in International Politics*. Ithaca: Cornell University Press.

Keohane, Robert O. 1982. "The Demand for International Regimes." *International Organization* 36 (2): 325–355.

Kibreab, Gaim. 1994. "Migration, Environment and Refugeehood." In *Environment and Population Change*, edited by Basia Zaba and John Clarke, 115–129. Liege: International Union for the Scientific Study of Population, Derouaux Editions.

———. 1997. "Environmental Causes and Impact of Refugee Movements: A Critique of the Current Debate." *Disasters* 21 (1): 20–38.

King, Gary, Robert O. Keohane, and Sidney Verba. 1994. *Designing Social Inquiry: Scientific Inference in Qualitative Research*. Princeton, N.J.: Princeton University Press.

Kinsey, Bill H. 2010. "Who Went Where . . . and Why: Patterns and Consequences of Displacement in Rural Zimbabwe after February 2000." *Journal of Southern African Studies* 36 (2): 339–360.

Kiwanuka, Monica, and Tamlyn Monson. 2009. *Zimbabwean Migration into Southern Africa: New Trends and Responses*. FMSP Research Report. November. Johannesburg: Forced Migration Studies Programme, University of the Witwatersrand.

Kleist, Nauja. 2004. *Nomads, Sailors and Refugees: A Century of Somali Migration*. Sussex Migration Working Paper, no. 3. Brighton, U.K.: Sussex Centre for Migration Research.

Koremenos, Barbara, Charles Lipson, and Duncan Snidal. 2001. "The Rational Design of International Institutions," *International Organization* 55 (4): 761–800.

Krasner, Stephen D. 1982. "Structural Causes and Regime Consequences: Regimes as Intervening Variables." *International Organization* 36 (2): 185–205.

———. 1999. *Sovereignty: Organized Hypocrisy*. Princeton, N.J.: Princeton University Press.

Landau, Loren B. 2003. "Beyond the Losers: Transforming Governmental Practice in Refugee-Affected Tanzania." *Journal of Refugee Studies* 16 (1): 19–43.

———. 2004. "Challenge without Transformation: Refugees, Aid, and Trade in Western Tanzania." *Journal of Modern African Studies*. 42 (1): 31–59.

Landau, Loren B., and Jean Pierre Misago. 2009. *Towards Tolerance, Law and Dignity: Addressing Violence against Foreign Nationals in South Africa*. February. Johannesburg: IOM Regional Office for South Africa.

Lange, Maria. 2010. "Refugee Return and Root Causes of Conflict." *Forced Migration Review* 36: 48–49.

Lefko-Everett, Kate. 2004. "Botswana's Changing Migration Patterns." Migration Information Source. www.migrationinformation.org/Profiles/display.cfm? ID=246.

Legro, Jeffrey W. 2005. *Rethinking the World: Great Power Strategies and International Order.* Ithaca: Cornell University Press.

———. 2007. "Which Norms Matter? Revisiting the 'Failure' of Internationalism." *International Organization* 51 (1): 31–63.

Lemarchand, René. 2004. "Exclusion, Marginalization and Political Mobilization: The Road to Hell in the Great Lakes." In *Facing Ethnic Conflicts: Toward a New Realism*, edited by Andreas Wimmer, 61–77. Lanham, Md.: Rowman & Littlefield.

Lemke, Douglas. 2002. *Regions of War and Peace.* Cambridge: Cambridge University Press.

Lesetedi, Gwen N., and Tirelo Modie-Moroka. 2007. Reverse Xenophobia: Immigrants' Attitudes towards Citizens in Botswana. In *African Migrations Workshop: Understanding Migration Dynamics in the Continent.* Legon-Accra: Centre for Migration Studies, University of Ghana.

Lieberman, Robert C. 2002. "Ideas, Institutions, and Political Order: Explaining Political Change." *American Political Science Review* 96 (4): 697–712.

Lindley, Anna. 2010. *The Early Morning Phone Call: Somali Refugees' Remittances.* New York: Berghahn Books.

———. 2011. "Between a Protracted and a Crisis Situation: Policy Responses to Somali Refugees in Kenya." *Refugee Survey Quarterly* 30 (4): 14–49.

Lischer, Sarah Kenyon. 2003. "Collateral Damage: Humanitarian Assistance as a Cause of Conflict." *International Security* 28 (1): 79–109.

———. 2005. *Dangerous Sanctuaries: Refugee Camps, Civil War, and the Dilemmas Of Humanitarian Aid.* Ithaca: Cornell University Press.

———. 2007. "Causes and Consequences of Conflict-Induced Displacement." *Civil Wars* 9 (2): 142–155.

Loescher, Gil. 2001. *The UNHCR and World Politics: A Perilous Path.* Oxford: Oxford University Press.

Lututala, Bernard Mumpasi. 2010. "The Role of Governance and Research." *Forced Migration Review* 36: 8–9.

Mahoney, James, and Kathleen Ann Thelen. 2010. *Explaining Institutional Change: Ambiguity, Agency and Power.* Cambridge: Cambridge University Press.

Mail and Guardian. 2010. "Humanitarian Crisis Close to Home." 14 December. http://www.mg.co.za/article/2012-12-10-humanitarian-crisis-close-to-home.

Marques, Rafael. 2011. *Blood Diamonds: Corruption and Torture in Angola.* Lisbon: Tinta da China.

Marques, Rafael, and Rui Falcão de Campos. 2005. *Lundas: The Stones of Death; Angola's Deadly Diamonds, Human Rights Abuses in the Lunda Provinces, 2004.* Lisbon: Apoios.

Martin, Susan. 2010. "Forced Migration, the Refugee Regime and the Responsibility to Protect." *Global Responsibility to Protect* 2 (1–2): 38–59.

Mawowa, Showers, and Alois Matongo. 2010. "Inside Zimbabwe's Roadside Currency Trade: The 'World Bank' of Bulawayo." *Journal of Southern African Studies* 36 (2): 319–337.

McAdam, Jane. 2006. *Complementary Protection and Beyond: How States Deal with Human Rights Protection.* New Issues in Refugee Research, no. 118. August. Geneva: UNHCR.

————. 2007. *Complementary Protection in International Refugee Law*. Oxford: Oxford University Press.

————. 2011. *Climate Change Displacement and International Law: Complementary Protection* Standards. Geneva: UNHCR.

————. 2012. *Climate Change, Forced Migration and International Law*. Oxford: Oxford University Press.

Médecins Sans Frontières (MSF). 2004. "Angola: MSF-Belgium Monthly Situation Report." May.

————. 2007. *Angola: Systematic Rapes and Violence against Congolese Migrants, the Women Testify*. December. Brussels: Médecins Sans Frontières.

————. 2008. *Refoules congolais: Informations recoltée par le Pool d'Urgence Congo de MSF— Mission d'évaluation et prise en charge des refoues entre le 02 et le 06 Juin 2008*.

————. 2009. "No Refuge, Access Denied: Medical Needs of Zimbabweans in South Africa." June. South Africa: Médecins Sans Frontières.

————. 2011. "Kenya: Humanitarian Crisis on the Outskirts of Overcrowded Dadaab Camp." July 13. http://www.doctorswithoutborders.org/news/article. cfm?id=5438.

————. 2012. "Dadaab Refugee Camps: Back to Square One." February 16. http://www.doctorswithoutborders.org/publications/article. cfm?id=5774&cat=special-report.

Menkhaus, Ken. 2010a. "Stabilization and Humanitarian Access in a Collapsed State: The Case of Somalia." *Disasters* 34: 320–341.

————. 2010b. "Non-state Actors and the Role of Violence in Stateless Somalia." In *Violent Non-state Actors in World Politics*, edited by Kledja Mulaj, 343–380. New York: Columbia University Press.

Meredith, Martin. 2002. *Robert Mugabe: Power, Plunder and Tyranny in Zimbabwe*. Johannesburg: Jonathan Ball.

Merry, Sally Engle. 2006. "Transnational Human Rights and Local Activism: Mapping the Middle." *American Anthropologist* 108 (1): 38–51.

Milner, James. 2009. *Refugees, the State and the Politics of Asylum in Africa*. St. Antony's Series. Basingstoke, U.K.: Palgrave Macmillan.

Mixed Migration Task Force (MMTF). 2008. *Mixed Migration through Somalia and across the Gulf of Aden*. Nairobi: MMTF.

Moret, Joëlle, Simone Baglioni, and Denise Efionayi-Mäder. 2006. *The Path of Somali Refugees into Exile: A Comparative Analysis of Secondary Movements and Policy Responses*. SFM Studies no. 46. Neuchâtel: Swiss Forum for Migration and Population Studies.

Mukumbira, Rodrick. 2003. "Citizens Turn on Zimbabwean Migrants." *African Business*. May. www.questia.com/library/1G1-101291137/citizens-turn-on-zimbabwean-migrants-countryfile.

Müller, Harald. 2004. "Arguing, Bargaining and All That: Communicative Action, Rationalist Theory and the Logic of Appropriateness in International Relations." *European Journal of International Relations* 10 (3): 395–435.

Murphy, Martin N. 2011. *Somalia, the New Barbary? Piracy and Islam in the Horn of Africa*. New York: Columbia University Press.

Musoni, Francis. 2010. "Operation Murambatsvina and the Politics of Street Vendors in Zimbabwe." *Journal of Southern African Studies* 36 (2): 301–317.

Myers, Norman. 1993. "Environmental Refugees in a Globally Warmed World." *BioScience* 43 (11): 752–761.

————. 1997. "Environmental Refugees." *Population and Environment* 19 (2): 167–182.

———. 2005. "Environmental Refugees: An Emergent Security Issue." Paper presented at the 13th Economic Forum, May 22, Prague.

Myers, Norman, and Jennifer Kent (1995), *Environmental Exodus: An Emergent Crisis in the Global Arena*. Washington, D.C.: Climate Institute.

Oded, Arye. 2000. *Islam and Politics in Kenya*. Boulder, Colo.: Lynne Rienner.

Odhiamno-Abuya, Edwin. 2004. "United Nations High Commissioner for Refugees and Status Determination Imtaxaan in Kenya: An Empirical Survey." *Journal of African Law* 48 (2): 187–206.

Office for the Coordination of Humanitarian Affairs (OCHA). 2007. *Rapport de la mission d'évaluation des besoins humanitaires des refoules de l'Angola a Luiza et Kamako en province du Kasai Occidental*. April 12–14.

———. 2009. "Angola-DRC Expulsions: Regional Situation Report No. 1." October 14. http://ochaonline.un.org/rosa/HumanitarianSituations/AngolaDRCExpulsions/tabid/5800/language/en-US/Default.aspx.

Office of the High Commissioner for Human Rights (OHCHR). 2010. "DRC Mapping Report: Democratic Republic of the Congo, 1993–2003." http://www.ohchr.org/EN/Countries/AfricaRegion/Pages/RDCProjetMapping.aspx.

———. 2012. "UN Report Exposes Mass Killings in Eastern DR Congo." http://www.ohchr.org/EN/NewsEvents/Pages/KillingsInEasternDRCongo.aspx.

Olson, Mancur. 2000. *Power and Prosperity: Outgrowing Communist and Capitalist Dictatorships*. New York: Basic Books.

Orchard, Phil. 2013. "Implementing a Global Internally Displaced Persons Protection Regime." In *Implementation and World Politics: How International Norms Change Practice*, edited by Alexander Betts and Phil Orchard. Under review.

Ostrom, Elinor. 1990. *Governing the Commons: The Evolution of Institutions for Collective Action*. Cambridge: Cambridge University Press.

Partnership Africa-Canada (PAC). 2007. *Diamond Industry Annual Review: Republic of Angola*. Ottawa: PAC. http://pacweb.org/Documents/annual-reviews-diamonds/Angola-AR2007-eng.pdf.

Patrick, Stewart. 2011. *Weak Links: Fragile States, Global Threats, and International Security*. Oxford: Oxford University Press.

Pearce, Justin. 2004. "War, Peace and Diamonds in Angola: Popular Perceptions of the Diamond Industry in the Lundas." Institute for Security Studies Working Paper.

———. 2005. *An Outbreak of Peace: Angola's Situation of Confusion*. London: David Philip.

Perouse de Montclos, Marc-Antoine, and Peter Kagwanja. 2000. "Refugee Camps or Cities? The Socio-Economic Dynamics of the Dadaab and Kakuma Camps in Northern Kenya." *Journal of Refugee Studies* 13 (2): 205–222.

Pierson, Paul. 2004. *Politics in Time: History, Institutions, and Social Analysis*. Princeton, N.J.: Princeton University Press.

Piguet, Etienne. 2008. "Climate Change and Forced Migration." *New Issues in Refugee Research* no. 153. January. Geneva: UNHCR.

Polzer, Tara. 2008. "Responding to Zimbabwean Migration in South Africa: Evaluating Options." *South African Journal of International Affairs* 15 (1): 1–15.

Polzer, Tara, Monica Kiwanuka, and Kathryn Takabvirwa. 2010. "Regional Responses to Zimbabwean Migration, 2000–2010." *Open Space, On the Move: Dynamics of Migration in Southern Africa* (3): 30–34.

Pottier, Johan. 2008. "Displacement and Ethnic Reintegration in Ituri, DR Congo: Challenges Ahead." *Journal of Modern African Studies* 46 (3): 427–450.

Price, Matthew E. 2009. *Rethinking Asylum: History, Purpose, and Limits*. Cambridge: Cambridge University Press.

Prunier, Gérard. 2009. *From Genocide to Continental War: The "Congolese" Conflict and the Crisis of Contemporary Africa.* London: Hurst.

Rafti, Marina. 2006. *South Kivu: A Sanctuary for the Rebellion of the Democratic Forces for the Liberation of Rwanda.* Discussion Papers, no. 2006.05. March. University of Antwerp, Institute of Development Policy and Management.

Ramji-Nogales, Jaya, Andrew Schoenholtz, and Philip Schrag. 2009. *Refugee Roulette: Disparities in Asylum Adjudication and Proposals for Reform.* New York: New York University Press.

Regional Mixed Migration Secretariat (RMMS). 2012. "Regional Mixed Migration Summary for December 2011 & January 2012." Nairobi: Regional Mixed Migration Secretariat. http://www.regionalmms.org/fileadmin/content/rmms%20monthly%20summaries/RMMS_Mixed_Migration_Monthly_Summary_Dec_2011___Jan_2012.pdf.

Reyntjens, Filip. 2007. "Briefing: Democratic Republic of Congo; Political Transition and Beyond." *African Affairs* 106 (43): 307–317.

Richmond, Anthony. 1993. "Reactive Migration: Sociological Perspectives on Refugee Movements." *Journal of Refugee Studies* 6 (1): 7–24.

Risse-Kappen, Thomas, Steve C. Ropp, and Kathryn Sikkink. 1999. *The Power of Human Rights: International Norms and Domestic Change.* Cambridge: Cambridge University Press.

Rodríguez, Maria. 2011. "The FDLR as an Obstacle to Peace in the DRC." *Peace Review* 23 (2): 176–182.

Rutinwa, Bonaventure. 1996. "The Tanzanian Government's Response to the Rwandan Emergency." *Journal of Refugee Studies* 9 (3): 291–302.

———. 2005. *Identifying Gaps in Protection Capacity in Tanzania.* Geneva: UNHCR.

Rwegayura, Anaclet. 2011. "Time Running Out on DR Congo Refugees in Tanzania." Panpress. www.panapress.com/Time-running-out-on-DR-Congo-refugees-in-Tanzania-(News-feature)--12-774683-101-lang2-index.html.

Salehyan, Idean. 2009. *Rebels without Borders: Transnational Insurgencies in World Politics.* Ithaca: Cornell University Press.

Sandholtz, Wayne, and Kendall Stiles. 2008. *International Norms and Cycles of Change.* Oxford: Oxford University Press.

Schmidt, Anna. 2006. *From Global Prescription to Local Treatment—the International Refugee Regime in Tanzania and Uganda.* Berkeley: Department of Political Science, University of California.

Schreier, Tal Hanna. 2008. "An Evaluation of South Africa's Application of the OAU Refugee Definition." *Refuge* 25 (2): 53–63.

Shacknove, Andrew E. 1985. "Who Is a Refugee?" *Ethics* 95 (2): 274–284.

Sharpe, Marina. 2012. "The 1969 African Refugee Convention: Innovations, Misconceptions, and Omissions." *McGill Law Journal* 58 (1): 95–147.

Shay, Shaul. 2008. *Somalia between Jihad and Restoration.* New Brunswick, N.J.: Transaction Publishers.

Shue, Henry. 1980. *Basic Rights: Subsistence, Affluence, and U.S. Foreign Policy.* Princeton, N.J.: Princeton University Press.

Simmons, Beth A. 2009. *Mobilizing for Human Rights: International Law in Domestic Politics.* Cambridge: Cambridge University Press.

Skran, Claudena. 1995. *Refugees in Inter-War Europe: The Emergence of a Regime.* Oxford: Clarendon Press.

Solidarity Peace Trust. 2012. *Perils and Pitfalls: Migrants and Deportation in South Africa.* Johannesburg: Solidarity Peace Trust. http://www.solidaritypeacetrust.org/perils-and-pitfalls.

Stark, Oded, and Edward Taylor. 1989. "Relative Deprivation and International Migration." *Demography* 26 (1): 1–14.

Sundstrom, Lisa McIntosh. 2005. "Foreign Assistance, International Norms, and NGO Development: Lessons from the Russian Campaign." *International Organization* 59 (2): 419–449.

Stearns, Jason K. 2011. *Dancing in the Glory of Monsters: The Collapse of the Congo and the Great War of Africa.* New York: Public Affairs.

Stone Sweet, Alec, Wayne Sandholtz, and Neil Fligstein. 2001. *The Institutionalization of Europe.* Oxford: Oxford University Press.

Suhrke, Astri. 1994. "Environmental Degradation and Population Flows." *Journal of International Affairs* 47 (2): 473–496.

Talley, Leisel, Paul B. Spiegel, and Mona Girgis. 2001. "An Investigation of Increasing Mortality among Congolese Refugees in Lugufu Camp, Tanzania, May–June 1999." *Journal of Refugee Studies* 14 (4): 412–427.

Tayler, Letta, and Chris Albin-Lackey. 2009. "Kenya Recruits Somali Refugees to Fight Islamists Back Home in Somalia." *Huffington Post.* November 10. http://www.hrw.org/en/news/2009/11/16/kenya-recruits-somali-refugees-fight-islamists-back-home-somalia.

Teff, Melanie. 2012. "Attacks Bring New Risks for Kenya's Urban Somalis." *Refugees International Blog.* February 17. http://www.refintl.org/blog/attacks-bring-new-risks-kenyas-urban-somalis.

Throup, David. 2012. "Kenya's Intervention in Somalia." Center for Strategic and International Studies (CSIS). http://www.csis.org/publication/kenyas-intervention-somalia.

Tshisela, Namhla. 2010. "Zimbabweans Face Permits Bottleneck." *The Sowetan.* December 15. http://www.sowetanlive.co.za/news/2010/12/15/zimbabweans-face-permits-bottleneck.

UN Conference on Trade and Development (UNCTAD). 2008. *World Investment Report, 2008: Transnational Corporations and the Infrastructure Challenge.* New York: United Nations.

UN High Commissioner for Refugees (UNHCR). 2005. *The Framework for the Comprehensive Plan of Action (CPA) for Somali Refugees.* September. Geneva: UNHCR.

———. 2010. "Protection Gaps and Responses." *Background Paper: High Commissioner's Dialogue on Protection Challenges.* Geneva: UNHCR.

———. 2011a. *Safe at Last? Law and Practice in Selected EU Member States with Respect to Asylum Seekers Fleeing Indiscriminate Violence.* July 27, 2011. Geneva: UNHCR.

———. 2011b. *East & Horn of Africa Update: Somali Displacement Crisis at a Glance.* November 24. Nairobi: UNHCR Regional Support Hub, East, Horn of Africa & Great Lakes Region.

US Committee for Refugees and Immigrants (USCRI). 2009. *World Refugee Survey, 2009.* Washington, D.C.: U.S. Committee for Refugees and Immigrants.

US Department of State. 2010. "2010 Human Rights Report: Tanzania." April 8. http://www.state.gov/j/drl/rls/hrrpt/2010/af/154373.htm.

Vale, Peter. 2003. "Sovereignty, Identity and the Prospects for Southern Africa's People." In *What Holds Us Together: Social Cohesion in South Africa*, edited by David Chidester, Phillip Dexter, and Wilmot Godfrey James, 23–41. Pretoria: Human Sciences Research Council.

VanDeveer, Stacy D., and Geoffrey D. Dabelko. 2001. "It's Capacity, Stupid: International Assistance and National Implementation." *Global Environmental Politics* 1 (2): 18–29.

van Kersbergen, Kees, and Bertjan Verbeek. 2007. "The Politics of International Norms: Subsidiarity and the Imperfect Competence Regime of the European Union." *European Journal of International Relations* 13 (2): 217–238.

Verdirame, Guglielmo. 1999. "Human Rights and Refugees: The Case of Kenya." *Journal of Refugee Studies* 12 (1): 54–77.

Verdirame, Guglielmo, and Barbara E. Harrell-Bond. 2005. *Rights in Exile: Janus-Faced Humanitarianism*. Studies in Forced Migration, vol. 17. Oxford: Berghahn Books.

Victor, David G., Kal Raustiala, and Eugene B. Skolnikoff. 1998. *The Implementation and Effectiveness of International Environmental Commitments: Theory and Practice*. Edited by Analysis International Institute for Applied Systems. Cambridge, Mass.: MIT Press; Laxenburg, Austria: International Institute for Applied Systems Analysis.

Vigneswaran, Darshan, Tesfalem Araia, Colin Hoag, and Xolani Tshabalala. 2010. "Criminality or Monopoly? Informal Immigration Enforcement in South Africa." *Journal of Southern African Studies* 36 (2): 465–485.

Vlassenroot, Koen. 2002. "Citizenship, Identity Formation and Conflict in South Kivu: The Case of the Banyamulenge." *Review of African Political Economy* 29 (93–94): 499–516.

Vrasti, Wanda. 2008. "The Strange Case of Ethnography and International Relations." *Millennium—Journal of International Studies* 37 (2): 279–301.

Waters, Tony. 2009. "Assessing the Impact of the Rwandan Refugee Crisis on Development Planning in Rural Tanzania." *Human Organization* 58 (2): 142–152.

Weyland, Kurt. 2008. "Toward a New Theory of Institutional Change." *World Politics* 60 (2): 281–314.

Whitaker, Beth Elise. 2002. "Refugees in Western Tanzania: The Distribution of Burdens and Benefits Among Local Hosts." *Journal of Refugee Studies* 15 (4): 339-358.

Wiener, Antje. 2009. "Enacting Meaning-in-Use: Qualitative Research on Norms in International Relations." *Review of International Studies* 35 (1): 175–193.

———. 2010. "Cultural Validation: Examining the Familiarity Deficit in Global Governance." In *Arguing Global Governance: Agency, Lifeworld, and Shared Reasons*, edited by Corneliu Bjola and Markus Kornprobst, 103–116. London: Routledge.

Wood, Tamara. 2012. "Legal Protection Frameworks." *Forced Migration Review* 39: 8–9.

Zetter, Roger. 1991. "Labelling Refugees: Forming and Transforming a Bureaucratic Identity." *Journal of Refugee Studies* 4 (1): 39–62.

Index